HARRY
STYLES

Also by Sean Smith

Meghan Misunderstood
Spice Girls
Ed Sheeran
George
Adele
Kim
Tom Jones: The Life
Kylie
Gary
Alesha
Tulisa
Kate
Robbie
Cheryl
Victoria
Justin: The Biography
Britney: The Biography
J.K. Rowling: A Biography
Jennifer: The Unauthorized Biography
Royal Racing
The Union Game
Sophie's Kiss (with Garth Gibbs)
Stone Me! (with Dale Lawrence)

HARRY STYLES

THE MAKING OF A MODERN MAN

BY SEAN SMITH

SUNDAY TIMES BESTSELLING AUTHOR

HarperCollins*Publishers*

HarperCollins*Publishers*
1 London Bridge Street
London SE1 9GF

HarperCollins*Publishers*
Macken House, 39/40 Mayor Street Upper,
Dublin1, D01 C9W8, Ireland

www.harpercollins.co.uk

First published by HarperCollins*Publishers* 2021
This edition published 2022

7 9 10 8

A catalogue record of this book is
available from the British Library

ISBN 978-0-00-835956-0

Printed and bound in the UK using 100%
renewable electricity at CPI Group (UK) Ltd

MIX
Paper | Supporting
responsible forestry
FSC™ C007454

This book is produced from independently certified FSC™ paper
to ensure responsible forest management.

For more information visit: www.harpercollins.co.uk/green

To Joma –
wishing you a wonderful future

'... If you are black, if you are white, if you are gay, if you are straight, if you are transgender – whoever you are, whoever you want to be – I support you. I love every single one of you.'

Harry Styles, Ericsson Globe, Stockholm, 18 March 2018

CONTENTS

PART THREE:
A MODERN MAN

FIRST IMPRESSIONS

It wasn't the eye-catching cover of *Vogue* that did it for me. It wasn't the envy-making cavorting with beautiful people on an idyllic, sun-kissed Malibu beach for the video of 'Watermelon Sugar'; it wasn't two number one albums or his role in *Dunkirk*.

No, what triggered a fascination with Harry Styles and made me want to write a book about him were just a few words from the actor and director Olivia Wilde, who described him as 'very modern', and observed, 'I hope that this brand of confidence as a male that Harry has – truly devoid of any traces of toxic masculinity – is indicative of his generation and therefore the future of the world.'

Wow, that's quite an endorsement of a man who just ten years earlier had done his best to impress Simon Cowell with a version of Stevie Wonder's sentimental chestnut 'Isn't She Lovely'. Did he deserve such praise from Olivia, I wonder?

Like fifteen million others I had watched the entire seventh series of *The X Factor* in the days when it was compulsory Saturday night viewing. You literally weren't part of the Sunday conversation if you hadn't seen Matt, Rebecca, Cher and the boys from One Direction battle it out every week to stay in the competition.

The five members of One Direction had sparkle and youthful exuberance, but I had no idea they were going to rule the pop world in such a short space of time. The stars aligned for them: the world was ready for a new boy band; they had a brilliant team looking after them day to day and they had the unswerving support of the corporate board room where careers were made or broken.

The boys were only together for five intense, mad years – becoming multi-millionaires – before going on indefinite hiatus in December 2015. With a few exceptions, five years seems to be the average life span of a boy or girl band – especially one put together by a third party. That was true of Take That and the Spice Girls, for example.

Zayn Malik had left One Direction before the official hiatus, which was a nice way of describing a full stop. Harry, though, was already looking different from the others. He had longer rock-star hair and an eye for the fashionable and flamboyant.

But nice hair and the ability to look good in a Gucci suit did not make him modern. My task in this book is to see if the description of Harry Styles as a modern man is justified. Is Olivia right or is referencing toxic masculinity just a neat soundbite? You don't just arrive ready-made as a beacon of the present and future, so who are the friends, the role models and the influencers that have helped Harry on his journey? And what does it actually mean to be 'modern' anyway?

These are the questions I hope to answer in a serious look at a superstar: *Harry Styles: The Making of a Modern Man*. See you on the other side …

PART ONE

FINDING DIRECTION

1

DRESSING UP

———————

Harry Styles was nearly born in the back of a car. His dad, Des, confessed that he and his heavily pregnant wife, Anne, only just made it to the Alexandra Hospital in Redditch before their son was on his way. It was a twenty-mile dash up the A46 in Worcestershire from their home in Evesham. There wasn't even time to 'call the midwife'. Instead, Harry Edward Styles said hello to the world at 2am on 1 February 1994.

There's a memorial statue in Redditch that honours a very famous name in world music. But it's not Harry. Instead, pride of place in the town centre belongs to John Bonham, the legendary drummer with Led Zeppelin.

The local papers and media always refer to Harry as Redditch-born whenever the more-recent superstar does anything noteworthy, but in reality he has no connection with the town half an hour south of Birmingham other than noting it as his place of birth on the official paperwork.

A month after his second birthday, the Styles family moved. Des and Anne sold the three-bedroom semi-detached house in St Philips Drive, Evesham, an estate close to the main road, and relocated a hundred miles north to rural Cheshire. They were a family of four: Harry had an elder sister, Gemma, who was three when he was born.

They settled into a spacious four-bedroom house in Chestnut Drive, Holmes Chapel, a large village that enjoyed a rural atmosphere despite being close to the motorway, and an easy twenty-mile commute into Manchester. The town of Crewe was even closer – just eight miles south.

If there is going to be a statue of Harry Styles in the future then it should be in Holmes Chapel, probably in the main square near St Luke's Church, or there's plenty of room outside his local secondary school in Selkirk Drive. Harry once said that nothing much happened in Holmes Chapel. That may be true, but it's not a sleepy village and these days it is a bustling place, more like a small town than the gentle setting for an Agatha Christie whodunit or an episode of *Midsomer Murders*.

The proximity to Manchester was ideal for Harry's dad, who was a committed supporter of Manchester United, and these were the best of times for the club enjoying the glory years of Alex Ferguson and a first team that included Eric Cantona, Roy Keane, Paul Scholes and David Beckham. There was always plenty of football memorabilia dotted around the Styles' house. At the time, Des, who was ten years older than his then 28-year-old wife, worked in financial services as an operational manager for HFC bank, primarily responsible for arranging loans and credit.

Anne had her hands full with two young children. They could scarcely have been more different. Harry's elder sister was the quiet, studious one, an A-grade student throughout school who found the academic side of things much easier than standing up in front of the class, and could only look on a little jealously as her cheeky and precociously charismatic kid brother sailed through life.

Harry did secure an A once, for his very first English essay, and he was proud of his achievement – but perhaps the top mark lived long in his memory because it was all downhill from there and he never matched it. He was always the boy getting told off by the teacher for chatting away to his friends at the back of the class.

His first pre-school nursery was called, sweetly, Happy Days, and it was just two minutes' walk from their detached house in Chestnut Drive, a smart new-build with a large garden for their dog, Max, to patrol. He was a cross between a border collie and a lurcher, who could sometimes look a bit fierce but wasn't, and he loved the children to bits. Gemma had chosen him from a litter because he was the outsider – the only puppy who was not pure black.

Ironically Harry's very first word was not dog but 'cat'. Anne had driven the children to visit their grandparents, Brian and Mary Selley, in Hampshire. As they were walking up the path to the front door, the family feline appeared. Little Harry pointed and declared 'cat', which made everyone's day.

When he was old enough, Harry joined his sister round the corner at the Hermitage Primary School. As was usual on these occasions, Mum came too to make sure her five-year-old was going to be alright. She sat in the class for an hour or so before slipping away. Harry may have been a bit of a 'mummy's boy', as Anne has always affectionately said, but she didn't leave a child weeping and wailing for his mother. He settled down to enjoy the day until she was back to walk him and Gemma home.

From a young age Harry was one of the boys *and* one of the girls. He never seemed limited by gender stereotyping or, as he memorably put it, 'I wasn't one of those boys who thought girls were smelly.' Just to prove it he gave one little girl, Phoebe, a teddy bear as a present when they were six.

Right from the start, Harry was an enthusiastic performer in the school plays, confident enough, it seemed, to get up on stage and sing, whatever embarrassing costume he had to wear. For the Christmas musical in December 2000, he played the title role of Barney, a church mouse; he sported a pair of Gemma's grey tights, a headband with oversized ears sticking out the top and a long string tail. Looking back on his starring role aged six, he observed, 'I like to think I was a good mouse.'

Often, enthusiastic mums can light the fire for their children – perhaps taking them to dance classes or booking piano lessons before they could barely walk. Anne loved playing dressing-up games with her children, painstakingly making elaborate papier-mâché outfits, including one that featured Harry as the World Cup. He also had a *101 Dalmatians* outfit, which was a particular favourite and the one he wore all the time around the house. Anne explained, 'I was always a big fan of doing fancy dress when my children were small … which Gemma hated but Harry always embraced.'

Harry would carry his love of dressing up into adulthood, and in his now-famous *Vogue* interview in 2020 he acknowledged, 'There's so much joy to be had in playing with clothes. I've never thought too much about what it means – it just becomes this extended part of creating something.'

In the primary school favourite, *Chitty Chitty Bang Bang*, he played Buzz Lightyear, who obviously did not feature in the original musical. In his school's adaptation, the children hid from the scary Child Catcher in a toy store where Buzz and Woody from *Toy Story* were living.

Harry also played the Pharaoh in a production of *Joseph and the Amazing Technicolor Dreamcoat*. The character's big number is 'Song of the King' and he delivered it as if Elvis Presley had been transported back to biblical times. The first pop song that Harry learned all the words to was 'Girl of My Best Friend', a number that 'the King' originally recorded for his 1960 UK number 1 album *Elvis is Back*. The track was one of his dad's favourites.

None of the family was especially musical, but Des at least loved a wide variety of past and present records and his son grew up hugely influenced by not just Elvis but also The Beatles and Coldplay – not forgetting a smattering of Fleetwood Mac and the peerless 'Shine on You Crazy Diamond' by Pink Floyd, the epic tribute to the band's original lead singer, Syd Barrett.

Harry was able to practise his inner rock star with the help of a karaoke machine his grandpa Brian had bought him for Christmas. Harry remained particularly close to Brian over the years, describing the man who picked him up and told him to be brave when he fell over and scraped his knee as 'the coolest guy ever'.

The admiration was mutual: recalling his grandson as a small boy, Brian observed that he always had a smile on his face.

The famous smile left Harry completely, however, one dreadful evening when he was seven and his parents sat him and Gemma down in the lounge and told them gently that they were splitting up. Everyone was in tears. Des later recalled, movingly, 'It was the worst day of my life. Harry wasn't a cry baby or generally emotional but he cried then.'

Although Des and Anne had agreed to separate, he didn't move out immediately, which perhaps made the situation a little easier for their children. There was even a memorable family summer holiday to Cyprus when Harry, according to both his father and his sister, became the mascot of the teenage girls at the resort hotel. While Gemma was a bit of a loner, Harry was the centre of attention around the pool, entertaining everyone with his now-trademark cheeky grin and boisterous nature.

To Des's astonishment, when it came for them to leave on the shuttle bus to the airport, a crowd of young women gathered to wave goodbye to his young son. 'Bye, Harry, we love you,' they shouted as the bus sped away. 'He's very charming,' said Des, simply.

Eventually, and inevitably, Des moved out of the family home and the divorce was finalised. He still saw the children every couple of weeks, doing his best to make sure everything was alright with both of them, supporting them financially and, when he could, with any emotional problems.

Des was not a million miles away, moving to the outskirts of Manchester. 'I'm not an estranged dad,' he said, and he wasn't, as would prove to be very much the case in the future. He was always close enough to take his son to football or buy him a club jersey or two for the bedroom wall.

Anne, meanwhile, met someone, a man who really would become estranged from them in the future – in his case, a future stepfather. John Cox was the good-looking landlord of the Red Lion pub in Pickmere, a village twenty minutes' drive past the town of Northwich.

Anne was a vivaciously attractive woman of thirty-three when they met, although they didn't start going out until they had known each other for a year. They were soon making plans for a life together, setting a wedding date for April 2003, not long after Harry's ninth birthday.

They chose a swish local venue, the Mere Golf Club – now the Mere Golf Resort and Spa but still known in this part of rural Cheshire as 'The Mere'. For the big day, Harry looked immaculate in a dress suit complete with a black bow tie, an early indication of a young man who was born to wear a suit well. After the wedding, Harry and Gemma were dropped off at Des's to allow the newlyweds to jet off to Mauritius for their honeymoon.

Before the celebration, the happy couple had already joined forces to take over the Antrobus Arms, a large country pub on the main A558 Warrington Road. The premises formerly run by Lancashire brewers Greenall Whitley needed a lot of work, so they set about the refurbishment and decorating to turn it into a sparkling new local for the village of Antrobus. It was a large building, so it made economic sense for the new landlord and landlady to live upstairs with Harry and Gemma.

John and Anne didn't want to lose the feel of a traditional Cheshire pub, making sure the Antrobus Arms retained a tap room and a back room where charities and societies could hold evening events. Half a mile away was the Antrobus post office, run by two regulars at the pub, Trevor and Sandra

Collins. They became firm friends of Anne in particular. They also had a son, Reg, who was nearer Gemma's age but was Harry's best buddy when the family moved into the pub.

Harry stayed at the Hermitage Primary School in Holmes Chapel but during the holidays he was pleased to have a good friend nearby. They went on long bike rides together, exploring the country lanes but always making sure they popped in for a cornet on the way home at the Ice Cream Farm in Great Budworth, two miles away.

The parlour, run by June Wilkinson and her family, is one of the hidden gems of this part of rural Cheshire, but once discovered it becomes a habit that's hard to break, as was the case with Harry when he discovered their christmas pudding flavour one chilly December afternoon.

Even more important than ice cream, Harry started having informal guitar lessons when he was ten from a pub regular who had once been in a rock band. Harry has never shouted about his early musical training but it gave him a start that would be valuable when he picked up a guitar as a career musician and songwriter.

Harry seemed to settle in well to life at the pub, although he was notorious in the household for being untidy. He sang in public for the first time – apart from performing in school plays – when he joined John at The Elms, another pub in Pickmere. When John got up to sing, Harry insisted he join him and the pair gave a rousing rendition of 'New York, New York', the Frank Sinatra favourite.

For the moment, though, Harry was more interested in sport than crooning. He enjoyed badminton, taking it up because his dad played. He was also keen on football, playing for a boys' team on a Sunday, although he was never going to be signed up by a United scout.

John Cox completely disappeared out of Harry's life when he and Anne split up in 2006. He is no longer part of the Harry Styles story and hasn't seen him since Anne moved back to Holmes Chapel. He has been erased from the family history. Neither Harry, his mother nor his sister have ever mentioned him, although Anne continued to be known as Anne Cox right up to the heady days of *The X Factor*.

John was eventually tracked down by the investigative journalist Sharon Feinstein. He was still living in Cheshire but was no longer in the pub business. He spoke warmly of Harry and hoped that one day they might meet up for a drink.

In the small world of this part of Cheshire, the Antrobus Arms was sold to Trevor and Sandra Collins, who would keep up the tradition of a thriving country pub for the next twelve years One of the regulars was a local businessman called Robin Twist, a sociable and popular chap who would be a significant figure in Harry's life in the years to come.

Anne, meanwhile, bought a modest three-bedroom terraced house in London Road, Holmes Chapel, within walking distance of the local comprehensive school. Harry would soon be a teenager.

2

WHITE ESKIMO DAYS

————

Harry's football career was not going well. He was playing for the Holmes Chapel Hurricanes FC, a junior team set up in 2000 by local businessman Chris Rogers so that his son and his friends could enjoy a game on weekends. According to Chris, Harry wasn't the most physical of players, although he did score a few goals.

The lowest point of his footballing days, however, was when he had to stand in for the regular goalkeeper. The Hurricanes lost the game 8–0. He wasn't asked to play in that position again. The plus side of his weekly ordeal was that the mums and sisters on the touchline were always charmed by Harry, who was quick with a little quip to cheer up everyone.

He may not have impressed with his soccer skills but at least he was having fun with his mates away from school. One in particular, Will Sweeny, would be a significant friend. Will was the closest thing to a celebrity at Holmes Chapel Comprehensive School because his mum, Yvette Fielding, was a familiar face on television.

Yvette had been the presenter of *Blue Peter* when she was just eighteen and subsequently appeared in a host of TV programmes, including as the presenter of the cult show *Most Haunted*, which also featured her second husband, Karl Beattie. They lived on a farm not far from Holmes Chapel. Harry was a regular visitor after school, scoffing pizza and chips in the kitchen with her son.

Will and Harry often went on double dates together away from school. Harry's social life as a young teenager was going well, although he was in danger of drifting a little when he first started secondary school. He had always assumed he would end up as some sort of entertainer when he grew up, but that ambition seemed to fade for a year or two. He still played badminton and spent time in the school gym, especially enjoying the dancing classes under the enthusiastic guidance of Miss Brocklehurst – Miss Brock to the students – but that was not a career.

Living locally was a bonus. He didn't have to stand around outside the school gates every afternoon to be assigned a seat on the bus home. This daily bussing ritual was presided over by the headmaster, Denis Oliver. He was a familiar sight, clipboard in hand and always wearing a well-used high-vis jacket. Away from his gaze, Harry and his friends would slip away across the field to the river behind the school to hang out before it was time to go home.

Harry's gang of girlfriends, who were fun, loyal and not especially serious, included Lydia Cole, Ellis Calcutt and, most importantly, Emilie Jefferies. Harry was just twelve when he first started dating Emilie but they were too young to get carried away with romance. She has remained one of his close friends from the 'old days' and she looked stunning in her ball gown on Harry's arm at their leavers' prom at the end of Year 11.

Harry has always said his first serious girlfriend was another very pretty girl at school, Abi Crawshaw, who was a key member of the school hockey team. She would go on to become head girl in the sixth form after Harry had left.

The fascinating aspect of Harry's early friendships with the opposite sex throughout his school days is that none of the girls have come forward to sell lurid tales to the tabloids. Lydia once said, 'We all love Harry to bits,' but that was all. The nearest Harry has got to revealing something juicy was to point out the place where he had his first snog. It was up against a tree down by the river. 'It was quite steamy,' was all he would say.

His dad Des recalled that he never had to sit Harry down for an excruciating 'birds and bees' conversation about sex. They would chat about things from time to time as if it were a natural part of growing up – no embarrassment.

One girl, Felicity Skinner, who wasn't from Holmes Chapel, was more forthcoming about Harry, but not in a salacious way. She said, 'He was really sweet. He was a really good boyfriend, very romantic. He was good-looking and obviously I found him very attractive.'

Felicity, who was introduced to Harry by a mutual friend in Holmes Chapel, lived in Solihull, south of Birmingham, so it was never a case of popping over to each other's houses after school. It was a long-distance teen romance that was played out mainly on the phone, although Fliss, as he called her, observed, 'It was puppy love and we were definitely each other's first love.'

Will Sweeny recalled how early on in the relationship Harry announced, 'Let's go and find her.' So they headed off to Birmingham without knowing her exact address. They knew she lived in Solihull, and that was all. 'It was pouring with rain and it took hours to find her,' Will said.

When he was with Fliss, Harry would finish work in the bakery and, instead of meeting up with his friends in Holmes Chapel, would spend his wages on a train fare south to see her. Will pointed out that she was his first very serious girlfriend: 'He really cared about her, but they were both young and it didn't work out.'

Will confirmed that Harry was not the sort of guy to play around and was not a womaniser at school. He was thoughtful where girls were concerned, and a very good listener. 'His girlfriends were long term. He was dead caring,' he said. Another close friend at school, Nick Clough, thought Harry had a precociously romantic streak where girls were concerned, a hearts and flowers boy, who preferred a candlelit dinner at his house to a can of cider by the river.

Sometimes Harry would cook a meal for his mum or run her a hot bath. She was dating Robin Twist and that was going well. They had become a settled couple, although still living in separate houses. Anne was very careful not to take her teen-age children for granted and to make sure they didn't come home from school to find Robin with his feet up watching *Countdown* on TV.

Harry thought Robin was a 'really cool guy', so he was always happy to see him, sometimes texting him to come over without asking Anne first. The home in Holmes Chapel was a happy one, a tribute to his mum, who when asked about her parenting skills remarked drily, 'I make it up as I go along – like everyone else.'

On Saturdays, Harry was up before the sun, leaving the rest of the household to snooze away while he ambled down for his shift at W. Mandeville, the bakery in the centre of the village. The shop had been a fixture in Holmes Chapel since 1900, when it was founded by the great-grandfather of the present owner, Simon Wakefield. The building in Macclesfield Road even has a vintage sign on the side declaring that it is a 'Maker of HOVIS'.

There was always plenty to do before the shop opened every morning – packing orders, making sure all the shelves were correctly stocked and clearing up if any of the loaves or cakes had spilled onto the floor. Harry worked there for two and a half years, always greeting the customers with a winning smile as he stood behind the till. 'He's our boy!' said one, remembering him fondly.

At least Harry never went hungry at work. There was always some treat to try. Simon had already been baking for at least two hours before his Saturday staff arrived. His brunch pasties were especially popular as he seemed to be able to cram in a filling of bacon, sausage, scrambled egg and cheese.

Harry wasn't the only pupil from Holmes Chapel Comprehensive earning some extra cash at the bakery – there were usually three others working there too, including his close friend Nick Clough. They were teenage partners in crime, not that there was much to get up to in the village. The height of rebellion was a Chinese takeaway on a Friday night from Fortune City, which was conveniently situated two doors down from Harry's house. Harry favoured sweet and sour or crispy beef in Cantonese sauce. Then the pair of them would meet up with friends. They were too young to go to the pub so they would gather by the river and drink beer.

Nick would usually stay over at Harry's so that they could stagger bleary eyed into work together the following morning. Not many people had heard the teenage Harry sing but one memorable afternoon Nick was serving a customer when they heard Harry singing away while he was sweeping up out the back. They couldn't miss it because he hadn't realised there was anyone in the shop and was singing very loudly, as if he was in the shower at home.

'Who's singing?' asked the customer. Nick went to fetch Harry: 'I brought him out and the customer said, "Have you ever thought about singing professionally? If you ever consider it, give me a call."'

Nick knew Harry could sing because most evenings he would stroll round to the house in London Road with his guitar and practise his chords. Harry was shy about his musical ability so he usually limited himself to bashing a tambourine or singing along. By this time Harry's teenager bedroom had morphed into something out of a sitcom – cans of Lynx deodorant, clothes tossed casually onto the floor and an old Manchester United shirt pinned to the wall. His mum was fighting a losing battle shouting at him to 'TIDY UP HIS ROOM!'

Harry hadn't taken singing seriously despite both his mum and dad complimenting him when he sang in the car. Fate, however, was about to play a part when Will Sweeny decided to form a school band. He would be the drummer and he enlisted Nick to play bass and another friend, Haydn Morris, to play lead guitar. Now, they just needed a singer.

At first Harry wasn't keen. He fancied playing bass guitar, but that position was already taken. Nick recalled, 'Harry didn't think he could sing and was worried people would laugh.' The boys wouldn't take no for an answer so Harry had to get over his misgivings. Nick added, 'There was a born performer in there – he just had to find it. But when his confidence grew, he was amazing.'

The new band wanted to enter the school's Battle of the Bands competition in the summer of 2009 when Harry was fifteen. They needed a name, so Will came up with Cheese and Crackers, in honour of the legendary American band Red Hot Chili Peppers. The others gave that idea a fast thumbs down. At the time, the four of them were waiting outside a music room at school and, for reasons lost in the fog of time, the name White Eskimo popped into Will's head.

White Eskimo only had two weeks to rehearse before the big night. At least they would look the part. They all thought they were rockers or, more precisely, devotees of emo. The term standing mostly for 'emotional hardcore' embraced a punk culture that was as much about fashion as it was about music. Emo swept through the teenagers of Holmes Chapel and you couldn't pass a street corner without noticing the glint of a studded belt and a pair of tight skinny jeans, topped off with a belt made from shoelaces.

They all thought they were very cool, naturally. For once Harry was influenced by his elder sister, Gemma, although he probably loved the fashion more than the music that blared from her attic bedroom. He even let her cut his hair. She told the magazine *Another Man*, 'I had no idea what I was doing.' She did get the floppy fringe right, though, and Harry seemed pleased.

If he wasn't going to Solihull when work finished at the bakery on Saturday at 3.30 or 4pm, Harry and Nick would dash to the station a few hundred yards away to catch a train into Manchester Piccadilly. It usually took no more than three-quarters of an hour, which gave them plenty of time to hit the shops and spend their wages on a new pair of chequered trainers.

One of the fashion statements associated with the emo culture was a piercing. Nick suggested that they had their ears pierced one afternoon when they were in Manchester. Harry wasn't keen, concerned that his mum might not approve. He didn't even have a discreet tattoo until he was eighteen.

For the big evening at Holmes Chapel, Harry looked the part, choosing to wear a plain white shirt and black tie – more Robert Palmer than My Chemical Romance. They were very accomplished for an inexperienced school band, performing just two songs: 'Summer of '69' by Bryan Adams and the evergreen 'Are You Gonna Be My Girl' by Jet, which was much rockier. The audience was very enthusiastic, with a host of schoolgirls gathering at the front. White Eskimo won, pocketing £100 in cash and getting the chance to perform at the local arts festival, Goosfest, based in the nearby village of Goostry.

In those very early days, Harry was already a natural front-man, even if he sang in a slightly strained manner with his neck strangling the sound, suggesting he could benefit from some vocal coaching. Harry is modest about his time with White Eskimo but they were popular locally, playing an eclectic mix of songs. At a White Eskimo concert you might hear The Beatles classic 'A Hard Day's Night', 'Valerie' by the Zutons – later made famous by Amy Whitehouse and Mark Ronson – 'First Date' by American rock band Blink-182 and Paolo Nutini's 'Jenny Don't Be Hasty'; and one they wrote themselves, 'Gone in a Week'.

The most they made from a gig was for the wedding party of the mother of one the girls from school. They had to learn a couple of extra Bob Marley songs that were the bride's favourites, but they were paid a handsome £400 for the occasion.

At school, GCSEs were looming and Harry was looking to the future, planning what he would study in the sixth form. Although he might not match the academic prowess of Gemma, he would have little trouble passing his exams and looking to continue with career-orientated subjects including law, business and sociology.

His mum, however, had other ideas for her son.

3

LOVELY NEWS

———

Harry asked Simon Wakefield for the day off. He wasn't just
working Saturdays now, he was swinging by the bakery after
school during the week to spend an hour or two helping to
clear and clean to earn some extra cash. His GCSEs were
imminent and, if they went well, he intended to go on to
college for further studies. He wasn't sure exactly what career
he wanted to pursue but there was talk of becoming a physio-
therapist somewhere down the line. It was a career Abi was
keen on, so they had talked about the possibility and Harry
thought it seemed promising if the rock-star plan didn't bear
fruit.

Simon readily agreed when Harry told him he was going
for an audition for *The X Factor*. Harry had been feeling a bit
unsettled since Gemma had left home to go to Sheffield
Hallam University, where she was studying Science
Education with a qualified teacher status. She was just as
academically brilliant as she had always been. She observed,
'It was only after I had left home that I realised he would
actually miss me.'

He couldn't ask the school's permission to miss classes for a TV audition, so he took the traditional solution – he skived off. Will Sweeny went with him on the day to offer moral support.

White Eskimo were still very much a band but perhaps it was time for Harry to strike out on his own. He's never properly explained why he decided to go it alone, but a casual look at the show's history (this would be the seventh series) revealed that groups had never won and, apart from JLS, hadn't done particularly well afterwards. Bands playing instruments were definitely nowhere to be seen.

In the finest traditions of mums, Anne encouraged him to fill out the application form. In the end, she did it for him and sent it off. He was given a date at the end of April 2010, along with literally thousands of others, to roll up to Old Trafford to meet the advance production staff. These were the unheralded judges who would decide who was going to go through to the next stage. It was never just a case of being able to sing well; contestants had to be good TV, so being quirky, amusing or possessing a twinkle were qualities as important as hitting the right notes.

The audition was bedlam, with more than 6,000 hopefuls jamming the car park, all wanting to be chosen. They had come from right across the north of England to queue up for literally hours, just hoping to be noticed. Will and Harry hung around for four or five hours. Like everyone else, Harry had to wait to hear if he had won through to the first televised audition stage when he would have to sing in front of the judges. It was good news.

Simon Cowell and co. were not there at this first stage but host Dermot O'Leary was on duty to give the crowd a rousing pep talk. The *Manchester Evening News* also sent along a reporter and photographer. They didn't see Harry but they did spot Emma Chawner, who seemed to enter every year, as well as a young woman from Liverpool who had failed to make the televised stages four years earlier. However, this time, Rebecca Ferguson, a twenty-three-year-old mother-of-two, sang 'River Deep Mountain High' and sailed through.

When Harry heard that he would be at the first televised audition in Manchester, he was sent a list of possible songs and told that he needed to choose and prepare two for the big day. He went for the Stevie Wonder standard 'Isn't She Lovely' with the back-up of 'Hey, Soul Sister', which had been a hit the previous year for the American rock band Train. Nobody knew it then but the latter was much more in keeping with the artist that Harry Styles would become.

For the moment, 'Isn't She Lovely' was the front runner. The classic was older than Harry. Stevie Wonder had written it for his *Songs in the Key of Life*, one of the great albums of the seventies. The lyrics refer to the birth of his daughter, Aisha, and might be regarded as either sweet or cheesy depending on one's taste. The song was quite a daring choice for a sixteen-year-old boy, because the performance could easily become corny if Harry overdid the saccharine and the smile.

He needed to practise, but to his mum and sister's surprise, he seemed quite shy when it came to rehearsing. The boy who had a karaoke machine in his bedroom and already sang in a group at school was suddenly bashful. He made sure the bathroom door was firmly shut as he wailed, 'Isn't she won … dur … ful.' He had no idea the two women were sat on the landing outside, excitedly listening to every note.

The reason for Harry's new-found reticence is simply explained. When he was part of White Eskimo he could be Bryan Adams singing 'Summer of '69' or John Mayer performing 'Free Fallin''. In his bedroom, enjoying karaoke, he was Bowie, Jagger or Elvis. In front of the *X Factor* judges, though, there would be no hiding place: he needed to be Harry Styles from Holmes Chapel and show them he had what it took to be a star.

This was the golden age of *The X Factor*, a top-rated show that made stars not just for lucky finalists but also for the judges, who up until now were more famous than the artists they discovered. Some of the winners, including Alexandra Burke, Joe McElderry and, especially, Leona Lewis, had become household names, but they were all eclipsed by Simon Cowell.

Simon may not have spent his Saturdays in a bakery, but he left school at sixteen and was a tea boy, a runner and then worked in the post room at EMI before edging his way up the record-business ladder. He had been a senior A&R consultant responsible for the cringeworthy Robson & Jerome hits before *Pop Idol* began in 2001. He had brokered an agreement whereby the winner would release their first record on his label, S Records, and, keen to protect his investment, he was persuaded to become a judge – a role, it soon became apparent, he was born to play. His famous clash with eventual winner Will Young was television gold.

By the end of the first series, Simon was on his way to becoming a television institution. He was not especially witty or clever in addressing the hopefuls but he had a style and method that was essential viewing on a Saturday night. We expect Simon Cowell to be rude and are genuinely pleased when he is.

After a couple of series of *Pop Idol*, Simon was able to introduce his own series, *The X Factor*, to British TV. A complicated legal case involving the mastermind behind *Pop Idol*, the former Spice Girls' manager Simon Fuller, ended with a financial settlement that allowed Cowell to pursue *The X Factor* in the UK while working for Fuller in the US on *American Idol*. Together, these shows propelled Simon Cowell into superstar status on both sides of the Atlantic.

Behind the scenes, Simon was known as The Dark Lord, but in reality he is one of the most charming men in the business. The radio host and former television critic Kevin O'Sullivan observed, 'He is great company and he kind of loves you, that's his charm. You are sucked in.'

Simon is, however, primarily a businessman not a TV personality. Behind the scenes in 2010 he had formed the Syco Entertainment Group, a joint venture with Sony Music that gave him enormous fire power for cross-promoting between television and records. Having this power behind you almost guaranteed success for the acts he wanted to promote.

He understood, though, that he needed to keep *The X Factor* fresh in order to maintain its success. He had, for instance, introduced an audience for the televised auditions and so Harry, in 2010, faced that additional pressure.

But he was not a clairvoyant, and he could not have foreseen the path that Harry Styles would take when he was confronted by the sixteen-year-old boy from Holmes Chapel at the Manchester Central Hall, on the site of the city's old railway station.

Harry had dressed very carefully for the occasion. He chose a plain white t-shirt, a light-grey cardigan and a slightly darker-grey, patterned scarf hanging loosely in casual bohemian style around his neck. 'The outfit spoke volumes,' observed fashion commentator Alison Jane Reid. 'Harry is clearly interested in fashion and in making a statement. A scarf is a good place to start. It shows individuality from the moment he stepped into the public gaze. Few men would choose to accessorise a classic white t-shirt with a scarf, which he has chosen to wear in an artful, interesting way. It hints at what is to come.'

Harry radiated good health, but that had not been the case the previous day: he couldn't stop throwing up. When he started coughing up blood as well, it was time for a trip to the local hospital in Northwich. There didn't seem to be an explanation, so perhaps it was an acute case of old-fashioned nerves. He gradually felt calm enough to go ahead and on the day itself there was no outward sign of any apprehension.

Team Styles was there to support him, including Mum, Gemma and Robin Twist, who was now a welcome family fixture and much appreciated by Harry. To begin his day, Harry and his crew had to speak to Dermot O'Leary, who pretended he had just stumbled across them in a crowd of people.

Harry stood out but his 'team' were distinctive as well, wearing t-shirts that declared 'We Think Harry Has the X Factor'. He told Dermot, 'I'm Harry Styles. I'm sixteen and I'm from Holmes Chapel in Cheshire. It's a bit boring. Nothing much happens. It's picturesque.'

He revealed that he was in a band with school friends called White Eskimo, which was a great plug for the group, and mentioned their Battle of the Bands triumph. He also explained the experience of that competition had prompted his singing ambitions: 'I got such a thrill when I was in front of people singing that it made me want to do it more and more.'

Harry seemed a natural in front of the camera, cracking a joke: 'People tell me I can sing – it's usually my mother.' Dermot, laughing, added, 'They always say that.'

Anne gave her son a kiss and a hug before he went on stage to meet the judges and face a young crowd of some 3,000 *X Factor* fans. Harry was still a teenage boy but there was no sign of embarrassment about receiving a kiss from his mum … in public!

The judges panel for that year was Simon Cowell, Cheryl Cole, Dannii Minogue and, old favourite, Louis Walsh, but there were some early problems. Dannii had missed all the auditions around the country because of her first pregnancy and had given birth to her son Ethan earlier in the month. Cheryl Cole, as she was then, was arguably the most famous woman in the country that year – and certainly the most photographed. While Harry caught the train into Manchester for his first *X Factor* experience, Cheryl was named the World's Sexiest Woman by *FHM* for the second year running. The magazine said, 'No one was even on the same continent in terms of votes.'

The following month she was headline news when she filed for divorce against footballer Ashley Cole, citing his unreasonable behaviour as the grounds. In July, just before she was due to judge Harry's first performance in front of the television cameras, she returned from a break in Tanzania with a dose of malaria that meant she needed complete rest and would not be on the panel in Manchester.

Her stand-in was the Pussycat Dolls singer Nicole Scherzinger, then just starting out on British television. She was a natural, though, and would prove to be very popular, taking on the role of a permanent judge in subsequent years. To begin with she needed to give her opinion on Harry.

He hadn't seemed at all nervous when he told Simon that he was planning to go to college. He sang a soupçon of 'Isn't She Lovely' a cappella and was robustly in tune. He finished and did a little bow to the audience. Nicole was impressed, saying, 'You could really hear how great your voice was.'

On this occasion, Louis Walsh was the Grinch. He thought Harry was too young, which prompted Simon to play the good cop and encourage the audience to boo his fellow panellist. Even Harry gave a boo to Louis when he decided that it was a 'no from me'. At least the famed boyband manager didn't come out with one of his well-worn clichés: 'You remind me of a young Cliff Richard.'

Simon did suggest that Harry might benefit from some vocal coaching – perhaps reflecting that Harry was trying a little too hard. 'You actually could be very good,' said Simon. He cast his deciding vote in Harry's favour. The outcome never really seemed in doubt, but Harry didn't know that and described it as 'one of the best moments of my life'.

The problem now was not being able to shout his progress from the rooftops of Holmes Chapel. His support team were all sworn to secrecy and Harry went back to working in the bakery, knowing that in a couple of months' time he would be on his way to London for the Bootcamp stage.

As before, he asked Simon Wakefield for the day off. But this time, he didn't go back.

4

A SECOND CHANCE

Gemma drove Harry down to Wembley Arena for the start of Bootcamp and left him when she saw he was in his element chatting and laughing with the other contenders still living the dream in the car park – so far so good. Clearly, it was just going to be a nice day out. That was before Simon Cowell addressed everyone.

The first day of Bootcamp is the most brutal. Simon told the hopefuls: 'Today, you're going to be put into your categories and you're going to sing one song. There are literally no second chances today.' The Boys had to perform 'Man in the Mirror' from Michael Jackson's 1987 album *Bad*. The song had been re-released in 2009 following Jackson's death and had reached number two in the charts – so for many it was very much a modern track.

It's a serious song that's wasted on a lot of young men hoping to progress on a Saturday night variety show. 'Man in the Mirror' is a call for change; the need for all of us to look at ourselves in tackling prejudice and discrimination. Jackson's video had featured images of starving black children in Africa, the homeless, and important figures from our immediate past including Dr Martin Luther King Jr., President Nelson Mandela and Archbishop Desmond Tutu – cut powerfully against images of the Ku Klux Klan and Hitler. It wasn't subtle, but it was more effective because of that. One can only imagine the images that would be included if the song were re-released today, in the wake of George Floyd's murder.

The song's message was the least of Harry's worries on this warm July day in north-west London. Michael Jackson songs are very hard to sing but he did a passable version and was invited back the following day. More than 200 contestants had already been trimmed by half.

That evening he enjoyed celebrating with other contenders at the hotel in Wembley where they were all housed during Bootcamp. Reports suggested that Harry had a few drinks before heading off for an early night. They didn't suggest that he might not have been alone, although later it was revealed he enjoyed a Bootcamp fling with a young blonde singer from Stroud in Gloucestershire called Katie Smith.

Next morning, it was dancing day, which always makes for good television as those hapless contestants with two left feet do their best Fred Astaire impression. Some of them are born dad dancers. Harry, however, was a natural. He may not have been ready to join Diversity, the inspiring street-dance troupe who had won *Britain's Got Talent* in 2009, but he had rhythm.

Harry didn't broadcast it but he loved dancing at school. That was not the case for Zayn Malik, a seventeen-year-old from Bradford, though. It may or may not have been a set-up but he refused to join the other boys on stage, claiming to camera, 'I hate dancing.'

Zayn had form when it came to being the reluctant pop star. He had to be pushed out of the door by his mum Trisha to go to his judges' audition: 'He chickened out, saying, "Can't I just leave it?"' She had to softly persuade him that he had nothing to lose and he should just see what happened.

Trisha had converted to Islam when she married Yasser Malik and they settled into a rented terrace house in the East Bowling district of the city. She made sure Zayn and his three sisters read the Koran and attended the local mosque. She worked as a halal chef in the kitchen of a primary school, where she prepared meals for the Muslim children.

Zayn had three yeses from the judges in Manchester, one better than Harry, for singing the smooth, Grammy Award–winning hit 'Let Me Love You' by Mario. The song perfectly suited his crystal-clear, soulful voice. While he was obviously very good-looking, Zayn seemed to lack Harry's twinkly charisma – and that was before he 'felt like an idiot' when the dancing began.

Simon Cowell personally had to go and find him backstage, sitting by himself. Simon persuaded him to continue, telling him 'the only person he was hurting was himself'. It was great TV. Zayn clearly wasn't as good a mover as Harry but he wasn't totally useless either, and the episode made sure he was noticed.

Harry, dressed in his favourite purple hoodie, danced immediately behind Zayn so we noticed him as well. The choreographer in charge of the day was, as usual, Brian Friedman, and he later observed, 'Zayn was better than he thought.' He was also in no doubt about a seldom-publicised fact about the boys who would eventually form One Direction: 'Harry was definitely the best dancer.'

Having navigated his way through the dancing, Harry had to choose a song from a list of forty to perform for the panel the following day when the final six for Judges' Houses would be chosen. He went with 'Stop Crying Your Heart Out', a top-ten hit for Oasis in 2002. The Noel Gallagher-written song had enjoyed a revival when Leona Lewis recorded it in 2009.

Unsurprisingly, her version was on the Syco label, so giving it a free plug on his TV show demonstrated once more Simon Cowell's astute commercial awareness: never miss an opportunity to make money. The Oasis version featured Liam Gallagher's unique vocal style, while Leona gave it a touch more emotion. Undoubtedly it's a beautiful song, but it was too mature for a sixteen-year-old boy. Harry had picked it because it was one he could perform without fear of making a mistake. 'My performance was so boring,' he said, truthfully. He also drew the short straw of being first on among the boys. Another hopeful, Liam Payne from Wolverhampton, also sang it – unmemorably.

Decision time had arrived. Simon read out the final list of boys chosen to go to Judges' Houses. Cranking up the tension, just two spots remained and Harry had still not been picked. The next successful candidate was Matt Cardle, a singer from Essex. Matt was twenty-seven, so in previous years would not have been eligible for the Boys' category, but in 2010 the producers changed the goalposts and made the age limit twenty-eight. Apparently it was Nicole Scherzinger's idea but it made good commercial sense. If Matt happened to win the competition, he would appeal immediately to a younger audience than if he was stuck in the older category.

At this point, Matt's good fortune was Harry's loss. The final choice was a sixteen-year-old from South Wales called Tom Richards. Five young men in particular, including a tearful Harry, were left heartbroken … but it was the best thing that ever happened to them.

Harry was sitting disconsolately on his suitcase in the car park of Wembley Arena. He was chatting to another contestant, Niall Horan, who had travelled over from County Westmeath in the Republic of Ireland and had just had the same crushing disappointment. Niall had been one of the most popular among the other contestants at Bootcamp, always strumming away on his guitar and leading a group sing.

Niall had been a natural entertainer as a youngster, playing the title role in the musical *Oliver* at school, teaching himself guitar by watching YouTube videos, singing in the back of the car and being told by relations that he would be famous one day. Like Harry, his parents had split when he was very young and he had grown up dividing his time between the two of them.

Before his audition he had explained that he had been compared a few times to Justin Bieber. He was a cute sixteen-year-old, which was definitely not how he wanted to be viewed, but the judges, in particular fellow Irishman Louis Walsh, thought he had the likeability factor after he sang 'So Sick' by singer-songwriter Ne-Yo, who, in the small world of music, had also written Zayn's audition song 'Let Me Love You'. Simon brought Niall down to earth by observing, 'You are not as good as you thought you were,' before giving him a yes. Guest judge Katy Perry noted that 'likeableness is not going to sell records,' which was almost certainly not true.

Niall had also been sunk at Bootcamp by a weak version of an Oasis song – in his case, 'Champagne Supernova' – before joining Harry as a reject. Both boys really had no idea that they were not finished after all. The groups were not that strong in 2010, so behind the scenes it was decided to place some of the boys and girls who had nearly made it into two new bands. Simon Cowell explained the reasoning: 'The groups that year were actually pretty bad.'

Both Nicole Scherzinger and Simon Cowell have claimed the credit for suggesting a boy band of also-rans. It was Simon. He explained to *Rolling Stone* magazine that he was relying on his gut instinct, taking just fifteen minutes to decide which five boys he was going to bring back as a group.

They were Niall, Zayn, Liam Payne, Louis Tomlinson from Doncaster and Harry. They were called back on stage but they genuinely had no idea why. Simon gave Nicole the task of telling them that they weren't out of the competition after all.

As ever, it was classic *X Factor* television, especially when Harry sank to his knees in delight at the news that they would be going to Judges' Houses when the series returned in September The boys all jumped around and hugged each other – lottery winners in life.

Simon told them to take five minutes to think about it and what this news meant for their futures. They needed five seconds, although Liam, who had invested so much time and energy on being a singer, probably needed a little longer.

The major surprise was not that Harry was chosen for the group but that he had not been picked as a solo artist for the

Boys' section in the first place. Simon was once asked how he could *not* put through someone with such obvious charm and presence, not to mention talent, as a solo act. He admitted that the biggest single factor was his age. Harry was a sixteen-year-old boy from Holmes Chapel who might have been lost if he had gone up against Matt Cardle, ten years older and a seasoned professional.

From the very beginning, at the first audition, Simon had seen something in Harry, declaring enthusiastically: 'This kid's got everything: he's really confident, he's got unbelievable charisma, and he's a good singer. He wasn't a great singer on his first audition, but he was a *good* singer and everyone gravitated towards him. He was exactly what you're looking for when you make one of these shows: memorable and a natural frontman.'

He almost revealed too much. Simon had been around long enough to understand stardom. Kevin O'Sullivan confirmed, 'Cowell does have a serious talent for spotting what the masses will love.' All five boys had an edge, a talent that added to the collective but Harry was the one who, in his words, had 'unbelievable charisma' and was a 'natural frontman'. Simon is far too shrewd to admit it openly but it's easy to conclude that the boy band was actually formed *around* Harry Styles.

Manufacturing a boy band or girl band was nothing new, so this wasn't a 'eureka' moment patented by *The X Factor*. In the nineties, both Take That and the Spice Girls were put together by forward-thinking managers. Robbie Williams' entire career began when he spotted an advertisement in a local paper that stated simply, 'Singers and dancers wanted for a new boy band.'

The Spice Girls followed the same formula – although this time the ad was in *The Stage* in amongst the jobs for dancers in Dubai and cruise ship cabaret entertainers. If members of both these iconic groups had been ten years older then it's a racing certainty they would have been trying to impress Simon Cowell.

He himself had form when it came to manufacturing a boy band. Back in the late nineties, he had joined forces with Chris Herbert, the man who put together the Spice Girls, to find a boy band. This time the ad placed in *The Stage* said, 'Spice Boys Wanted'. They were put up in a house in Camberley, Surrey, to see if they gelled as a unit and to prepare.

They were called 5ive, and, before disbanding in 2001, had achieved a dozen top ten hits, including topping the album charts. They sold ten million records worldwide and, perhaps just as significantly, were on twenty-three magazine covers and secured some lucrative commercial deals, including a link-up with Pepsi.

They were a useful template for Simon Cowell's next boy-band venture, although Chris Herbert's philosophy for 5ive was perhaps not right for good-looking teenage boys on Saturday night prime time TV. He explained what he was looking for with 5ive: 'Take That would give you roses but I wanted a band that would fuck you up against a garage door.'

What was needed was something in between – a blend of romance and naughtiness – that Simon thought he had found in the cheeky yet winning smile of Harry Styles.

When 5ive disbanded in 2001, television was about to transform the search for fame. Now, stardom could be grasped instantly and the gradual progress of Take That, the Spice Girls and 5ive was, for the moment at least, a thing of the past. The show *Popstars* in 2001 was the game changer. Talent shows, it seemed, hadn't much evolved since the 'good old days' of *Opportunity Knocks* and *New Faces*. But now, after just six weeks, three girls and two boys were chosen by a panel of judges to be the members of a new British band called Hear'Say.

The power of TV was seldom so well illustrated as when their easy-listening single 'Pure and Simple' became the fastest-selling debut record of all time. The attraction of a reality pop show was clear – big ratings and a guaranteed number one hit record with something inoffensive and middle of the road.

The short-lived career of Hear'Say revealed some flaws in the idea. First, you can't have much of a future if the group don't have a connection. Secondly, a mix of boys and girls thins the fan base rather than expands it: far better to have one or the other. When the all-male Take That first disbanded in the nineties, it was the all-female Spice Girls who slipped into the empty chair.

These lessons were soon learned. When the next 'discover a new band' series, *Popstars: The Rivals*, was broadcast in autumn 2002, it was promoted as a rivalry between a boy band and a girl band. The idea was clever and commercially astute – auditions, Bootcamp, judges' visits and live shows would create excitement throughout the series, which ended with the final group of boys going up against the girls to see who would have the Christmas number one.

Looking back, one could be forgiven for not even remembering the name of the winning boy band. They were called

One True Voice, a cheesy name, and fittingly they recorded a saccharine-heavy version of a Bee Gees' song, 'Sacred Trust'. The girls, on the other hand, became Girls Aloud and their single 'Sound of the Underground' was an instant classic. The renowned music critic Alexis Petridis observed, 'It was a reality pop record that didn't make you want to do physical harm to everyone involved in its manufacture.'

Surprisingly, the bookies initially had One True Voice as favourites to be the seasonal number one, but it soon became clear that Girls Aloud would win and step into the shoes recently vacated by the Spice Girls. One True Voice split up within a year, perhaps hinting that there wasn't room for two *Popstars'* bands.

By the time Simon Cowell was putting together an *X Factor* boy band in 2010, Girls Aloud had achieved twenty-one hit singles and Cheryl was on her way to becoming the most successful female solo artist in the UK.

But, just as One True Voice are all but forgotten, so are the all-girl group of also-rans that Simon picked at the same time as the boys who would form One Direction. At this early stage, Belle Amie, as they would become, had every chance of being *the* winning combination. The public would soon have the chance to make known their preference. The four girls were just as surprised to be selected and as enthusiastic as the boys.

The next significant event for the boys was discovering which judge would be their mentor. Simon was handed the groups – again, a fortunate break for the five. They might have stood a better chance of winning with Cheryl or Dannii, but Simon's influence was far-reaching and global, something that would be of huge benefit to Harry's future. It was no coincidence that Simon had been the mentor of Leona Lewis, the biggest act to date to come out of the UK *X Factor*.

The first consideration for the as-yet-unnamed boy band was a discussion about what they were going to wear. Louis Tomlinson, as always, looked immaculate, so they could just copy what he was wearing. Harry needed to ditch the beanie that seemed to be glued to his head. Then they had to measure each other's heights to make sure they would all fit nicely into team photographs and wouldn't have one person disappearing out of shot.

More importantly, they needed to properly get to know one another. Louis was the oldest at eighteen and Harry, at sixteen, was the youngest, so there wasn't a huge age difference. These two teenage boys had got on well from the outset but now the *X Factor* team needed to see if there was any chemistry between all five.

They hit upon the unoriginal plan of the five of them staying together in a house for a week – a chance to bond and to create some footage for when they went to Judges' Houses. Harry told *The X Factor* that his mum's partner, Robin, had a bungalow in the grounds of his house near Congleton. He could check but they could probably have the place to themselves.

The *X Factor* producers liked this idea, so a week or so before Judges' Houses, four teenage boys arrived in Cheshire to see if they would get on. Zayn was the last to arrive, perhaps already a hint that he would be the one to find it the most difficult to blend with the others.

Harry was ready to show them around his home patch. It was like freshers' week at university – slobbing out and making friends before proper work began. Anne and Robin sensibly left the teenage boys to get on with it. The accommodation was a step up from student digs, especially because they had the use of a swimming pool in the garden, which also doubled as a 'jumpers for goalposts' football pitch. Anne popped some sensible food in the fridge but this was ignored in favour of Super Noodles and supplies from the nearest KFC.

The most important aspect of the week was that the boys got to know one another – they were just lads having a laugh. Harry, in particular, had an instant rapport with Louis Tomlinson, who was even more boisterous than him and could break any tension in the room with a jokey remark. He was also the best at football and a lifelong supporter of his hometown team, Doncaster Rovers.

Like Harry, he had been brought up primarily by his mother, Johannah, who split from his father when Louis was just two. He was estranged from his dad throughout his childhood and took the name Tomlinson from her second marriage.

Despite his obvious good looks, Louis wasn't the brooding teenage heartthrob at school, preferring instead to be the class clown. His teenage journey was remarkably similar to Harry's, initially gaining a love of performing through drama and he too was in a school band, playing songs by Oasis and Green Day and generally being more rock-oriented than White Eskimo.

Initially, it looked as if acting might be the way forward for him. His younger twin half-sisters, Phoebe and Daisy, were in demand for roles at a very young age and he would accompany them to various sets, acting as big brother chaperone for the day and earning £30 for sitting around.

Occasionally he would be roped in as an extra, which he found 'super-exciting'.

He was only eleven when he was given one line to say in *Fat Friends*, an ITV drama about a weekly slimming club. Among others, it starred James Corden, who would become one of Harry's best friends in showbusiness. Phoebe and Daisy were cast as babies.

He joined a drama society in Barnsley when he was at Hall Cross school, but could only go when his mum, who everyone called Jay, could afford the fees. He appeared occasionally on television; in 2006, aged fourteen, he was uncredited in the one-off crime drama *If I Had You*, which starred Sarah Parish and Paul McGann. Louis was one of four boys who found a dead body floating in a lake.

More relevantly for his future career, he starred in a production of *Grease* at Hall Cross, dressed all in black in the John Travolta role of Danny Zuko. A high-school musical was probably the best training for being in a boy band and helped to engender a love of performing in the teenage Louis.

He auditioned for *The X Factor* in 2009 but didn't make it past the first producer's assessment. Undaunted, he had another go the following year and offered something extra to the new group, even if he was arguably the weakest singer. After performing 'Hey There Delilah' by Plain White T's at his live audition he said simply, 'I sang terribly.'

The one potential hurdle for the new band was that Louis and Liam did not get on. They had very different personalities. Louis was bumptious and Liam was more serious, aware that this was his big chance – the others would joke that he was the dad of the band. He acknowledged, 'I was a bit too grown up. I needed to grow down.' He also didn't have any crazy mates – all his friends were quiet, so being with a group of rowdy boys was a jolt.

Liam nearly had a career as an athlete. He was a member of his local Wolverhampton and Bilston Athletic Club and, as a boy, would run five miles before school. He might have ditched performing altogether if he had been selected for the England national schools' team.

That disappointment encouraged him to move from karaoke to stage productions and he joined a local theatre group for which he dressed all in white to play the John Travolta starring role of Tony Romero in *Saturday Night Fever*. His career was already the most advanced of the newly formed boy band – he had sung in front of the crowd at Molyneux before a Wolves' home game against Manchester United.

Liam had also come close to progressing in a previous *X Factor* series, and he was determined not to squander the opportunity this time round. In 2008 he made it to Judges' Houses in Barbados, having just turned fifteen. He wasn't chosen for the Live Shows, but Simon had suggested he try again in two years' time.

Liam was installed as one of the favourites for the whole competition after his 2010 audition when he sang the Michael Bublé version of the old standard 'Cry Me a River' and Simon had stood up to applaud. But, like Harry, he should have steered well clear of a Liam Gallagher song at Bootcamp.

The problem going forward for the new band was that both Louis and Liam wanted to be its leader. The two came to an unwritten understanding that they would keep that animosity within the group and not let on to potential fans or Simon.

Liam, however, revealed, 'We absolutely hated each other. It was so funny. Really bad. We hid it well.'

At least the lads were all keen on sport – Liam was talented at running and boxing; Zayn, too, was a decent boxer; Louis was the man for football; Niall was pretty good at football but golf was his game. Harry would have had no competition from the others on the badminton court.

Aside from the high spirits of a free holiday, the new band needed to rehearse for their trip to Judges' Houses and that presented yet another problem: how to decide who would sing each part. That 'cut-throat decision' was too difficult at this early stage and so, to start with, they sang each number in unison. 'It was a horrible thing,' said Liam.

They managed to come up with a name they all liked. Harry suggested One Direction because they were all heading in one direction. Someone else came up with USP and another idea was Status Single. Fortunately these alternatives were quickly put in the bin and One Direction was born. It just stuck, so if nothing else came of it, at least they had a good name.

The reality had yet to sink in that at some point soon they would have to impress Simon Cowell – that would be make or break.

5

TORN

———

They hadn't actually performed one song together but the newly named One Direction were swanning around by yet another swimming pool, this time in the sun-drenched resort of Marbella, in Southern Spain. For the moment, *The X Factor* seemed to be nothing more than a summer camp.

Even Liam and Louis were putting on a united front, realising the opportunity they had been given depended on them being 'all for one, one for all'. In the short term, they were told by the producers to prepare an acoustic version of 'Torn', one of the biggest hits of the nineties. Originally the song was written and recorded by the Californian rock band Ednaswap, but it became a million-seller after it was released as a single in 1997 by former *Neighbours* star Natalie Imbruglia.

The general public were used to 'Torn' being sung by a female singer, so it would offer something different to hear it performed by a boy band. The rehearsals hadn't gone smoothly because Louis had been stung by a sea urchin when they were splashing around by the beach, so he was in casualty while the other four practised in the villa grounds.

Louis was trying not to grimace with pain when, nursing a red and swollen foot, he joined the others to sing in front of Simon and his usual guest judge, Sinitta, who was looking fabulous. Louis was hardly needed because, in effect, it was the Harry show, as the 'natural frontman'.

Liam sang two verses before Harry, wearing the same lucky audition white t-shirt and scarf, took over for the rest of the song, with some background oohs from the others and a sweet harmony from Zayn. Afterwards Simon said, 'See you later,' and had a chat with Sinitta. They agreed the boys were cool, although Simon thought they were a 'little bit timid'.

That was just for the television filming. In reality, he was already seeing the pound signs where One Direction was concerned. As soon as the cameras were switched off, he sprang up and declared, 'These guys are incredible!' In reality, he had taken 'one-millionth' of a second to realise that this was the group he would be backing – and not just for the next week or two.

Back on television he cranked up the tension by declaring that it was a tough choice: 'My head is saying it's a risk and my heart is saying you deserve a shot.' It was no surprise whatsoever when he concluded, 'Guys, I've gone with my heart – you're through!'

Once more there was a gap between Judges' Houses and the beginning of the live finals, when it was practically impossible for Harry to conceal his excitement. He stopped using Facebook, kept a low profile in Holmes Chapel and ventured out just to go to Manchester to shop for clothes. He had to borrow some money from his mum to brighten up his wardrobe for what he hoped would be a much longer stay in London.

He opted for his favourite well-known brands, including Topman, Hollister and Jack Wills, responsible for his much-worn purple hoodie. Alison Jane Reid was unimpressed: 'I wouldn't call the purple Jack Wills hoodie stylish. It screams, "I am a Jack Wills hoodie!" It's loud. It's the logo uniform of teenagers obsessed with consumerist status symbols. The most interesting thing is that Harry chose to wear it in purple. That's daring. It shows already his love of experimentation with fashion and desire to stand out through the choices he makes.'

At sixteen, Harry was yet to be inducted into the fashion world, but there was already an adventurous edge to what he chose to wear. That was evident when he paraded around the latest *X Factor* house wearing nothing but a gold leopard-print thong that a friend had given him for his birthday back in Holmes Chapel.

Apparently, Harry would have considered the thong being overdressed, often lounging around the house naked if he felt like it. He explained, 'Stripping off is very liberating. I feel free. It's always a spur of the moment thing, but no one seemed to mind.'

Perhaps Harry was fortunate that nobody cared. Ten years on and it would only take one complaint for his stock to fall rapidly – from cheeky, mischievous chap to weird perv who would flash his bits in front of the telly. The actor John Barrowman was axed in 2021 as a judge on *Dancing on Ice* when allegations surfaced of him flashing numerous times on the set of *Doctor Who* and *Torchwood*. He called it 'tomfoolery'.

That excuse doesn't wear so well when you are a middle-aged man, but it's ok to be high-spirited at sixteen.

Fortunately for Harry, everyone realised he was just a scamp of a teenager having a laugh. He volunteered, 'I think Mary secretly liked it.'

The Mary in question was the Irish singer Mary Byrne, the Tesco check-out cashier who made it to *The X Factor* finals at the age of fifty. She and Harry became great friends and she really didn't mind her daily eyeful. She recalled, 'Every morning One Direction would come into the studio where we rehearsed and they always gave me a kiss. But Harry went further, he'd moon at me, the cheeky little boy! And it wasn't as if I wanted to see his bottom – it's just like a baby's bottom.'

The studio Mary mentions was a large room in the house that was given over to musical practice. The boys spent most of their time in the 'bean bag' room, their name for the relax-ation area, the common room of the house where they could play table tennis or Nintendo Wii.

So far, the *X Factor* experience seemed to be moving from one slice of five-star accommodation to the next. The 2010 mansion was a stunning Spanish-style villa with seven bedrooms close to Borehamwood, just north of London. The previous year had been a nightmare for neighbours when the house between Hampstead and Golders Green was mobbed daily by excited fans of the show and its contestants.

The teenage boys of One Direction did not seem to appre-ciate their luxurious surroundings, complaining that they had to share the smallest room. The producers gave them a list of rules, which they promptly put in the bin. The first was to keep their room tidy, which was never going to happen with five teenage lads. If you lifted up a t-shirt casually scrunched up and thrown onto the floor, you were more than likely to find the remains of the previous night's takeaway. Nobody bothered making a bed.

The former *Blue Peter* host Konnie Huq, who this year had taken over from Holly Willoughby to present the companion show *The Xtra Factor*, described it simply as a 'pigsty'. The girls from Belle Amie, who had also made it through to the Live Finals, gamely tried to tidy it a little but had to give up. At least they didn't have to share a bathroom with the boys. That room was almost as bad and made public conveniences seem like four-star luxury. Liam, in particular, said he found it hard sharing with the others, especially as his old enemy Louis was the messiest.

The biggest drawback regarding the room, however, was Harry's snoring; the others would complain and tell him to shut up – with little success.

The theme of the first live show at the Fountain Studios, Wembley, in October 2010 was Number Ones. The producers in consultation with Simon handed One Direction the multiple Grammy Award-winning 'Viva la Vida', the 2008 classic from Coldplay. The track is not a simplistic Spanish holiday song – 'Long Live Life' – but a title inspired by the great Mexican painter Frida Kahlo.

Her 1954 work 'Viva la Vida' was her last painting before her death that year, aged forty-seven. It depicts watermelons in various shapes and shades of green, symbolising perhaps the passing of time in one's life. Frida had spent a lifetime dealing with chronic physical pain – a result of childhood polio and a crippling bus accident at the age of eighteen. She was in rapidly declining health after having a leg amputated. She scrawled 'Viva la vida' on the flesh of one of the melons.

The significance of the painting was not lost on the accomplished songwriters of Coldplay, a group that had long been one of Harry's favourites. They used it as a starting point for their own reflections on the passage of time and the ending of life. From the point of view of lyrics, it's not an easy song to learn. There are just so many lines.

One Direction knuckled down under the guidance of Texas-born vocal producer Savan Kotecha, who would play a leading role in their musical development, especially as a songwriter. They were the second group on and Harry had little to do this time, other than sing the chorus and thrust his shoulder provocatively at the audience, for some reason.

Most importantly, and this was true of any week, they needed to stay in the competition. They were never going to win. Within a couple of weeks, it was clear that Matt Cardle was miles ahead. He was always a commanding favourite with the bookies and would come first in eleven out of twelve public votes across the series. The only week when he did not receive the highest number of public votes was the very first one, when Mary Byrne won after singing 'It's a Man's Man's Man's World'. Her victory was perhaps a mirror image of the support for Susan Boyle in the previous year's *Britain's Got Talent* – a vote for the middle-aged female singer. Like Susan, Mary – with her hard-working and humble background – was a great story.

Simon had seen and heard enough from young girl fans to believe his gut instinct about One Direction had been entirely correct. He also confided to Konnie Huq that Harry was his favourite member of the group: 'I'm drawn to him. I just think he gets it. He is charming and the easiest to talk to.'

The young man himself wasn't feeling too charming the following week when he felt ill as they were preparing for their sound check. They were due to perform Kelly Clarkson's 'My Life Would Suck Without You'. Nobody was sure at first if it was something he ate or just what is simplistically known as stage fright. He would later reveal that it was chronic anxiety brought on by being constantly scared he would sing a wrong note: 'I felt so much weight in terms of not getting anything wrong. I felt like if I'd sung I would have been sick.' He had to take time out and go back to the *X Factor* house to relax and eventually be given the all-clear by the show's medical advisors.

Savan revealed that everyone was worried about him but that it turned out to be an attack of nerves. In the end he coped well, although once again he didn't have any solo lines. A pattern seemed to have been established that Liam would sing the opening verse – rather like Shane Filan in Westlife – before the others came in. For this song, Zayn was the other soloist, so Harry only had to belt out the catchy chorus.

The audition scruffiness had completely disappeared. Each of the boys now had an immaculate haircut styled by Adam Reed, as well as clothes that better suited them. On a television show like *The X Factor*, how you looked was just as important as how you sounded, at least in the beginning rounds.

Their look impressed Cheryl, now happily restored to good health after her bout of malaria, who said, 'I can't even cope with how cute you are.' Simon Cowell was delighted, claiming pompously, 'You are the most exciting pop band in the country today,' which was not exactly what the remaining groups wanted to hear, especially as both Diva Fever and Belle Amie were in the bottom two, with the former going home.

The third week took in the orchestrated hysteria of a trip to Topshop in Oxford Street where hordes of girls shouted 'I love you' at them. During the show, they sang 'Nobody Knows' by Pink, a ballad that brought Harry more to the fore with a solo, although once again the trusted formula of Liam beginning the lead vocal worked well. The judges were enthusiastic and Cheryl declared the band was 'her guilty pleasure'. A few years later, in 2017, she would give birth to Liam's son, Bear.

More significantly, Louis Tomlinson revealed a significant characteristic of Harry that could easily have been ignored in the context of boys having a laugh. He knew when to work and when to play. 'He knows where the line is,' said Louis.

Unsurprisingly, the media ran stories about possible flings between contestants. Harry was linked with Cher Lloyd, arguably the most interesting and individual of the acts that season. Harry put their friendship into perspective: 'If anyone talks to anyone on *The X Factor* they are immediately dating.'

Matt Cardle, still readily winning the series, was reported to have been caught in bed with singer Katie Waissel. He was far from delighted at the stories, although such unfounded rumours generated more publicity for the show. Zayn, meanwhile, was said to be dating Geneva Lane, one of the members of Belle Amie. Niall faced rumours about him and another member of that girl group, Sophie Hardman.

Harry would have to get used to rumours of romances, true and false, as interest in the group grew. Time was up, however, for Belle Amie, who didn't make it past Halloween-themed week four. Their exit left One Direction as the only group standing. That suited Simon Cowell, who could then focus completely on their development.

Belle Amie were not happy at the lack of attention they had received. Sophie observed, 'You could put the boys out there in bin bags and sing "Baa Baa Black Sheep" and they'd go through with flying colours.'

Even Louis Walsh noticed that Simon had all but abandoned the girls. He told them, 'You've got a problem because you're on your own in this competition.' The other issue for the girls was that they didn't really get on. The show's stylist, Grace Woodward, observed, 'I feel Belle Amie are pulling in different directions. They are four solo girls and I am not sure they have gelled well enough.'

It was the Hear'Say scenario repeating itself. Matt Cardle noticed it and predicted they would split up within a few months because they 'simply do not get on well enough'. He was right – Geneva left the group after Christmas.

Fortunately, that was not going to happen to One Direction anytime soon, although there was an ironic reminder for Harry that he had actually abandoned his first group, White Eskimo; he suggested 1D sing 'Summer of '69' in the quarter-finals. *The X Factor* was no Battle of the Bands, but they performed it slickly and exuberantly, more in the style of *Glee* than Green Day. The noise from the audience was deafening. Simon pointed out that the choice had been Harry's idea, just another hint that the youngest member of the group was the 'natural frontman'.

Their second choice that night was the wonderfully soppy Joe Cocker classic 'You Are So Beautiful', a performance that revealed how much they had improved vocally during the weeks on the show thanks to some rigorous coaching. Their performance followed the established order of Liam leading, Zayn singing a solo and Harry doing the same. Perhaps a song with 'beautiful' in the title might work for the band in the future, if they secured a record deal.

More immediately, Harry topped the UK charts for the first time when the contestants joined together to record the *X Factor*'s annual charity single. This year it was a version of David Bowie's evocative 'Heroes'. Sales would benefit Help for Heroes, which provides lifelong support for military personnel bearing the scars of war and had already raised more than £70 million for wounded soldiers since it was set up in 2007.

The song was recorded while Belle Amie were still on the show, so at least they shared in the kudos of its success. Sales in the first week alone topped 144,000 copies. Matt Cardle and Rebecca Ferguson had the key roles singing the opening, revealing the producers knew back in October that they were the two who would be the frontrunners in the whole competition.

Harry had one line – 'Nothing could keep us together' – and would have been pleased not to have 'got anything wrong', but the most striking aspect of the collective performance was how good they all were. They had outstanding voices; Aiden Grimshaw, Treyc Cohen and Paije Richardson were just three of the finalists who demonstrated that it was a very thin line between success and failure on the show.

* * *

Holmes Chapel had never seen anything like it. Hundreds of screaming young fans gathered outside Harry's house in London Road, shouting 'Harry, Harry, Harry', hoping to catch a glimpse of their local hero. What a change it was from earlier in the year when they could have caught him shuffling along the street to school or to and from work. They could have queued behind him in the Chinese take-away, but those days were gone forever now that he was a bonafide pop star on the telly.

He rolled up to the front door in a limousine with blacked-out windows. Niall, Liam, Louis and Zayn were with him and they signed autographs while Harry gave his mum the biggest hug under a homemade banner that declared, 'One Direction to the Final'. He said all the right things to the press: 'I can't believe the number of people outside. It's amazing. Every week we are in total disbelief that we have got through.'

The group found time to make a 'surprise' visit to the W. Mandeville bakery. Security had already checked that it was safe for the five boys to enter unseen and be filmed. They chatted to Simon Wakefield who had made his special brunch pasties just for them.

For the final, the producers played it very safe with One Direction. First, they sang 'Your Song', which is about as daring a choice as 'Isn't She Lovely'. Liam and Harry had the solo verses and made no mistakes, but it did seem a pity to perform another Elton song. He had been the theme of the show just four weeks earlier when they had chosen the schmaltzy 'Something About the Way You Look Tonight'.

More excitingly their star duet was with Robbie Williams, until then the ultimate example of a successful solo career after boy-band fame, at least in the UK. Robbie is almost exactly twenty years older than Harry and was also sixteen when he joined Take That as their youngest member. He walked on after Liam and Harry had sung the opening verses of his number one 'She's the One' and looked a million dollars. Robbie is a big bloke and his stage presence did make the boys appear like the teenagers they were, but it was a performance to bring a smile to the faces of the most cynical. The boys themselves were clearly delighted and Simon confirmed that 'it was the night of their lives'.

The noise in the theatre was completely deafening, especially when Dermot spoke to Harry, who was centre stage in an elegant purple suit that was a step up from his hoodie. Intriguingly, Robbie has always employed a slight mid-Atlantic twang to his singing voice – a characteristic that might suit Harry looking forward. With hindsight, the song would have better complemented the sweeter, clearer tones of Zayn, but One Direction still made the final three, alongside Matt and Rebecca, who remained firm favourites, in that order. Afterwards Robbie advised them to be nice to everyone they meet and to stay away from drugs.

The following night was their final performance and they sang 'Torn', which, again, was unadventurous as the audience had already seen them sing that at Judges' Houses. Apparently the boys were particularly keen to revisit the song, but it seemed lightweight alongside Matt Cardle's interpretation of Katy Perry's 'Firework' and Rebecca doing her best Annie Lennox for 'Sweet Dreams (Are Made of This)'. Despite the noisy appreciation of One Direction from the live audience, they only received half the votes that Matt did.

One Direction were eliminated and so forfeited the chance to perform their 'winner's song', a quite obscure eighties' track called 'Forever Young' by the German synth band Alphaville. That was a pity as its anthemic quality suited them and became an enduring favourite during their future concerts.

Matt won, unsurprisingly, and his song 'When We Collide' would be UK number one in the blink of an eye. Although they never placed higher than third on any show, the boys could not contain their disappointment. It's the nature of competition that you always think you have a chance of beating Usain Bolt if you are in the race.

This seventh season was *The X Factor*'s finest hour. More than 17.7 million viewers switched on for the final alone, making it the most-watched TV show of the year. The following year the figure for the final, won by Little Mix, had slumped to a little over 12 million. That may have had something to do with Simon, Cheryl and Dannii taking a break from judging duties.

The rumours had been flying around that Simon planned to sign One Direction to his Syco label, now part of the Sony group. They were true. After the show had finished and before everyone gathered for the afterparty, he told the boys the good news. The deal was reputed to be worth £1 million, or some said £2 million – although that's a figure that makes an enticing headline. In reality, he had given each of them an early Christmas present of £8,000. The only downside was that the contract wouldn't be confirmed until the morning.

Harry was in tears but couldn't share the happy news, not even with his mum and Robin, who were there to support him on the night. He acknowledged, 'If this works out, it's going to totally change my life.'

6

NUMBER ONE
DIRECTION

Harry realised he had arrived when the Jack Wills store in Covent Garden rang up and asked if he would like to wear one of their t-shirts on *The X Factor*. 'I'll be in tomorrow,' said Harry, chuffed to bits. It was the first time he had been asked to wear anything, although it would not be long before designers were queuing up to invite him to model their latest creations. His life as a celebrity was beginning.

Part of the *X Factor* journey is turning unknowns into celebrities by taking them out into the world. One week One Direction would be at the Pride of Britain Awards at the Grosvenor House Hotel in Park Lane, the next being interviewed on the red carpet at the premiere of *Harry Potter and the Deathly Hallows: Part 1* at the iconic Odeon, Leicester Square.

Interest in them did not wane when the show was over. In fact, the opposite was true, as the band was surrounded by mounting hysteria wherever they went. Ronan Keating couldn't believe his eyes when he arrived at Heathrow Airport on a flight from Los Angeles and was greeted by hundreds of screaming young girl fans. It was pandemonium. They weren't there for the Boyzone heartthrob, though. He observed wistfully, 'Sadly not for me. Ha ha! One Direction were on the flight ... Those were the days.'

To be fair to Ronan, Boyzone had been a huge boy band in the nineties and he had become part of the group at sixteen, the same age as Harry when he joined 1D. He had watched fellow Irish band Westlife overtake him in the fast lane, and now it was the turn of the next big thing. He was only thirty-three but a veteran in pop terms.

Ronan had been in the States to record with the legendary Burt Bacharach. One Direction was there to shake hands, be sociable and introduce themselves to those who might be important to them as Simon Cowell prepared to launch their US career. He wanted them to meet top songwriters and producers and spread the word that they were in the market for a substantial record deal in the States.

Christmas had been a quiet time for Harry back in Cheshire, a chance to recharge batteries and spend some quality time with his family. He caught up with old buddies including Will and Nick, but was disappointed to discover some friends treated him differently, perhaps simply jealous or waiting for him to act superior. One disgruntled classmate described him as an 'arrogant prick'.

After that rural interlude, visiting Los Angeles for the first time was exciting. They stayed at the W Hotel in West Beverly Hills, conveniently close to the fashionable boutiques of Rodeo Drive. They were driven a couple of miles away for a photo opportunity at The Grove, the scenic Hollywood shopping precinct in Fairfax District, which, at the time, boasted an Abercrombie & Fitch flagship store. That suited Harry, who still loved a t-shirt with a logo on it. He raced around like a child in the candy store at Christmas. Louis joked that he had bought every t-shirt in the place. Harry did sheepishly admit that he had grabbed quite a few.

More significantly for the future, they were introduced to some key people in their recording future. Producers could listen to them in the studio and form some ideas of how they might sound for the vital first record. The weeks were about to pass very quickly so plans needed to be made early.

They laid down some early tracks with some of the current Swedish kings of chart music. Leading producers including RedOne, Carl Falk and Rami Yacoub were much in demand, dividing their time between LA and Stockholm. They had developed their expertise in the footsteps of Max Martin, the grandmaster of Swedish pop. Rami, for instance, had worked with Max at his Cheiron Studios in Stockholm on some of the best-known hits of recent years, including '… Baby One More Time' and 'Oops! … I Did it Again' for Britney Spears and many songs for Backstreet Boys and Westlife.

One Direction had dinner with Max and he was happy to pass on some tips. They met up with Cher Lloyd, who had also been shipped off to LA to make a start on her album. She was photographed strolling around The Grove with the boys. Harry was sporting a newly purchased polo shirt with the A&C logo. For a while Cher's career progressed in tandem with One Direction as she too was working with RedOne and other Swedish producers including Shellback and Savan Kotecha from *The X Factor*, who was a well-respected song-writer in his own right.

Quite clearly, the plan was to start One Direction at the very top. Time was blocked off in their diary to travel to Stockholm, to work more seriously on their debut album. The first commitment, however, was back in the UK for the annual *X Factor* tour. This was a Simon Cowell money-spinning exercise that was expected to raise upwards of £10 million by the time merchandise and all the spin-offs were added to ticket sales.

They didn't have long to rehearse before the opening night at Birmingham's LG Arena in February. Fortunately, they had already learned their set during the *X Factor* series: Rihanna's 'Only Girl (in the World)'; the elegiac classic 'Chasing Cars' by Snow Patrol; 'Kids in America', the Kim Wilde oldie from 1981; Kelly Clarkson's 'My Life Would Suck Without You'; and finally 'Forever Young', the winner's song they didn't have the chance to perform in the final. They were allotted five songs, the same as the actual winner Matt Cardle.

The front of the programme featured prominently the four acts that Simon Cowell had signed to Syco. He may have envisaged One Direction as the potential superstars, but he had taken the precaution of also giving contracts to Cher Lloyd, Matt Cardle and Rebecca Ferguson, who were pictured across the top with the five members of One Direction occupying the next row. Harry was in the middle.

The reviews of the tour were very mixed, although the *Belfast Telegraph* noted that One Direction was the 'young boy band with a big future'. The *Independent* described their reception from the audience as 'supersonic'.

When the show reached Wembley Arena, the *Guardian* critic Michael Cragg was perhaps not entirely empathetic with the thousands of young girls who were only there to shout, scream and swoon at One Direction. He observed, 'The noise levels go beyond human hearing capabilities for One Direction, an old-school boy band who only ever seem to harmonise by accident.' He was complimentary about Cher, Rebecca and Aidan Grimshaw, with whom Harry had always got on well; this was their last chance to catch up before they took very different career paths. Matt closed the show and Michael suggested pessimistically that Matt should 'enjoy it while it lasts'.

The nine acts returned to the stage to perform their charity number one, 'Heroes'. By the end of the year One Direction would have eclipsed them all.

When the tour ended at the Motorpoint Arena in Cardiff in mid-April, there was a week for a short break before recording the first album would begin in earnest. Harry went skiing with Louis and a couple of mates to Courchevel, in the French Alps. He hadn't skied before so he relied on his bandmate to help with basic technique – namely not falling over and breaking a leg.

Harry and Louis were the closest among the five members of One Direction. It helped that their mums had become firm friends as they watched their sons achieve fame so quickly. Both Anne and Jay combined to create a public platform to promote the causes about which they felt most strongly.

The boys also decided to share a luxury apartment in the suburb of Friern Barnet, just north of London. They moved into a flat in Princess Park Manor, named in honour of Princess Diana, which was home to many pop stars and footballers over the years. Simon Cowell's company, Syco, had a deal with the property developers that he could house his artists in the building that had been converted from a Victorian mental hospital. The rent was £5,000 a month.

The advantage of the secure location was that celebrities could come and go without having the prying lenses of paparazzi snapping them every time they went for a swim or popped to the tennis courts. The other three boys also moved into the Manor, but the luxury complex is so big that you might never meet another tenant.

Louis and Harry's new home used to be occupied by the England footballer Ashley Cole, who lived there while his eventual wife, *X Factor* judge Cheryl, shared another flat with Girls Aloud bandmate Nicola Roberts. By chance Ashley had spotted Cheryl when she walked by one day when he was visiting a friend in another apartment. She recalled, 'I walked past and he shouted, "Hey hot lips." I hate stuff like that so I rolled my eyes and was like, "Piss off."' It was a start. That opener from Ashley, though, was not in the Harry Styles dictionary of chat-up lines.

Living with Louis was an early indication that Harry much preferred sharing with other people than being on his own. For the moment he had to fly out to Stockholm to begin serious work on their debut album. Harry stood out when they started recording at the Kinglet Studios in Stockholm; not because he was a better singer than the others, he was just different. Carl Falk explained, 'He's got a very raspy voice. It's a good compliment to have to some of the others who are a bit more "clean". Harry brings a raspy, raw character to the recording process.'

Carl had nothing but praise for the band's work ethic, each of whom were taking everything very seriously. He reflected, 'They listen to what we say and our suggestions and there's never been an argument or any bullshit with them.'

The very first track they worked on was one that Savan Kotecha had brought in. Harry was in no doubt when he heard the early demo that it was perfect for their debut single. He sent Savan a text message that read simply, 'I think you got it. I think you got the one here.' He was right: 'What Makes You Beautiful' was perfect – the sweet sentiments of a romantic ballad dressed up in an infectious danceable rhythm. Savan was so chuffed he kept the text.

He had first thought of the catchy melody the previous year but needed inspiration for the lyrics. That came unexpectedly one day when he and his wife were staying at the five-star Royal Garden Hotel, close to Hyde Park. He was in the bathroom when he heard his Swedish wife, Anna Gustavsson, complaining that she felt so ugly that morning.

He shouted out, 'No you're not!' and had a lightbulb moment that he later explained, 'I was thinking "Wow, one of the great things about you is that you don't know how beautiful you are and that's what makes you beautiful."' He wrote the thought down before he left to go to the studio and shared it with Carl and Rami, as well as the original melody to the line, 'Baby you light up my world like nobody else.' It's easy to see how romantic old Harry would love the sentiment.

Both Carl and Rami loved it too, not just a 'beautiful' title but a 'really smart concept' that teenagers would appreciate. They set about finding the right sound for One Direction – an updated version of the original Swedish melodies of the nineties that had provided huge hits for the Backstreet Boys, NSYNC and Britney.

They were concerned, however, that the music that had been so popular in that decade would appear dated for a new generation, so they ditched the synths and pianos and replaced them with good old-fashioned guitars. They weren't looking to make Eric Clapton or Jimmy Page jealous, however. Carl Falk explained, 'The guitar riff had to be so simple that my friend's fifteen-year-old daughter could play it and put her cover up on YouTube.'

Their strategy worked perfectly with 'What Makes You Beautiful'. The two-finger guitar intro was copied in a million bedrooms. The trio of Swedish maestros crafted three songs for the album. As well as the first composition, they co-wrote and produced 'I Wish' and 'One Thing', which was originally two songs – one had a good verse, the other a winning chorus. They merged them together. Carl thought it was actually a better song than 'What Makes You Beautiful'.

When Roisin O'Connor, the *Independent*'s music writer, ranked all ninety-six songs in the 1D catalogue, she placed 'One Thing' at number five, by far the highest position of any track from the first album. She called it a 'preppier version' of 'I Want It That Way', which was no bad thing as the Backstreet Boys' signature song reached number one all around the world, including in the UK, in 1999.

The *X Factor* shows and subsequent tour did not prepare One Direction for life in the studio. Carl observed, 'They were searching for themselves.' Despite being the most affected by pre-stage nerves, Harry was brimming with confidence in the recording booth. He was up for anything and they could have just recorded him, which would have ruined the concept of a boy band. The most important thing was that they were all willing to learn and improve.

Sweden did not have a monopoly on the album, although RedOne also contributed two tracks. Harry was keen to involve other songwriters to prevent the album from becoming too samey. He asked Ed Sheeran if he had any songs he wanted to put up. They had been introduced by one of Ed's collaborators, the guitarist Chris Leonard. As ever, Ed was always happy to write songs for other acts. He always had songs. He enjoyed a process that improved his profile in the days before he became a one-man pop juggernaut.

Ed popped in to see Tyler Brown, then head of A&R at Syco, and left some tracks for consideration. They included a song called 'Moments' that he had written some time before with another collaborator, Si Hulbert, who was horrified when Ed told him he had included it: 'It was probably the shoddiest demo I had ever done with him if I'm honest. It actually started off as a drum and bass track.'

Ed was busy with promotion when Tyler emailed to say they wanted it. He also suggested how it could be reworked. Si recalled, 'Basically I totally changed it into a boy band sort of epic ballad.' One concern Si had was whether the content was suitable for a boy band. 'Moments' was actually inspired by the sad death, aged fifteen, of his younger sister. The poign-ant lyric is about missing her: 'If I could only have this life for one more day.'

Si once asked Ed Sheeran if One Direction knew what the song was about and he replied that he didn't think so. It didn't matter because it was a track that you could relate to personally in different ways. 'If you are a fourteen-year-old girl, it's about losing your boyfriend.'

As was customary, Liam sang the opening solo. His voice suited songs that began in a lower register. Harry would then provide a striking contrast, singing the bridge into the often anthemic chorus. 'Moments' did not make the final listing on the album but was a bonus track and available on deluxe editions worldwide. Louis, whose solo was particularly melancholic, said it was by far his favourite track on their first album. The song is also one of the most cherished among devoted One Direction fans, performed by the boys on all three of their world tours.

That would be in the future, though. The next task in this year's masterplan was making the video for 'What Makes You Beautiful'. So they literally flew in and out of Los Angeles to film on the beautiful beach in Malibu. The director was John Urbano, who didn't have a long history of pop videos but had already been chosen as the photographer for their first album cover. The result was an impressive depiction of the sheer energy and vitality of One Direction.

The video was more of the same – a three-minute frolic splashing about in the waves with three lovely young women. Harry, in particular, turned on the megawatt charm for one of them, aspiring actress and model Madison McMillin. Days out filming pop videos were just part of trying to get ahead for someone like Madison. She was like the girl next door, not dissimilar to Jennifer Aniston in *Friends* and, as such, more relatable to the thousands of teenage girls who dreamt of being serenaded by Harry Styles.

At least the actress didn't suggest there was anything between her and Harry. That innuendo was left to Alan Carr when the boys appeared on his television show *Chatty Man*, at the start of their promotional campaign for the single. Harry had mumbled that the girls in the video were 'lovely', whereupon a picture of Madison appeared behind him and Alan asked, 'So Harry, what happened between you and Madison? Did you take a trip down Madison Avenue?' Everyone laughed at the joke, which Madison must have heard a thousand times and more.

The band was always asked about girls, literally in every interview from the very first one on *The Alan Titchmarsh Show*, an affable afternoon chat on ITV. In the recent past, the strategy was always to make sure the fan base thought the boy band was available. Take That, for example, had to smuggle their secret girlfriends into hotels when they were touring.

Simon Cowell appeared completely relaxed about girls as far as One Direction was concerned. He declared that he was not a Svengali-type figure lecturing the boys on what they could or could not do: 'If I were their age in this group, I'd want to have a good time.' He also confirmed that all the boys liked girls.

That sounded good when it was banter about Madison or when Harry pointed out that his dream girl was Frankie Sandford of The Saturdays, who was twenty-one and gamely played along by suggesting she would date him if he was older.

At this stage, nobody had taken seriously Harry's actual preference for older women. While he was happy to embrace some light-hearted larks, he kept completely quiet about a real fling he was having. The woman in question was married, fourteen years his senior and a popular radio personality.

He met Lucy Horobin when the band popped in for a promotional chat at the Key 103 Radio station in Manchester. While she played the record, he flirted in Harry fashion, held his heart and mouthed 'I love you' to her. They kept in touch on social media and by text and met up again when he was back in Manchester in September.

Lucy is a brunette with a winning smile, rather reminiscent of Harry's mum. She didn't breathe a word about their relationship, and neither did he. The world would never have known that they hooked up again after an Ed Sheeran concert if it hadn't been for her estranged husband spilling the beans to a tabloid newspaper the following summer.

By the end of 2011, however, Harry had embarked on something more serious with a more famous broadcaster, born the same year as Lucy. The relationship would become his most notorious and one that was forever tinged with sadness.

PART TWO

HARRY & CO.

7

AN INNOCENT
RELATIONSHIP

───────

When Harry was snapped by paparazzi leaving Caroline Flack's North London home on a wintry morning in early December 2011, it would change his life – and hers – forever. Until then, his blossoming relationship with the new host of *The Xtra Factor* had been the subject of light tittle-tattle in the newspapers but now it faced the full glare of vitriolic opinion.

Harry had first flirted with the popular television personality back in August when he told the official *X Factor* website, 'If Caroline Flack is reading this, say "Hi" from me. She is gorgeous.' Subsequently, he enlisted the help of one of the producers to send DM messages on Twitter to Caroline, letting her know that he was up for a date.

She was flattered and amused in equal measure. Harry was seventeen and she was thirty-one, three weeks older than Lucy Horobin. The age gap bothered neither of them. In her autobiography, *Storm in a C Cup*, Caroline memorably described him as 'a man/boy with a captivating smile who got what he wanted'.

Like Harry, Caroline, or Carrie as her family called her, was brought up in rural surroundings. Although she and her twin sister, Jo, were born in Enfield, they moved to the quiet village of Great Hocking, in Norfolk, aged four when her father was promoted to a management job with Coca-Cola that gave him responsibility for the whole of the county.

They moved again when Caroline was seven, to the more remote village of East Wretham, to the north of Thetford Forest. They were a family of six and needed more space. Caroline and Jo had an elder brother and sister, Paul and Elizabeth. The setting for their new home was an idyllic slice of Breckland landscape, but Caroline dreamed of a life on the stage.

She was very petite and slim as a child and her 'absolute idol' was Kylie Minogue. The twins would be glued to the telly every night watching *Neighbours* after getting in from school. Later on, their party piece was singing 'Especially for You' in the lounge, when Caroline played Kylie and Jo was Jason Donovan.

Caroline went to secondary school in Watton, ten miles away. She thought the market town was a dump, was excruciatingly bored and couldn't wait to get away. Salvation came when her childhood dance classes paid off and she was given a bursary to attend the Bodywork Dance School in Cambridge. She was there from the age of seventeen until she was twenty.

Moving to London, she was working at the Medicine Bar in Islington when she made her movie debut playing a tiny role in a made-for-TV film called, ironically, *Is Harry on the Boat?* This is an obscure cockney rhyming slang reference to spunk on the face – Harry Monk, Boat Race. Caroline, and the majority of those who saw the comedy-drama about holiday reps, had no idea that was the meaning.

Caroline's character didn't have a name. She was just on the cast list as 'Blonde'. The film wasn't porn in the slightest, although she did have to go topless. Blink and you miss her in a scene with the star, Danny Dyer. The big plus was a week's filming in Ibiza.

Her moment on screen did not lead to a flood of offers. Instead, she won a role alongside Leigh Francis in his ribald sketch show *Bo' Selecta!* In the days before he rebranded himself as Keith Lemon, Leigh would dress up as various pop stars and indulge in some outrageous behaviour. When he pretended to be Michael Jackson, Caroline was his glamorous assistant Bubbles, in a low-cut top and shorts, an outfit the tabloids would describe as 'raunchy'.

The show hasn't aged well and Leigh would later apologise for his portrayal of black people, calling it 'offensive'. Caroline called him a mentor and a friend, 'He is gentle, supportive and honest. He watches everything I do and will say if I was brilliant or not too good. Leigh is the opposite of what he's like when he's in character, which is really ballsy.'

To a certain extent that was true of Caroline herself as she moved up the television ladder, improving her profile presenting shows including a revival of the hit eighties' series *Gladiators* and *Big Brother's Big Mouth*. Her biggest show was *I'm a Celebrity, Get Me Out of Here! NOW!*, the companion to the Ant and Dec's ratings blockbuster *I'm a Celebrity, Get Me Out of Here!*, probably the only one that could rival the popularity of *The X Factor*.

The annual trip to New South Wales was a dream job for any presenter – escaping the British winter and not having to engage in any Bushtucker Trials. She also met a fellow presenter making a name for herself in television. Dawn Porter, as she was then, was the same age and the two women became best friends. Dawn recalled, 'We laughed all week, told each other everything and bonded for life. The absolute greatest of times.'

Behind the façade of success, however, Caroline struggled to handle criticism, especially when the media sharpened their knives. She first faced the full glare of media scrutiny when it was revealed she was dating Prince Harry. They had met at a club in Chelsea in 2009. All she would say on the matter was, 'I was photographed with him and we did have a friendship.'

Caroline was totally unprepared for the onslaught from the Sunday papers. One front-page headline shouted, 'Harry's Girl in Three-in-a-Tub romp'. The source of the story was an unnamed 'pal'. Caroline, it claimed, was a 'wild child party animal' who once 'romped' in a tub with Sharon Osbourne's son Jack. Female celebrities, it seems, are always going to be targeted with this sort of headline. Before she became a national treasure, Cheryl woke up to the *News of the World* shouting, 'I Had Rub-a-Dub in the Tub with Girls Aloud Cheryl'.

Nothing seemed to change. It was depressingly similar to the headline the first week Meghan Markle was revealed as Prince Harry's new girlfriend. That read: 'Harry's Girl on Pornhub'. A subsequent apology does not cancel the original story.

As well as the scrutiny she herself received, Caroline's entire family was door-stepped and investigated. Again, it was very similar to the methods used six years later in Meghan's case, with so-called representatives of the papers sent out with chequebooks ready. According to Caroline, all her Facebook friends were offered money 'for dirt'.

Prince Harry understood the pressures any woman would face if they were linked to him. He was not photographed with Caroline again. Caroline explained that they had to stop seeing each other because neither wanted to face that level of press intrusion. Sadly, it would not be the last time she made the front pages for a relationship.

Caroline later revealed that she lost two stone in weight and would spend hours alone in her North London flat, just crying. The other famous Harry was blissfully unaware of such dramas, studying for his GCSEs in Holmes Chapel. He didn't meet Caroline during his time on *The X Factor*. She had gone up for the job as presenter of *The Xtra Factor* but had lost out to Konnie Huq. She had impressed Simon Cowell, however, and he took her on the following year when Konnie decided not to return.

To begin with, the rumours were flying that she was involved with co-presenter Olly Murs – nothing to see there. The reality was that she and Harry had got together after meeting up at an *X Factor* party at the W Hotel in Leicester Square. They were seen having a snog and left together.

While the media were fascinated by Caroline's love life involving the two Harrys and other possible or probable romances, she had been involved in an on-off relationship with drummer Dave Danger from the indie band The Holloways. That was over by the time she began dating Harry Styles, who tweeted, 'Sometimes things happen and you suddenly get a whole new outlook on life.' To begin with, it seemed like no big deal to the media – they would just make the odd comment about Harry already having an eye for the older woman.

The following month, in September 2011, 'What Makes You Beautiful' went straight to number one in the UK, selling more than 150,000 copies in its first week of release. They had a little way to go to match Adele, who was the queen of the charts with 'Someone Like You' and 'Rolling in the Deep', but the track crept into the top twenty of the biggest-selling singles of the year; it ended up with sales of more than a million and remains their biggest ever hit.

Its success was the final piece in the jigsaw for One Direction before they signed a lucrative American contract with Columbia Records, who were already enjoying great success across the Atlantic with Adele. British boy bands had not done particularly well in the US up until that point, but the record label could see a gap in the market left by the disbanded Backstreet Boys and NSYNC.

While the campaign for One Direction in the UK had been very old school, the American strategy was more modern, tapping into social media and the internet. The approach was groundbreaking and One Direction was arguably the first act to properly cash in online.

The problem with harnessing social media to generate publicity and commercial success was that the platforms made it very difficult for celebrities like One Direction to enjoy any privacy without the whole world seemingly having a view on what you, your friends or your lovers were up to.

Caroline and Harry had been seeing each other for a month before One Direction were guest stars on *The X Factor* performing their second single, 'Gotta Be You', in mid-November. By the time the band sang 'What Makes You Beautiful' during the December final, the rules of the game had completely changed.

It was the previous week that Harry had been photographed leaving Caroline's Muswell Hill flat early one Wednesday morning. In the subsequent stories, Harry was described as a 'school leaver', leaving no room for doubt as to the direction the press accounts were going to take.

References were made to him arriving the night before, having an overnight bag and looking tired the next day. The press were tying themselves up in knots to avoid stating categorically that Harry had clearly been up all night having sex.

In her own memoir, Caroline would lay the blame for the social media backlash at the door of the columnist Jan Moir, who next day in the *Daily Mail* described Caroline as a 'classic me-first cougar' and a 'predatory female', while Harry was 'basically still a child'. Jan highlighted the age gap: 'No wonder people find their liaison inappropriate; even slightly creepy.'

Caroline concluded, 'Once that was out, it was open season.' Passers-by felt empowered to shout out to her in the street: 'Paedophile' or 'Pervert'.

Jan had also suggested, 'And I don't imagine his mother is best pleased with these rather off-key romantic developments with a predatory older woman.'

In fact, Anne and Caroline were following each other on Twitter and Harry's mum had wished her a happy birthday earlier in November. Harry had taken Caroline to Cheshire to meet his mother and stepfather and, in turn, he had met her family. Her sister Jo was even spotted dropping him at King's Cross station to catch a train north.

For a while they tried to ride out the media storm but it seemed everyone had an opinion on whether the age gap made the relationship unsuitable. Anne, who was ten years younger than Harry's father, was calm about everything: 'I never really thought it would be a problem,' she said, before adding, 'Personality is more important than anything else.'

Des Styles, apparently, was less enthusiastic: 'It seemed a bit ridiculous – thirty-two or whatever she was and Harry seventeen. That's a bit extreme.' In his defence, Des did point out that he had been married three times 'so I wouldn't say anyone should take a leaf out of my book'.

Old friend Will Sweeny was asked about it. He observed, 'All his mates think he is a bit of a legend. It's classic Styles.'

Caroline and Harry went to see her agent, John Noel, for some advice and, for the moment, they decided to ignore the newspaper and social-media storm. In effect, that just prolonged the agony and made her a daily target. One Direction already had security and a private living environment. Caroline, however, lived in a maisonette that opened onto the street.

She opened the door in the morning and was greeted by a flurry of flashbulbs. On one morning she went across to the car and discovered that her tyres had been slashed. Nobody offered to help her. At Christmas, Caroline whisked herself off to the beautiful destination of Goa on the coast of India for a girls' holiday with Dawn Porter and others. Harry posted a tweet on 22 December that said simply, 'Work Hard, Play Hard, Be Kind.'

Only one or two people were being kind about him and Caroline. She faced a barrage of death threats, some more sinister than others. One message hoped that she would be 'eaten by an angry elephant'.

In January they tried to pick things up again, but the pressure became too much and they decided to call it a day. Harry was due to fly with the band to the US, so there was a chance for a natural break. There was an air of jubilation among fans, so much so that Harry was again moved to write on Twitter: 'Please know I didn't "dump" Caroline. This was a mutual decision. She is one of the kindest, sweetest people I know. Please respect that.'

Significantly, this is the one and only time that Harry has taken to Twitter to defend or even comment on a former girlfriend. Caroline was brittle as well as beautiful. She somehow never learned the art of saying nothing. A couple of months later she told a Sunday newspaper that Harry was adorable and that they were 'very close' for a time. She added, 'He is a nice person. He was nice to me – we were nice to each other. He's brilliant, he is so much fun.'

In 2021 her other Harry – Prince Harry – produced a series of programmes about mental health called *The Me You Can't See*. That certainly applied to Caroline, who left us in February 2020. She once said that celebrities expected there to be photographers at a public event because it was their job. It was an entirely different thing when 'they turn up at your mum's house, and when you are driving down your street and you have to swerve because there are three cars behind you and three motorbikes following you wherever you go'.

She said stoically, 'I have my dream job so I can't complain. If it got too much I would give it up, so obviously it hasn't got too much.'

Quietly, Caroline received support from an unexpected quarter. There had been some speculation that Simon Cowell had been less than pleased that a member of One Direction was involved with an older woman. That was not the case. He had been astounded, though, by the sequence of events involving his teenage 'frontman'.

Coincidentally Simon was himself seventeen years older than Lauren Silverman, the American socialite who gave birth to his son Eric in February 2014. Two years earlier, at the afterparty of the BRIT Awards, he went up to Caroline to check if she would be hosting *The Xtra Factor* again later in the year. He told her, 'I'd like to apologise for the way you were treated.'

The affection between Caroline and Harry during their three months together was real, if not exactly true love. In many ways, it was an innocent relationship. He had bought himself a swish Audi R8 Coupé, the perfect car for driving up to see his mum in Cheshire. On the journey, he would pop on a CD that Caroline had made of their favourite songs, a simple, romantic gesture that was something personal just for him; and he would sing along. It was a happy reminder of her and the music they enjoyed listening to at her flat.

One consequence of what happened between Harry and Caroline was that he retreated. Both would have more important relationships in the future but the scars from this one ran deep. Harry became secretive when not on official duty at those public events that Caroline mentioned or when he was out and about with fellow celebrities. He did not engage with tabloid media, preferring to give big exclusive interviews to publications he trusted. Nobody even knew where he lived!

8

CONNECTIONS

On his eighteenth birthday, Harry decided to do something for the first time: He was now old enough to vote, open a bank account, serve on a jury and, at least in the UK, order an alcoholic drink in a bar. He could also get a tattoo, and that was his present to himself to celebrate his coming of age.

He was in Los Angeles so he didn't have to worry about what his mum might say. Instead, he strolled into the famous Shamrock Social Club on Sunset Boulevard and asked tattoo artist Freddy Negrete to ink the outline of a five-pointed star on the inside of his left bicep.

Harry has not revealed what the star represented. One Direction fans speculated that it was a point for each member of the band, although it could also have been his personal walk of fame star, inspired by the legendary pavement in nearby Hollywood Boulevard. It was identical.

The star was a very low-key beginning for a man who now possesses more than fifty tattoos all over his body. He was in good company choosing the Shamrock; many British household names have been through the doors, including David Beckham, Russell Brand, Fearne Cotton and Adele.

Harry was back more than half a dozen times within the year, gripped by what Freddy later described as 'tattoo fever'. He explained, 'If you get a tattoo and you like it, you want more – it happens to a lot of people.'

They are also very fashionable and enduringly so. Fashion commentator Alison Jane Reid explained, 'Tattoos are all about rebellion but they are also now perceived to be an haute art form for the rich and famous.'

Harry was in the US with One Direction as part of the American strategy of embracing online coverage and social media to boost interest in the release there of 'What Makes You Beautiful' on Valentine's Day. The hype was in full swing with silly tunes and goofy posts, contests and fan petitions aimed at making the record the only tune in town. Radio stations across the country were being inundated with requests to play the song – and they didn't even have it.

In its first week the single reached number twenty-eight on the *Billboard* Hot 100 chart. That may not sound too impressive but the last British group to see its first US single debut in a higher position was the Spice Girls when their iconic 'Wannabe' made number eleven in 1997.

Just as significantly, 'What Makes You Beautiful' sold 132,000 downloads in seven days and that was before Columbia were going to make it available for radio airplay at the beginning of March. In the end-of-year round-up it was placed tenth in *Billboard*'s best-selling songs of the year.

Harry and the boys were back in London in time for the BRITs of 2012, held that year at the O2. He messed up spectacularly in the thank-you speech after One Direction had won their first major award, Best British Single, as voted for by listeners of Capital FM and iTunes users. Harry, looking immaculate in a three-piece grey suit and large black bow tie, gave a 'massive thank you' to *Radio 1*.

The bosses of Global Radio, which owns Capital, were in the audience and Harry's gaffe was not music to their ears. A planned appearance by the group at Capital in London was promptly dropped without explanation and for a day or two their music was, it seemed, not top of the station's playlist. A spokesman for the band called it an 'oversight as the boys were caught up in the excitement of winning'.

On the night, James Corden, who had become a good friend of Harry's, didn't notice and told the band, 'Go and ring your mums and tell them you'll be home late tonight.' Fortunately Harry was not the story of the evening. Notoriously, James interrupted Adele's big speech when she won Album of the Year for *21*. He was obviously embarrassed but only following instructions in his earpiece because the programme was about to overrun. As she turned to leave the stage, obviously furious, she flipped her middle finger towards a table of executives.

James's best mate, coincidentally, was the event's producer Ben Winston, a charismatic high-flyer in the world of television who had become friendly with One Direction when he began work on a film about their meteoric rise. He lived with his wife Meredith and a sweet cockapoo dog called Colin in upmarket Hampstead Garden Suburb.

Harry asked him if he could come and stay for a while. He explained that he had bought a house not far from Hampstead

Heath so it would be convenient to be close by while keeping an eye on the renovations that were under way. Then, he could move straight in.

He bought the house in a secluded cul-de-sac for an estimated £2.95 million, not bad for an eighteen-year-old. Harry would always make a point of investing part of his already growing fortune in property. His financial mantra was look after 70 per cent of every pound and be frivolous with the other 30 per cent. It helped having a father who was a financial advisor. Harry was part of the new sensible breed of pop star who put vast sums into the housing market knowing that their investment was unlikely to diminish. Ed Sheeran would do likewise and Taylor Swift already had a substantial property empire.

Ben was happy to oblige his friend. After all, it was only temporary; so he moved a mattress into the attic and told Harry to make himself comfortable. He did so for the next twenty months without the world knowing. He was able to slip in and out without running the gauntlet of photographers or fans lurking behind the bins.

Ben was popular with One Direction, who found him easy to get along with and good fun. That did not necessarily mean this new arrangement with Harry would work. Any misgivings on either side were quickly dispelled, however. Ben said simply, 'It was a really beautiful time. He is the most wonderful guy you could ever meet.' Ben and Meredith asked Harry to be godfather when they welcomed their first child, Ruby, into the world at the beginning of 2017.

This was the Harry Styles the world does not see. He does not have an entourage. He is not a cliché-driven representation of an old-style rock star, a throwback to the sex, drugs and rock-and-roll lifestyle favoured by so many in other eras. Quite simply, Harry preferred living in a stable and secure family environment with Ben, Meredith and Colin rather than going out on the town and then home to a soulless gated mansion.

He was seldom bothered by fans or press, even when he joined Ben and Meredith for a quiet meal out in a local restaurant. Ben explained that nobody really believed it was Harry so they left him alone. Occasionally Ben would see A-list stars he recognised slip unannounced up to his attic but stories of drunken nights – or passionate ones – never appeared subsequently in the press.

Harry became the youngest member of a network of close friends who are loyal and discreet. They don't gossip about each other or betray secrets. Ben, then aged thirty, was an integral part of this inner circle. His father, the medical scientist and Labour peer Professor Robert Winston, was a famous face on television, presenting many programmes, including *Child of Our Times* and the BAFTA Award-winning *The Human Body*. He is one of the few TV personalities over the years that have succeeded in making serious scientific and medical subjects accessible to the public. In the US, they call him the 'Daddy of IVF'.

The Winstons are also leading members of the Jewish community in London. Ben and Meredith were observant of the traditions that they had known throughout their lives. Friday night dinner, for instance, was the most important family occasion of the week, when Sabbath candles would be lit and families would come together.

Harry was always welcome to join them. He was respectful of their Jewish traditions, including keeping a kosher home, and was fascinated to learn more about Judaism while chatting over a hot drink before bed. Ben explained that orthodox rules such as not driving on the Sabbath were easy to follow for him because he had grown up with them and they were part of his life and lifestyle.

Ben had ambitions to follow his father into the world of television, inspired by the programmes he made. Lord Winston has always been a keen supporter of the arts and in his younger days had worked as a theatre director before embarking on medicine as his principal vocation.

During his gap year in 2000 Ben worked as a runner in Bristol on the set of a new comedy drama, *Teachers*. On his very first day, he met a young actor, James Corden, playing the role of a Year 11 pupil – although already in his twenties – who would become his closest friend as well an important figure in Harry's life. 'We instantly clicked,' said Ben. 'We recognised sheer ambition in one another.' They also both loved football, although bragging rights invariably went to Ben, who supported Arsenal, rather than James, a West Ham fan.

Their early friendship was sustained when James filmed the drama series *Fat Friends* in Leeds and would regularly hang out with Ben, who was at university there. In the world of weird showbusiness coincidences, James used to kick a football around on set with young teenager Louis Tomlinson, when he was helping his mother Jay chaperone his baby twin sisters.

Jay rang up James when Louis and Harry started living in Friern Barnet and asked if he could check that the teenage boys were coping. James spent the afternoon with them playing computer games and eating pizza and was able to report back to Mum that they were fine.

When Ben left Leeds, he moved back to London and went into partnership with three of his oldest friends, brothers Gabe and Ben Turner, and Leo Pearlman. They had grown up together from pushchairs in the park to enthusiastic members of Bnei Akiva, the UK's largest Jewish youth movement.

Their new production company was called Fulwell 73, named after the last year Sunderland won the FA Cup. The club's old Roker Park Stadium had a Fulwell End. The Turner brothers' mum and dad were from the north east, so watching all their games was compulsory growing up. From unpromising beginnings the business has grown into a resounding success story and one that would be particularly associated with One Direction and, subsequently, Harry.

The new partners had received many plaudits for their work on the 2007 documentary *In the Hands of the Gods*, about five freestyle footballers from different backgrounds in England who come together to pursue an ambition to meet their idol, Diego Maradona, in Buenos Aires. James worked with Ben again when he put his friend forward to direct the much-loved 2009 Comic Relief sketch in which Smithy, his character from hit comedy *Gavin and Stacey*, gives a rollicking to the England football team, including David Beckham and Peter Crouch.

Ben's production work on *Eyes Wide Open 3D*, a documentary about the life of *X Factor* runners-up JLS, brought him to the attention of One Direction. The two groups shared the same management company, Modest, who handled most of the show's stars. Ben met all five of 1D at the premiere at the Soho Hotel in London and instantly had a great rapport with them. As a direct result of getting on so well he embarked on the ambitious and ultimately phenomenally successful *One Direction: This Is Us*, a film that chronicled the boys' meteoric rise to fame from early *X Factor* days to Madison Square Garden in New York in December 2013. He enjoyed their company: 'We made each other laugh. They are always mucking around and there's an anarchic feel about them which makes my job much more fun.' He added, 'I look at them like they are my five little brothers.'

For television, he was the producer of both the 2011 and 2012 BRIT Awards shows at the O2 that his buddy James Corden hosted. In this very small world at the top of showbusiness, it was another step on the path to world domination for this unlikely duo whose rise throughout the next decade almost matched that of the pop stars James was introducing.

A couple of days before the 2012 ceremony, James was Harry's unlikely companion at the Savoy Hotel when Harry went to a London Fashion Week show for the first time without the other members of the band. James is not normally associated with sartorial elegance, but he was accompanying his glamorous fiancée Julia Carey, who he had met at a charity dinner in 2009 for Save the Children that she had helped to organise. Julia sat between the two friends in the front row of the Aquascutum runway show. Harry arrived wearing a timeless beige Aquascutum trench coat with the familiar check lining, which he placed on his lap during the show so that it was in the frame every time his picture was taken. The low-key occasion was early evidence that Harry was beginning to separate himself from the group in certain areas of his life.

They were back together in March when the US release of *Up All Night* was brought forward by a week to capitalise on the success of 'What Makes You Beautiful'. They played a one-off concert at the iconic Radio City Music Hall venue in New York, sharing the bill with the American boy band Big Time Rush, who were also signed to Columbia; they were the stars of a Nickelodeon TV series and very popular but were soon left trailing as One Direction moved towards world domination.

Columbia and Syco made the daring decision to cash in on this burst of popularity and release a second album for Christmas 2012. The boys were young, keen and fit but this would be challenging; and they were also growing up, not just obediently following the path that was being mapped out for them. They wanted a greater say in the sound and the songs they would be performing all over the world.

Savan Kotecha, Carl Falk and Rami Yacoub were again charged with setting the tone for the follow-up, which would be called *Take Me Home* – rather apt for a band that was on the road as much as One Direction was. When their schedule allowed, they would find a window to fly over to Stockholm and record again at the Kinglet Studios. This time they had writing credits on three of the songs, as well as several of the bonus tracks.

Nobody wanted to change a good thing too much so, largely, this was *Up All Night* part two. That was certainly what the record label bosses wanted, just in case the One Direction phenomenon was short-lived. That didn't look likely whenever the band were in the Swedish capital, though. On one occasion the whole street around the studio had to be shut down because of the sheer number of girls who had turned up, desperate for a glimpse of the boys. The city police even arrived clutching missing-person photos to see if any of the teenagers were runaways and had left home without telling their parents what they were doing.

Songwriters around the world were encouraged to submit their compositions for the new One Direction album. Simon Cowell put out an open invitation. Harry had already asked his new mate Ed Sheeran if he would like to offer another song. He did, and once again it became one of One Direction's most-loved songs. 'Little Things' wasn't something new and bespoke at all but a track Ed had worked on with struggling singer-songwriter Fiona Bevan. They had both wanted to write a love song and Fiona was inspired by the novelist Virginia Woolf: 'She always looked at the minutiae and emotion of a situation. I'd been thinking about that a lot, and how the little things really represent the big things.'

Ed thought it was a terrific idea. Fiona recalled, 'We were thinking of real people we loved, and the strange quirks and imperfections that made us love them. So everything in the song is real, which is a lovely thing to be able to say.'

As ever, One Direction could have been singing directly to any one of their adoring fans. That was a vital secret of their success. They had a once-in-a-lifetime knack of speaking directly to one person in a song. They could melt a million hearts when they sang, 'You're perfect to me.'

While they were absorbed in the next album, they still had a full touring diary. They began mixing with the superstars of pop, an indication that they were now in the premier league. Before they set off for Australia, Harry met Taylor Swift for the first time backstage at the Nickelodeon Kids' Choice Awards hosted by Will Smith at the USC Galen Center in Los Angeles. She was seen having a dance with her great friend, Selena Gomez, while the band performed 'What Makes You Beautiful'.

Taylor apparently mentioned to Justin Bieber that she thought Harry was hot. She said a quick 'Hello' to the boys, including Harry, backstage and then fanned herself afterwards, pretending she was overwhelmed by him. It was all good fun, although it did plant the seed that she fancied Harry, which would make future events more believable.

The First Lady, Michelle Obama, was the guest of honour and she presented Taylor with an award and chatted graciously with One Direction, who all thought she was lovely. Harry asked her if she and the president had trouble getting pizza delivered to the White House.

Perhaps as a cure for the hangover caused by the negativity that surrounded his relationship with Caroline Flack, Harry was cast as the lad about town when the *Up All Night* tour headed to Australasia. He was the one loudly cheering a wet t-shirt competition or photographed kissing a young, attractive blonde woman.

She turned out to be a Victoria's Secret model called Emma Ostilly, who was living in Auckland while on assignment in New Zealand. They had got on well apparently, when she appeared fleetingly in the video for 'Gotta Be You', which had been shot the previous year around Lake Placid, New York.

There was nothing in it, but that didn't stop speculation in the tabloids that they were an item. Harry was already learning that he only had to pass a woman in the street for them to be dating. More worryingly, Emma, who also modelled for Abercrombie & Fitch, was another victim of online abuse from One Direction fans and had to close her social media accounts.

Emma revealed she had been told not to say anything about Harry and she never has. She did not say why she had been told not to say anything or by whom. If it was all a publicity device aimed at demonstrating that Harry had moved on from Caroline Flack then it was not especially successful. As a rule of thumb, paparazzi tend not to just turn up – they are usually tipped off.

Emma flew back to the US and continued her modelling career. She remains best known, nine years later, for the Harry Styles kiss. Harry, meanwhile, continued the *Up All Night* tour in the US. The *Washington Post* captured the hysteria and the barrage of sound that greeted each of their 'puppy love anthems'. It reported that the noise was 'louder than an ambulance driving past a lawn mower in a thunderstorm'.

Returning to the UK in midsummer meant more work on the second album. Harry took time off with Liam and Niall to attend James Corden's wedding to Julia at Babington House near Frome, in Somerset. Ben Winston was best man and the couple's six-month-old son was the centre of attention.

Even James, a well-known celebrity, said he could not imagine what Harry's life was like. He had become so famous so quickly. James observed, 'The more normal people he has around, probably the better.'

He needed that normality when the previous year's fling with Lucy Horobin finally and belatedly made the Sunday papers. The year had been one of relentless triumph for Harry, but this was an unexpected downer. The negative publicity for him having assignations with another man's wife might have been much worse if they had been running at the same time as the Caroline Flack stories.

Lucy's marriage was all but over before she got together with Harry but that made no difference to the barrage of abuse and threats she received on Twitter – just as Caroline had done. She was called a 'paedophile', again, as Caroline had been. She posted, 'To clarify, I haven't said ANYTHING to any press, nor do I wish to. Thanks to those of you who have said kind words today. Xxx'

Lucy has been true to her word and has not spoken about Harry. Under the headline, 'Harry Styles slept with my wife', her soon-to-be ex-husband, a data analyst, stirred things further by declaring that he blamed Harry: 'He wasn't that into her but what happened between them ended our marriage.'

Clearly Harry was going to need something more than a kiss with a beautiful model to change the narrative about him. Five weeks later he was photographed holding hands with one of the most famous women in the world.

9

TAYLOR MADE

The first picture of Harry with Taylor Swift resembled a still from a rom-com movie. Of course it would be called *When Harry Met Taylor*. They looked a million dollars strolling through Central Park, New York, on a beautiful December afternoon. They were smiling easily, very much in step, wearing outfits to beat the chill that might have featured in a clothing catalogue. He had his hair pulled back under a favourite blue beanie; she sported a Fox sweater and maroon coat. They were the perfect couple and you could imagine the director yelling, 'Cut. It's a wrap. Let's go to the zoo everybody.'

A Sunday stroll in Central Park is like an announcement in *The Times*; formally letting everyone know you are an item. The photographs went all around the world. As is so often the case with well-chronicled romantic occasions, Harry and Taylor were not alone. They were with the One Direction stylist Lou Teasdale, singer Tom Atkin and their baby daughter Lux. Tom is the lead vocalist with Hull rock band The Paddingtons.

At the zoo, Taylor held Lux for a cuddle with Harry by her side as they watched the seals splashing around, while real mum and dad were out of shot watching on from the wings.

The walk in the park was just a week or so before Taylor's twenty-third birthday. Harry was still eighteen and had only been a star for a couple of years. Taylor, however, understood the pressures of being a teenager in the music business. She had released her first album, *Taylor Swift*, when she was sixteen and living in Nashville with her parents.

She wasn't from the home of country music, though. She had been brought up in Reading, Pennsylvania, with idyllic summers spent at a holiday home near the beach in New Jersey. Her parents had a business background but they encouraged their highly intelligent daughter to express herself and explore the pursuits she most enjoyed – acting and music.

The blot on her idyllic childhood was the bullying she suffered at school for being different. Unlike Harry, she was never very popular in class. Taylor's unhappiness with her peer group was one reason for her mum and dad's move to Nashville. Another was to enable their clearly talented fourteen-year-old daughter to pursue her musical ambitions.

Her first album won her recognition as a country artist and, more importantly, as a songwriter. Her second, *Fearless*, enabled her to cross over from country to mainstream. She won the Grammy Award for Album of the Year in 2010. At the age of twenty, she was the youngest ever recipient.

Intriguingly, bearing in mind Harry's future career path, she had also made her movie debut. She had a minor role in an ensemble romantic comedy and box office hit called *Valentine's Day*. She played a character called Felicia Miller and was involved in a subplot that revolved around kissing co-star Taylor Lautner, who had achieved heartthrob status through his role as vampire Jacob Black in the *Twilight* series of films.

The lip locks between them were so convincing that she was nominated in the Best Kiss category at the MTV Movie Awards. Predictably, the two Taylors were linked romantically for a month or two and were known as Taylor Squared, but it soon fizzled out. As she always seemed to do, she wrote a song about him – 'Back to December' – which featured on her *Speak Now* album.

Taylor spent a year performing the *Speak Now* world tour in support of her third album. Finishing in early 2012, she played 110 dates around the world before an estimated audience of 1.64 million. The figures were boggling, with tour receipts totalling more than $123 million. This was the first time Harry had been linked with someone even more famous than he was.

The UK had been surprisingly sluggish in its commercial appreciation of Taylor Swift, however. *Speak Now* had been a US number one and sold many millions there but in the UK, the album had been a bit of a flop, peaking at number six in the charts and selling less than 250,000 copies. The lead single from that album, 'Mine', only scraped to number thirty. Her school report for the UK read 'must do better'.

Much better was hoped for from her next album, *Red*, which she had spent most of the year writing and recording when her marathon tour had ended. One of her co-writers was another British star on the rise, Ed Sheeran. She had loved his song 'Lego House' that had been a hit in March. Unlike Harry and Ed, she wasn't a devotee of Lego bricks and didn't spend hours assembling tricky models. Harry bought his friend an Imperial Star Destroyer and the pair of them stayed up until 3am until it was complete.

Ed ended up co-writing outstanding tracks for both One Direction and Taylor: the sweet ballad 'Little Things' for *Take Me Home* and 'Everything Has Changed' for *Red*, which they wrote at her house in Beverly Hills, bouncing around on a trampoline in the garden. Across town Ed was with Harry for pizza day. Harry had a rare day off so he decided to buy lots of Domino's pizzas to hand out from his car to the homeless living in the Skid Row neighbourhood. Ed thought the take-aways ended up costing his friend between two and three thousand dollars. He said, 'People write about Harry in a negative way because of his love life but he does stuff like that a lot. He's a pretty genuine guy.'

'Little Things', the band's second UK number one, was on the set list when One Direction played Madison Square Garden in New York one day after the Central Park date. The concert in front of an 18,000-strong, predominantly female, teenage audience was 1D's most prestigious of the year. Ed came on stage when they performed 'Little Things' and sang a few lines with Harry. The concert was a triumph, with Dory Larrabee-Zayas in *Hollywood Life* noting how well the boys interacted with the fans, even jumping into the crowd at one point and posing for photos. Dory observed, 'I saw so many girls crying so hard, they looked like they were in pain, but they were tears of joy.' Taylor joined Harry at the after-show party where they were photographed and subsequently left together.

They were all back at Madison Square Garden a few days later for the annual Jingle Ball that featured eleven of the biggest acts of the year. During the week Harry had been photographed several times leaving the hotel in Tribeca where Taylor was said to be staying. Reports at the time suggested he looked pleased with himself, an unsubtle implication that he had been enjoying a night of passion with Taylor.

The set lists for the concert were an indication of where everyone was in their career at the time. One Direction opened the show and performed four numbers, including 'Little Things'. Ed sang just two, 'Lego House' and 'The A Team'. Taylor was top of the bill, sang six and closed the show, Ed joined her on stage for 'Everything has Changed'.

The *New York Times* reviewer, Ben Ratliff, said One Direction had 'bright smiles and uncoordinated body movements', whereas Taylor was the grown-up act of the night. Her set was 'several fathoms more elegant and sophisticated than anyone else's'. Ben added, 'The boss was in the house.' He did, however, repeat the speculation about a romantic link between Taylor and Harry. The fact that their connection was even mentioned demonstrated that the photo opportunities had done a good job.

The only one of Harry's close friends back in the UK to comment on the possible romance was the Radio 1 DJ Nick Grimshaw, with whom he used to speak frequently on the phone. Nick revealed, 'Harry really likes Taylor. At first I wasn't sure if the relationship was a real one but I talk to him a lot and it seems to be that she is the one – for now, anyway.'

Harry and Taylor barely had time to catch their breath before they were bound for London on her private jet. One Direction was appearing at London's equivalent Jingle Ball at the O2. And then they were at Manchester Central Arena as guests for the final of that year's *The X Factor*, when they performed 'Kiss You', another track from *Take Me Home*.

There would be plenty more photographs, especially when Harry took Taylor to Cheshire, where they wandered around Tesco in Manchester Road, Northwich – as superstars do. Harry bought some hair gel while excited shoppers, scarcely believing their eyes, watched as Taylor wandered up and down the fresh vegetable aisle.

The supermarket was one stop on a mini-break that included a trip with Harry's mum over to Bowness-on-Windermere, although it's a one-hundred-mile trek from her home, so not exactly down the road. Taylor joined in to feed the pigeons and swans and bought half of the gift store when they went to visit Beatrix Potter's house, Hill Top. Taylor loved the Lake District and would subsequently write a track called 'The Lakes' in its honour.

Harry and Taylor, who the media had named 'Haylor', also travelled to The Rising Sun pub in the Peak District, ten miles from his sister Gemma's university in Sheffield. Taylor nibbled some black pudding for the first time, although she was apprehensive when told the staple ingredient was pig's blood. For her twenty-third birthday, Harry gave her twenty-three custom-made cupcakes from a speciality shop in Warrington. He did not place the order himself, though. For good measure, he gave her two handbags, a pair of antique earrings and a photo frame containing a black and white picture of a famous pop star – himself, of course. For a man as discreet as Harry about relationships that matter, there was a surprisingly large amount of information about this one in the public domain.

If success is measured in column inches, then this whirl-wind mini-break had been a triumph. There was more to come. This time Harry was the one visiting home territory when he accompanied Taylor to Nashville, where he met her family. Back in Los Angeles, she joined him on some tattoo trips to the Shamrock Social Club, although she chose not to have one done at the same time.

He was having his striking galleon tattoo inked onto his left arm, again by Freddy Negrete. Harry didn't choose the design until he arrived at the salon and flipped through a book of old paintings of ships. He told Freddy that he wanted something to represent sailing home: 'We're always on the road but my heart is at home and I want a ship.'

The image, which many thought resembled Nelson's flag-ship HMS *Victory*, was a complicated tattoo that took several visits. Freddy was very happy with the results. He thought that Harry and Taylor seemed more like friends than two young people in love. He later said, 'There wasn't a sparkle in Harry's eye. They were kind and respectful to each other but didn't have stars in their eyes.'

The tattoo is on his left arm placed underneath his sister Gemma's name in Hebrew, a gesture acknowledging his inter-est in what Ben had told him about his Jewish culture back in Hampstead Garden Suburb. Harry had carefully written out the translation, realising that this was not something to get wrong.

Harry and Taylor didn't spend Christmas together – she was on a promotional trip to Australia and he was in Cheshire again. Naturally his family had asked him what present he wanted. He confided, 'I asked for socks and pants because if you're out on the road, you always run out.' His mum gave him a big beautifully wrapped box that wasn't full of underwear. When he finished carefully removing all the sparkly paper he discovered the small gift for the teenager who has everything – a belly button brush. Harry loved it.

He and Taylor did manage a New Year break in the British Virgin Islands but she left early amid reports of an 'almighty row'. He took a boat over to Necker at the invitation of the island's owner, Richard Branson, where he swam, sunbathed and was sociable. Then he flew back to Heathrow. Haylor was over.

During their briefest of time together, both *Red* and *Take Me Home* topped the *Billboard* album charts in the US. That was particularly significant for One Direction because it meant that they were the first British act to have their first two albums debut at the top of the US charts. Were Harry and Taylor ever going to be the next superstar couple following in the golden footsteps of Beyoncé and Jay-Z, Kim Kardashian and Kanye West or, looking further back, Justin Timberlake and Britney Spears?

The cynical answer is not a chance. But reflecting on that famous walk in Central Park, Harry said, 'Relationships are hard at any age. And adding in that you don't really understand exactly how it works when you're eighteen, trying to navigate all that stuff didn't make it easier. I mean, you're a little bit awkward to begin with. You're on a date with someone you really like. It should be that simple, right? It was a learning experience for sure. But at the heart of it – I just wanted it to be a normal date.'

He was still only eighteen and it seemed much of his life was a 'learning experience'. He surrounded himself with older friends who coloured the way he looked at the world. Taylor may have been only five or so years older but she was an enlightened young woman of the world. In the coming years both she and Harry would become strong supporters of the LGBTQ+ community and would have to answer intrusive questions about their own sexuality.

Harry's friendship with Nick Grimshaw, for instance, was a classic case of 'He's gay, therefore you must be too.' Nick was one of Harry's 'Thirtysomething' inner circle who was great fun on a night out or just an afternoon playing Frisbee in the park. 'Grimmy', as he is called by many, was once memorably described as possessing 'the air of a gossipy older brother with access to the best parties'. Harry was one of many who enjoyed his vivacious company.

Nick Grimshaw grew up in Oldham, just north of Manchester and wasn't officially 'out' until 2012. He spoke openly about his sexuality the same month that he was announced as the new host of the Breakfast Show on Radio 1, taking over from Chris Moyles – perhaps diffusing any lurid tabloid headlines before they were written.

Newspapers still tend to treat someone's sexuality as big news. Back in the eighties, George Michael was forever being pestered about it. He refused to confirm or deny the inevitable question about the gay rumours that seemed to slip into every interview. For a while, he liked the ambiguity, claiming that sort of thing had done no harm to the careers of David Bowie or Mick Jagger – two of the artists Harry greatly admired. George said, 'I don't think anyone should have to answer a "gay or straight" question.' But he kept being asked.

One of the triggers for the rumours that Harry and Nick were romantically involved appeared to be Harry's liking for floral shirts. During the coming months, they both responded to gossip that they were dating. Nick told *Now* magazine about their friendship: 'It seems totally normal to me; a DJ being mates with a pop star.'

Harry even had to respond to a direct question from *GQ* magazine. He answered simply, 'No, we're not dating. We're just friends.'

10

17 BLACK

Goodness knows how Harry and Nick made it to the Radio 1 studio for the DJ's breakfast show. They had literally been 'up all night' after the 2013 BRIT Awards the evening before. At least Nick had changed his shirt. Harry was still wearing the same smart suit that was looking a little bit more crumpled than it had done on the red carpet.

They had done the rounds of the after-parties, enjoying Champagne and Belvedere cocktails at the Warner Music Group event at the Savoy Hotel before going on to the Sony thrash at the Arts Club in Mayfair. The night was still young – maybe 4.30ish – when they piled into taxis with friends including the actress Jaime Winstone to continue the festivities at Nick's flat in Primrose Hill. Just before 6am they were on their way to BBC Broadcasting House in Portland Place.

Harry teased Nick on air, asking innocently: 'Grimmy, how many hours' sleep have you had since yesterday?' He certainly seemed in better shape than his older friend. Lily Allen tweeted, '@grimmers you sound hammered still.'

Harry didn't stick around long, leaving Nick to battle through, apologise for being unusually quiet on the show and admit he was in a 'pretty fragile state'. Then it was home for a 'very long sleep'.

The one party the pair had avoided was held by the Universal Music Group at Soho House. Taylor Swift was there. Several close friends were also present, including Ben Winston and James Corden, the consummate professional, who was completely at ease with Taylor when they messed around with some DJing.

James had earlier again been the host at the main event when both Taylor and One Direction had performed. Taylor sang 'I Knew You Were Trouble', which conveniently hinted she was referring to Harry, even though she had written and released it before they had taken their walk in Central Park.

When asked by the *Sunday Times* if it was difficult to perform the song on the night, she said, 'Well, it's not hard to access that emotion when the person the song is directed at is standing by the side of the stage watching.' There was, it seemed, still mileage to be had in the previous month's break-up, so it wouldn't have worked as well if they had been smiling and sharing a joke or two that evening.

They had avoided each other at rehearsal and on the night itself when One Direction followed her on to perform their Comic Relief single 'One Way or Another (Teenage Kicks)'. Three days later it entered the UK chart at number one. Taylor's single wasn't doing too badly either, going back up to number six. *Red* would finally become her first UK number one album in May.

One Direction was a big winner on the night, claiming the Global Success Award, recognising the group's impact around the world. The Damien Hirst-designed statuette was presented to them by Robbie Williams, two years and two months after he had shepherded them through the final of *The X Factor*.

Comic Relief was an enormous charity event and in 2013 raised more than £100 million. One Direction spent two days in Accra, the capital of Ghana, making a series of video diaries highlighting poverty and the need for improved medical facilities. Harry was seen crying in a hospital ward at the plight of a baby boy stricken with malaria: 'If you get involved in it and you don't cry, then you're superhuman.'

Harry explained how he felt about the reality of everyday life in a poor country and how he was unprepared for the hardship he witnessed firsthand: 'We thought we knew what it's like. But when you're there and you get the smells, your eyes hurt from the smoke, you cough, you're feeling it all. It's crazy how quick you get connections with children and the people who live there. You feel upset leaving them and saying goodbye to them.'

Away from the highly publicised charity life of One Direction, Harry was supporting the endeavours of his mum. Anne was creating her own future promoting charities that mattered to her and raising money for them. She would never have to worry about money for herself because her son was a multi-millionaire. But she didn't want him to just write out a cheque for her latest cause – where was the sense of achievement in that?

Instead, she decided to climb Mount Kilimanjaro in Tanzania for a charity she backed called Believe in Magic,

which helped seriously and terminally ill children. She under-
took her adventure with four friends, including Vicky
Sherlock, the mother of Ashley Sherlock, one of Harry's best
friends from Holmes Chapel Comprehensive. Robin Twist
boosted the fundraising by organising a sponsored chest wax.

The expedition raised nearly £28,000. Afterwards Harry
tweeted, 'Very proud of my mum today, she is on her way
home after reaching the top of Mount Kilimanjaro.'
Subsequently, Believe in Magic was mired in allegations of
financial irregularity and, after an inquiry, was removed from
the charity register in 2020.

Fortunately, the controversy did not deter Anne's philanthropic nature and she continued to promote the charities she
cared about, especially Parkinson's UK. Her father – and
Harry's beloved grandfather – Brian had been diagnosed with
the disease in his early seventies.

A week after Comic Relief, Harry ensured that Brian, then
aged seventy-seven, was his personal guest of honour when
One Direction played the O2 arena for the first time. Anne,
Robin and Gemma were also there to make sure Brian was
looked after during the concert. Before he went on stage,
Harry went up to chat to his granddad. 'He hasn't changed at
all,' said Brian. 'He always has a smile on his face and is very
loving and caring. I don't think of him as this well-known pop
star.'

Everyone was worried that Brian would find the noise of
the fans overwhelming, but he was a member of an older
generation who remembered Beatlemania and he took it in
his stride. He observed, 'The girls were screaming so loud – it
was deafening, but I would really like to go again.'

The extended Styles family were very close and remained so despite the pressure of fame. Harry slipped quietly into a hospital in Peterborough to visit another elderly member who had fallen ill. His grandmother Beryl, mother of Des and known affectionately as Nanny Styles, was unwell. It made her nurses' day to discover Harry Styles sitting by her bedside. Sadly, Nanny died the following year after a long illness when Harry was on tour in the US, but he flew straight over. The newspapers concentrated on what he was wearing when he arrived at Heathrow.

A happier family occasion was the wedding of Robin and Anne. They seemed to have been engaged for years before they married quietly at the upmarket Pecks restaurant in Congleton. The wedding was arranged for the break in the *Take Me Home* tour between the last gig on the European leg in Lisbon and the first concert across the Atlantic in Mexico. The occasion was kept so secret that the fifty guests weren't told of the location until the last minute so that the ceremony wouldn't be hijacked by over-enthusiastic Directioners. A decoy bus with fake wedding guests on board was even sent to Doncaster racecourse eighty miles away to fool any fans loitering in the area.

Harry shared best man duties with his new elder step-brother, Mike Twist, who was Robin's son from a previous marriage. This was Anne's big day and the bride was the centre of attention in an exquisite, traditional, full-length white gown, trimmed with lace. The best men and the groom wore matching dark suits.

The wedding illustrated Harry and his family's ongoing attitude towards keeping their private lives private. They would post a tweet or two and the odd photograph but there was never any question of a photographer from *Hello!* or another glossy magazine turning such happy events into a media circus.

That may explain what happened to his close friendship with his high-school friend, bakery pal and fellow band member in White Eskimo, Nick Clough. He gave an interview to a Sunday newspaper which was flagged as revealing 'all about the beer, the band, the girls, the tattoos …'

The revelations seemed harmless enough and rather sweet. He recalled driving Harry's Audi R8, which he loved: 'I'm more jealous of the cars than anything.' He did mention Caroline Flack and Taylor Swift briefly but the only off-colour anecdote involved Harry getting 'his k★★b out' and pressing it against the window of one of his friends' mum's car. No one was offended, recalled Nick.

The article was accompanied by a series of never-before-seen photographs of Harry as a teenager at school and playing with White Eskimo. They haven't been seen again. The words and pictures appeared a few weeks before the wedding. Nick wasn't invited. In fact, he hasn't spoken a word to Harry since the newspaper piece. He said simply: 'Unfortunately my article with the *Sunday Mirror* cost me my friendship with Harry.'

Nick is not alone in no longer being in contact with Harry. Will Sweeny, for instance, hasn't spoken to Harry since those days. Felicity Skinner last spoke to him the week before Judges' Houses on *The X Factor*.

Ed Sheeran was very much one of Harry's new friends who understood the line between privacy and public image where performers were concerned. Ed has never said a word about

112

Harry and Taylor's relationship despite spending time with both of them. He would meet up with Harry when his touring schedule with the latter allowed. He was drinking with him one night when they decided to get a tattoo together.

The following day Ed called Kevin Paul, his favourite tattoo artist in London, and asked him to meet them at one of Harry's houses the next Sunday morning. Kevin recalled, 'Harry and Ed had been out the night before, got pissed and started talking about their favourite childhood shows and Pingu was both of their favourite, which is why they both decided to get them.'

Ed opted for an illustration of the actual naughty penguin while Harry went for a more obvious PINGU lettering on his left bicep. Harry also wanted a tattoo of 17 Black, which became one of his best-known ones. Everyone assumed that it was a reference to James Bond's lucky bet in the 1971 film *Diamonds Are Forever*.

Harry loved roulette but he was not as successful playing 17 Black as Sean Connery had been in the film; far from it. He had first lost heavily when One Direction went to a casino in Perth, Western Australia, during their *Up All Night* tour. They all did except Niall, who won £100 and then stopped and watched the others keep digging. He said, 'Let's just say a lot of money was lost. A lot. When management found out, we got a serious dressing down.'

Harry lost on 17 Black so his new tattoo, high on the left side of his chest, was a reminder of that or perhaps heralding a change of luck. It didn't work. He wandered into the VIP area of the casino in Perth during their *Take Me Home* tour and had another unsuccessful night with his 'lucky' number.

At least the tattoo looked good, which is more than could be said for the one Ed inked on Harry's left forearm. Kevin set up the machine for them and Ed carefully drew a padlock, although Harry was later heard to remark that he thought it looked more like a handbag. Fortunately for Ed, they ran out of time before Harry was able to get his revenge.

Perhaps his best-known tattoo was already in place – a large butterfly across the middle of his chest. This time he went to Liam Sparkes at Old Habits Tattoo in Hackney, another of his favourite parlours. You couldn't miss the result. A butterfly is a popular symbol, representing the transformation of life from child to adult. Liam also pointed to the film *Papillon* as being an inspiration. In the 1973 version Steve McQueen plays Henri Charrière, a safecracker named Papillon because of the giant butterfly tattooed on his chest.

Harry's butterfly stood out proudly below a tattoo of two swallows facing each other. He explained that he particularly liked the old-fashioned type of tattoo that sailors would traditionally have: 'They symbolise travelling and we travel a lot.'

The aptly named *Take Me Home* tour was a marathon and a reminder that One Direction was a successful business and the five members were the majority shareholders. They performed 123 shows across the globe, including concerts in the US, Japan, Australia and six nights at the O2. More than 300,000 tickets were sold for the UK and Ireland leg in one day while 108,000 fans screamed at them at the Fara Sol stadium in Mexico City.

The public face of the band was that they were just five lads having fun – but the reality was very different. Andy Greene, an associate editor with *Rolling Stone* magazine, commented,

'It's insane; they're working them like dogs and printing money right now.' The tour generated well over $100 million.

Simon Cowell had already said that he did not want to introduce rules for the boys as if they were still at school, not least because they would just break them. He observed, 'They're good-looking guys and they all like girls.'

In practice, it was not a sex free-for-all. Lou Teasdale, who was responsible for make-up and style on all the tours since the *X Factor* days, revealed that sex with the band was strictly off limits. It was a no-tolerance policy. She explained, 'You can't sleep with them. It's kind of important if you want to keep your job.'

Occasionally a member of staff, perhaps a newcomer, crossed that line and they were swiftly shown the door. They might have thought it was true love but it wasn't. The boys and those looking after them did not want to provoke an embarrassing incident if a new girlfriend was on the scene.

In any case, there wasn't much time for anything extra-curricular. As well as performing, travelling between gigs on a tour bus or plane and checking into soulless hotels, they were busy recording their third album, literally on the road.

Hotel rooms were doubling as makeshift recording studios with beds flipped up against the wall. They would work on a new song for twenty minutes before having to leave for the show, then perform for a couple of hours, come back and put in some more time before bed. The recording was their winding up and winding down. The bonus from a musical point of view was that the boys were still in the zone. The demo vocal recorded in a hotel after midnight was often better than the version in a million-dollar studio.

Two LA-based writers and producers, Julian Bunetta and John Ryan, were largely responsible for steering One Direction's musical progress to the next stage. They had worked for Syco on *X Factor USA* and on *Take Me Home* and collaborated on more than half of the tracks on the new album.

Both Savan Kotecha and Carl Falk had young families, so it was left to Julian and John to step up and travel around the world, although most of the groundwork for what would become *Midnight Memories* was prepared in London. They both realised that the members of One Direction were moving forward as a band. Julian explained, 'They needed to grow up or they were going to go away – and they wanted to grow up.'

All five of One Direction had input into the writing of their third album, some more than others. Louis, for instance, had a credit on nine of the songs. Harry featured on only four but, more interestingly, he was the sole band member on two of the tracks, 'Happily' and 'Something Great', suggesting he was beginning to find his own songwriting identity. 'Something Great' was co-written with Gary Lightbody, the lead singer with Snow Patrol, and that band's long-standing producer, Jacknife Lee. In the very small world of the music premiership, they had collaborated with Taylor Swift on *Red*. Gary was also great mates with Ed Sheeran, who had toured the US supporting his band the previous year.

Harry was also more prominent in the lead singles from the album, 'Best Song Ever' and 'Story of my Life'. He was centre stage for both videos that were directed by his landlord, Ben Winston.

The 'Story of my Life' was a painstakingly put-together work of art, drawing on collections of old childhood photographs. Ben explained his use of the family album snaps: 'You are still from the same place. That is the story of their life.' The mums were enlisted as well and Anne couldn't stop smiling next to Harry singing away.

Ben was one of the producers of *One Direction: This Is Us*. Leicester Square had to be sealed off for the evening when a football-stadium-size crowd of teenage girls descended on central London, many camping out overnight to ensure their place at the front of the queue. A week later the same thing happened at the New York premiere at the Ziegfeld Theatre on West 54th Street in midtown Manhattan. The area was brought to a standstill.

Each fan seemed to have their favourite, although there did seem to be a lot of Harry in evidence. His name was painted on foreheads, Harry dolls and masks were waved and t-shirts proclaimed: 'Harry You Wanna Marry Me?'

The authorised 3D film was directed by Morgan Spurlock, who had sprung to prominence for his documentary *Super Size Me* about his existence on a diet of McDonald's food (and would later achieve notoriety after confessing to sexual misconduct). The final movie managed to keep everyone happy. The *New York Times* commented, 'The film catches the singers at their most adorable: adjusting to fame, marvelling at the devotion of the fans, and often taking off their shirts.'

The newspaper also observed that 'there is little indication of romance, and absolutely no alcohol, cigarettes, drugs or sex'. This was a documentary that reflected the enthusiasm and exuberance of five boys on a yellow brick road to adulthood. Ben, who had travelled with them remarked that the band was determined 'to squeeze every bit of fun and joy' out of their journey.

Obviously the target audience was their fans, the Directioners, the already converted who needed no persuading to go and see the film. Their devotion turned into box-office gold. *One Direction: This Is Us* earned more than $67 million dollars worldwide on a budget of $10 million. The DVD alone sold 270,000 copies within three days.

Ben neatly defined One Direction's philosophy on what was happening to them: 'We will always be part of the biggest part of each other's lives.'

1D was still very much part of Harry's life but as he prepared to leave his teenage years behind, there were already signs that the twenty-something man would be moving away from being just another member of a boy band.

11

THE ARCHITECTURE
OF HAPPINESS

———

When Harry met the philosopher Alain de Botton, one of the leading lights of London intelligentsia, they talked easily of Aristotle, Plato, love and beauty. Harry was never tongue-tied at parties. His life experiences and natural inquisitiveness made him an ideal guest. He wasn't fazed by money, reputation or intelligence.

A first, casual chat with Alain was not a eureka moment for Harry, but it would prove to be an indication of a man on a thoughtful and enlightened path. Alain was impressed: 'Reports of the death of culture in the young are much exaggerated: Harry is a real enthusiast of Greek philosophy.'

Alain was born in Switzerland, the son of the prominent international financier, multi-millionaire and art collector, Gilbert de Botton. He moved to England as a schoolboy, attending Harrow and then Cambridge before obtaining a master's degree in philosophy at King's College London.

He became well known first as a writer of both fiction and non-fiction before reaching a wider audience through broadcasting, lectures and workshops. His meeting with Harry prompted him to reach out to the pop world as a means of communicating important ideas to the next generation.

He urged pop stars to suggest to their fans that they should read the classical philosophers. He expanded on the thought: 'My plan is to shut the Arts Council and get people such as Harry Styles to go on television and recommend to everyone they read Proust and Hegel, which would achieve more in five minutes than the Arts Council achieves year in, year out.

'David Beckham could do Aristotle and Plato … and in an ideal world Harry Styles would be teaching his ten million Twitter followers a little more about Greek philosophy.'

To illustrate Alain's point, Harry responded by immediately tweeting a sentence from Wikipedia, 'Socrates, born in Athens in the 5th century BC, marks a watershed in Ancient Greek philosophy.' The post would be retweeted 56,000 times and liked by 47,000 users.

Newspaper columnists saw this exchange as an open goal to poke fun at Alain and Harry's expense. Sam Leith wrote in the *Guardian*: 'We are accustomed to thinking of him as an intellectual lightweight, a Twitter-addicted, sex-obsessed celebrity socialite quite incapable of holding his end up in a conversation about philosophy with Harry Styles.'

Alain, then forty-three, took it all in good part because he genuinely liked Harry and appreciated that he was an 'intelligent chap'. He said, 'It's important to try and bridge this gap between popular culture and what people see as highbrow. Hopefully, this will be the start of Harry engaging with more philosophy.'

It was. Quietly and with no fuss, Harry would stay in contact with Alain, reading his books, listening to his podcast,

The True Hard Work of Love and Relationships, and even discreetly attending his workshops. He has been an admirer ever since their first meeting. In his now celebrated 2020 *Vogue* cover story, Harry paid tribute to the philosopher: 'I just think he's brilliant. I saw him give a talk about the keys to happiness, and how one of the keys is living among friends, and how real friendship stems from being vulnerable with someone.'

Living with friends as a key to happiness helps to explain Harry's enjoyment of living in Ben and Meredith Winston's house. He was not just being eccentric, after all, and this would not be the last time that he chose a similar living arrangement. *The Architecture of Happiness* (2006) was one of the books written by Alain that Harry kept on his bookshelves. Again, it highlighted the importance of environment in well-being.

Harry would later mix the world of fashion with that of philosophy when he designed a hoodie that displayed three pictures of Alain across the front. He wore it to be interviewed by *Vogue*, the fashion bible. By this time, 2020, anything Harry wore was going to become a talking point.

That was not the case in the early days of One Direction but big-name brands identified him as the best member of the group to target. One of the true ironies of being so successful in the world of celebrity is being able to afford anything you want but never having to buy a thing because you receive it all for free. He could have opened his own designer-label clothing store with the amount of merchandise he was sent. It was always worth a punt to send him something just in case it took his fancy. If he was photographed wearing a particular t-shirt, for instance, it would be advertising gold.

Harry's bedroom resembled a stroll round the menswear department of Selfridges – Ray-Bans, Adidas and Nike trainers and Ralph Lauren polo shirts were just some of the brands competing for his attention. He always stood out as the classiest dresser in One Direction.

Harry spent most of 2013 touring but had a month off between *Take Me Home* shows in Los Angeles in mid-August and the resumption in Adelaide in late September, so he had the chance to ditch the band and attend various events at that year's London Fashion Week. He clearly loved being involved. He was in good spirits, laughing and joking in the front row next to Nick Grimshaw, Kelly Osbourne and Nicola Roberts at Henry Holland's runway show at Somerset House.

Harry was a late arrival but immediately became the centre of attention for the photographers. He chose to wear a label-free, plain white t-shirt and jeans, a neat gesture to avoid favouritism. Afterwards, he told *E! News* that he liked the hats.

After House of Hutton, it was over to Kensington Gardens for the Burberry Prorsum Show, where he was sat between two very glamorous blondes, Suki Waterhouse and Sienna Miller. The assembled media, however, were more interested in his reaction to watching supermodel Cara Delevingne on the runway. One reporter set a trap for him by asking innocently, 'Are you looking forward to seeing your girl Cara walk down the runway?' Harry responded, sharply: 'She's not my girl. I know what you're doing.'

Harry went backstage after the show to congratulate Cara and chat. He posed for pictures with her but had donned a black balaclava with the letters BS scrawled in white across the top – an abbreviation for bullshit – which may or may not have been aimed at photographers intruding on this occasion. They both well knew that these balaclava pictures could not be dragged out year after year as enduring proof of their relationship.

The rumours about Cara and Harry had been keeping the gossip pages interested for months. They seemed intent on never being photographed together – no walks in Central Park – although they were captured on camera by a member of the audience at the Prince of Wales Theatre enjoying the hit musical *The Book of Mormon*, a few days before London Fashion Week. Harry was clearly visible but the only way celebrity sleuths could deduce that Cara was the blonde woman sitting next to him in the dress circle was by the lion tattoo on her finger.

They were said to have been dating secretly for years and the most likely confirmation of that is that they were not 'spotted' together. Magazines and online diaries would cheat by running full-length pictures of them side by side, hoping that readers would not realise they were snapped on completely different occasions and they weren't actually *together* when the photographs were taken.

Cara, twenty, had quickly become fashion royalty, winning Model of the Year at the 2012 British Fashion Awards. She was brought up in the higher echelons of London society, but her early life was far from an upper-class glide. Her father, Charles Delevingne, is a property developer and her socialite mother, Pandora, is the daughter of the late Sir Jocelyn Stevens, a publishing magnate, and Jane Sheffield, lady-in-waiting to Princess Margaret. Pandora has been frank about her struggles with heroin addiction and a bipolar diagnosis. Cara's elder sister and fellow supermodel, Poppy Delevingne, tried to shelter her younger sibling from the worst of it by letting her sleep in her bed for years. Even so, Cara has admitted to suffering from a deep depression at the age of fifteen.

With the benefit of hindsight it's easy to identify the connection between Cara and Harry. They are kindred spirits both on their career paths and their willingness to embrace non-toxic criteria in their lives – and neither liked society's need to put a label on everything. Cara Delevingne was not 'Harry's girl' and he hated being linked to every girl who stood next to him.

Over the years she has patiently explained that she is not 'gay', she is sexually fluid, a young woman who enjoys relations with men and women. She observed, 'Once I spoke about my sexual fluidity, people were like, "So you're gay." And I'm like, "No I'm not gay."' She told *Glamour* magazine, 'I am very happy how sexuality has become easier and freer to talk about, especially for kids.'

More recently, in 2020, Cara, now a Hollywood fixture, was on the front cover of *Variety* magazine's Pride issue, in which she described herself as 'pansexual' – attracted to all genders. *Variety* observed that she is one of Hollywood's most visible queer actors.

Harry has had to bat away potentially explosive questions about his sexuality. His response to being asked if he was bisexual was, 'Bisexual? Me? I don't think so. I'm pretty sure I'm not.'

Cara and Harry were very much part of the same 'fashionable' London circle back in 2013, which included Poppy, Nick Grimshaw, Rita Ora, Pixie Geldof, Kelly Osbourne,

Jack Guinness and the uber-stylish Alexa Chung. Harry was with everyone for Alexa's thirtieth birthday party in November at the Edition Hotel in Soho and happily posed for pictures that ended up on Instagram.

Alexa, who was ten years older than Harry, loved his company. She enthused that he was amazing and radiated a magnetic quality: 'If he looks at you, it's like staring into the face of a lighthouse. I don't know what it is about that boy, he's just incredibly charming.'

Harry was readily accepted into this world. He even gate-crashed Poppy's hen party in early December at the Groucho Club, in Soho, when he donned a long blonde wig, pretending to be a member of former teen favourites Hanson. He danced around to the band's 1997 number one 'MMMBop', ending up sitting in the bride-to-be's lap.

Some commentators hinted that a member of a teenage boy band was perhaps not high end enough to mix in such exalted fashion circles, but that was proven to be nonsense two days later when Harry became the first man to win the British Style Award at the British Fashion Awards, the fashion equivalent of the BRITs or the BAFTAs. Alison Jane Reid observed, 'It's a big deal within the fashion industry.'

While the award, backed by Vodaphone, was voted for by the public, the fact that Harry was nominated in the first place demonstrated that he was a fully accepted face of fashion and not just a celebrity pop star brightening the front rows of runway shows or looking good with a supermodel on his arm. He was described as 'embodying the spirit of London' and as 'an international ambassador for London as a leading creative fashion capital'.

The nominations for his year included David Beckham, Kate Moss, Kate Middleton and, coincidentally, Cara Delevingne. For once the list did not include Alexa, who had won for the previous three years. This time she had to make do with co-presenting the award with the writer and former model Jack Guinness at the London Coliseum.

Harry was elegantly dressed in a Saint Laurent suit by Hedi Slimane. Suits suited Harry. Hedi Slimane, the creative director first at Dior and then at YSL, is responsible for what Alison Jane describes as 'the skinny silhouette in menswear since 2000'. He was heavily influenced by the music scene and youth culture that Harry, for one, represented.

The style winner kept his acceptance speech very short: 'Thank you for voting; this is very very kind. Thank you for having me here. I really appreciate it. Thank you.' The next day, Harry's success was the only fashion story in town.

More and more it was becoming clear that Harry would be the centre of attention wherever he went. The best he could hope for was to keep quiet until after the event. That was the strategy with his big sister's graduation at Sheffield Hallam University.

He was sat next to his mum and couldn't have looked any more delighted when Gemma went on stage to receive her degree from Professor Robert Winston, Ben's dad, who was chancellor of the university. She had achieved First Class Honours and Qualified Teacher Status in Science Education.

Afterwards, Harry posed for a picture with Gemma that he posted on Instagram with the short message: 'My sister graduated today. She's all clever and that.' And that was all he had to say — it wasn't about him and it wasn't his day. The university followed up by posting a couple of photographs on Twitter with the caption: 'A special guest attended today's graduation ceremony to see his sister collect her degree. Welcome @Harry_Styles.'

Privately, however, Harry was receiving some very unwelcome attention. He couldn't, it seemed, move without hearing the click of more than one paparazzi camera. It was time to take action. Quietly, he instructed David Sherborne, one of the most celebrated lawyers in the country, to institute legal proceedings on his behalf.

David was the go-to lawyer for A-list litigants, having represented Princess Diana, Michael Douglas, Sienna Miller, Kate Moss and many more. At the Leveson Inquiry into the British press he represented 'core participants' including the McCanns, J.K. Rowling and Hugh Grant.

In more recent times he has been instructed by Meghan Markle and Johnny Depp.

On Harry's behalf, he won a court order against a group of paparazzi. The unnamed photographers were ordered by Mrs Justice Nicola Davies to stop pursuing Harry by car or motorcycle, placing him under surveillance or loitering within fifty metres of his place of residence in order to monitor his movements.

Harry was mindful of not appearing precious and unaccommodating to his loyal fans. David told the court: 'This is not a privacy injunction. Mr Styles is not trying to prevent fans approaching him in the street and taking photos. He remains happy to do that as he always has. Rather, it is the method or tactics which have been used by a certain type of photographer.'

This was a significant victory for Harry, although he was not in court and made no comment about the case. He had hated the way Caroline Flack couldn't even open her front door when she was in a relationship with him. He was determined to put a stop to it as far as he was concerned.

Professionally, things could hardly have been going better. *Midnight Memories* had been released towards the end of November and was already astonishingly successful. One Direction became the first act to debut at number one on the US *Billboard* chart with its first three albums. In the UK, it was the fastest-selling album of 2013, clocking up sales in the first week of release of 237,000.

The demand was exceptional everywhere and by the end of year *Midnight Memories* was the best-selling album in the world, with sales of four million. The critics generally seemed on board with the slightly different, rockier sound – more guitar throwback than Euro pop synthesisers. *USA Today*'s Brian Mansfield was encouraging: 'The best songs, such as the current single, "Story of My Life," suggest the group's finest memories may still lie ahead.' Alison Stewart in the *Washington Post* noted, 'The songs are expertly made, impressively (sometimes very impressively) sung, nominally more adult and in every way quite decent, which is all they need to be.'

Tongue-in-cheek, Alison also wondered, 'Who might be the first to unwisely go solo? To be hospitalised for "exhaustion"? Which one is Justin Timberlake?'

One Direction's first stadium tour had been announced for 2014. They would be spending six months on the road performing at the largest venues throughout the world. How could they possibly keep up this pace?

12

KEEPING UP
WITH HARRY

Behind the scenes progress was being quietly made about Harry's future. He was proving to be very popular in important showbusiness circles in Los Angeles. He fitted in. He was charming, good company and very discreet. He was always the one in One Direction.

A very significant development had occurred without fanfare before One Direction had even released a record. Back in August 2011, Simon Cowell's Syco Entertainment had formed a partnership with Front Line Management, the largest management company in the world.

The deal was for Front Line to manage the winners of the American version of *The X Factor*, which was about to launch in the US. It was an arrangement totally separate from the UK where contestants, including 1D, were handled by Modest Management.

The chairman and CEO of Front Line was Irving Azoff, arguably the most influential man in the music business. He was also in charge at Ticketmaster and was executive chairman of Live Nation Entertainment. In 2012 he topped *Billboard*'s

Power 100, recognising him as the most powerful man in the industry. He was the ultimate behind-the-scenes player.

Since he started as a manager in the 1970s he had a long association with some of the biggest names in pop and rock, including the Eagles and Fleetwood Mac, two of Harry's favourites growing up.

His son Jeffrey was following in his father's footsteps, learning the business as a manager at Front Line with ambitions to strike out on his own at some point. His wife Shelli has been the best friend of reality matriarch Kris Jenner for more than thirty years; his daughter Allison Statter went to school with Kim Kardashian and is her oldest and dearest friend – one who shuns the limelight.

Harry stepped easily into this world. A social meeting of music folk in Los Angeles quickly led to Harry becoming part of the Azoff/Kardashian/Jenner circle. He and Jeffrey, who was eight years older, hit it off straight away. This was more than a possible professional interest somewhere in the future. Harry was soon practically part of the family and socialised with the Azoff friends, including the Kardashians and Jenners.

The nearest in age to Harry was Kendall Jenner, who was just a year his junior. The world knew of their friendship when they were photographed in November 2013 after having dinner at the renowned celebrity haunt Craig's in Melrose Avenue. The restaurant was a favourite of the Azoff and Kardashian clans.

This is not the place to go for a quiet meal if you are as well known as these two. It's not that you are going to be photographed dribbling spaghetti sauce down your chin. The hazard is when you arrive and leave as there is always the chance of paparazzi hanging around hoping to catch sight of Kim Kardashian looking fabulous.

Sure enough, Kendall and Harry were snapped leaving in his black Range Rover Sport. Kendall was in the passenger seat checking messages on her mobile phone. Harry was driving and looking straight ahead. Neither of them was smiling for the cameras. In fact, the opposite was true. They looked as if they were gritting their teeth in frustration at not even being allowed to grab some food without having their picture taken. Harry had already made it obvious through his High Court action that he hated this sort of intrusion.

The resulting photographs could scarcely have been less interesting but they still made the papers all around the world and became a hot topic on social media. Kendall was quickly sick of it – she tweeted, 'Enough with the rumours! I'm single, people.' Harry was even asked if they were dating on national television. He answered Piers Morgan's question, 'I mean, we went out for dinner, but no, I guess.'

The next night he was back at Craig's but this time he was meeting Jeffrey Azoff and they definitely weren't dating. He would dine there many times over the years but almost always as a guest of the Azoffs, the Kardashians or the Jenners – or all three.

At least Kendall was a more believable romance than some of his alleged flings. Harry was constantly being defined in the media by who he may or may not have been cuddling up to. He was described as 'Lothario Harry' and the 'floppy haired hunk'. It didn't matter where in the world he was.

Rod Stewart of all people sort of confirmed that Harry had been briefly involved with his daughter, Kimberley, who had been at school in LA with Kim Kardashian. This was entirely different from his low-key dinner with Kendall – a well-orchestrated, dressed-up encounter that was all celebrity smiles for the cameras when they left Dan Tana's on Santa Monica Boulevard.

It didn't seem remotely a thing, although Rod did say that Harry's car was still parked outside his Beverly Hills mansion the next morning. The encounter seemed to attract more publicity for Rod, who had a new album coming out.

There was even less evidence of a secret fling with Nicole Scherzinger, the *X Factor* judge who had been present when One Direction had been assembled on the show. The fact that she was sixteen years older than Harry seemed to be the only reason for believing a 'source'. He was now being described as a 'pop hunk'.

He had much in common with Kendall thanks to their love of fashion and mutual friends in that world. They were part of the same small network including Cara Delevingne, who saw Kendall often on modelling jobs around the world.

They were even pictured wearing the same t-shirt with the logo CaKe on the front, a gentle rebuke to the media who love to merge two celebrity names together. Kim Kardashian and Kanye West (managed at the time by Irving Azoff) were Kimye; Harry and Taylor Swift were Haylor; and Harry and Kendall were Hendall.

Kendall, like Cara, had started modelling at a young age. In Harry, she also found somebody who understood what it was like to be thrust into the limelight as a teenager. Kendall was fourteen when she began modelling and soon featured as the cover girl of *American Cheerleader*. She credited cheerleading with helping her to overcome a natural shyness. It also helped that she was a fixture in *Keeping Up with the Kardashians*, the biggest reality TV show in the world.

The show began in 2007 when Kendall was eleven and only her half-sister Kim Kardashian could properly be considered well known; but it quickly made stars of the whole family: Kendall's parents, Kris and Caitlyn Jenner; her younger sister Kylie Jenner; her half-sisters, Kim, Kourtney and Khloe Kardashian; and her half-brother Rob Kardashian.

Kendall grew up on the show. She appeared only sporadically in the early years because she was attending the Sierra Canyon School, ten miles from where the family lived in Calabasas, an upmarket suburb of Los Angeles. There seemed no hurry to rush her dramatically into the public eye. That changed when she was the subject of a coming-of-age episode entitled 'Kendall's Sweet Sixteen' that centred around her birthday party and obtaining her driving licence. This was her launch pad to stardom.

Optimistically she had said that she and her younger sister wanted to keep 'somewhat normal lives' for a while. But when she met Harry, she already had her own clothing line, had been on the cover of *Miss Vogue* and *Harper's Bazaar* and was on the books of Wilhelmina Models.

Her career seemed to be moving faster than her love life. Right from the start she preferred to be guarded about any romances, perhaps a side-effect of having to live in front of a TV camera for part of her day. Harry was the first high-profile man she was linked to and that might have been a damp squib if they hadn't been seen together a few more times over the next couple of months.

'Together' usually meant editing out the friends and security that were with them. When they went on a skiing holiday to the Mammoth Mountain ski resort in Eastern California, it was an Azoff adventure. The problem Harry faced wherever he went in the world was that someone was bound to take his picture and either post it online or, less preferably, give it to a picture agency. He tried his best to stay in the shadows or make any picture half-baked. When he was in the mountains he was wearing head–to–toe ski wear and huge mirror sunglasses that practically covered his face. When pictures appeared online, nobody seemed interested that Jeffrey Azoff was in shot next to Harry.

He was snapped again with Kendall by a member of the audience at a concert by the Eagles, long-standing Azoff clients. You could just about make out Harry with his arm around Kendall, but it could have been anyone and the photographer failed to notice her mum Kris and sister Khloe who were sitting next to them.

Coincidentally, Khloe and Kris have been the only family members who have confirmed that Harry and Kendall did date for a while. Kris was appearing by Zoom on *The Ellen DeGeneres Show* in 2021 to talk about the end of *Keeping Up with the Kardashians*. She played a game of 'Never Have My Kids Ever'. The question was, 'Never have my kids ever dated someone from a boy band'. Kris held up a sign declaring 'They have.' Ellen then said, 'Well, of course, Kendall right. And Harry.' Kris said, 'Yeah.' It wasn't exactly chapter and verse.

Kendall wasn't with him when he popped over to the Sundance Film Festival in Utah but Jeffrey, who had now joined CAA (the Creative Artists Agency), was, as were Harry's friends from London, Alexa Chung and Pixie Geldof. This time Harry was properly dressed up for the camera, posing on the red carpet before the premier of *Wish I Was Here* with the film's star and director Zach Braff. The movie world was one completely removed from One Direction and one Harry was keen to join. Perhaps Jeffrey could help?

Finally, Harry turned twenty. He was in the US on the day and reportedly Kendall threw a party for him at Caitlyn Jenner's Malibu mansion. His new Los Angeles 'family' were there. It seemed as if he had been a teenager forever, accomplishing so much in the five years – and earning £10 million – since he had taken the day off from Holmes Chapel bakery to go to an audition. To mark the occasion, Directioners donated more than £5,000 to the Believe in Magic charity. Harry tweeted in response: 'Just saw donations to believein-magicx for my birthday. Thank you. You're all very kind and nice. xx.'

Harry's gift to himself was rumoured to be a painting by the influential twentieth-century New York artist Jean-Michel Basquiat. All sorts of huge sums were floated about claiming to be the amount he paid for it at a Christie's sale but the art world decided it was £1.8 million. Harry was not tossing away his money on a whim. He was already renowned for being very smart with his fortune and art was recognised as a shrewd investment. Apparently the super-rich superstar Jay-Z had recommended it to Harry, but it could just as easily have been any of his new LA circle. They knew how to make a lot of money and how to hang on to it.

Basquiat has become one of the most sought-after artists, not least because he died tragically young at the age of twenty-seven in 1988. Cultural icons such as James Dean, Kurt Cobain and Jean-Michel Basquiat live forever if they leave us too soon. It's easy to see why the artist would appeal to Harry, because of his enduring reputation in the world of fashion. In 2005 he was listed in *GQ*'s '50 Most Stylish Men of the Past 50 years'; and in 2015 he was on the cover of *The New York Times Style Magazine*'s Men's Style Issue. In the 1996 biographical film of his life he was played by Emmy Award-winning actor Jeffrey Right while David Bowie took the role of Andy Warhol.

Harry has never confirmed that he owns a Basquiat but he was building up a private art collection. He had begun by reportedly buying a limited-edition portrait of Kate Moss by the peerless Banksy. He was conspicuous at the Art 13 fair at the Kensington Olympia. He was looking to decorate his London home with avant-garde pieces. He bought at least four random works, including a cast of a human skull placed upon a Bible, sat alongside a hypodermic needle; a work by renowned taxidermist Polly Morgan; some prints by south London artist Ben Turnbull; and, intriguingly, a sculpture for £20,000 depicting Jesus as a boxer, complete with boxing gloves and white shorts.

On another occasion Harry spent more than £33,000 on some twenty original pieces of artwork by Hayden Kays, the very collectable London artist said to straddle the gap between street art and high art. He is renowned for his typewriter works on love and sex and that's what Harry bought on a private visit to the Cobb Gallery round the corner from Nick

Grimshaw's place in London. As well as the world of fashion – and philosophy – Harry embraced the world of contemporary art in London.

Fashion was again the focus of his attention when he attended the 2014 London Fashion Show and watched Cara walk the runway at the Burberry Prorsum show. He deliberately gave Kendall's show a miss. She was the hit of the week when she walked in Giles Deacon's fall 2014 show. Her rising profile was clear when she was seated next to Anna Wintour, the Editor-in-Chief of *Vogue*, at the Topshop show.

Harry, it seemed, was mindful not to make he and Kendall the story at her big professional opportunities. They were about her. She did attend his belated British birthday at the uber-trendy Box Club in Soho, which Nick Grimshaw had helped to organise. For once the night out and the lurch home were not captured by the paparazzi. He wasn't pursued through the streets of London by men on motorbikes, so his legal fight seemed to be working.

He wasn't at the High Court in London the following month when his lawyer David Sherborne updated Mr Justice Dingemans on the legal action's progress. He was 'happy to inform' the judge that the four defendants involved had consented to permanent injunctions. The identity of other photographers that had harassed Harry was still being investigated. The solicitor added that it was hoped that because of the protection the courts had given the star, other individuals 'have in fact gone to ground and that is the last we hear of them'. Harry was keen for his legal team to emphasise again that he was not seeking a 'privacy injunction'; and he didn't want to stop fans approaching him in the street.

While this was a serious victory for Harry, he had been forced to confront the painful truth that certain aspects of celebrity life were not fun. The world contracted while friends you could trust became fewer. David Sherborne summed up what the legal success would achieve: '... an end to the crazy pursuit of the claimant when he is not on official duties.'

It would, however, soon be time to get back to those 'official duties'.

13

FOUR-D

Harry loves a flash car. When his pal Ed Sheeran passed his driving test and bought a Mini Cooper he told him not to be silly and to get an Aston Martin. He himself had splashed out $200,000 on a scarlet Ferrari California as soon as the money started pouring into his bank account. The convertible was the perfect ride for motoring around the streets of Beverly Hills.

He kept that car, along with his Range Rover Sport, for use in Los Angeles but in the UK he had invested, aged eighteen, in a dark grey Audi R8 Coupé that cost about £100,000 and was perfect for bombing up to Cheshire. It was the car he let his friends drive.

Harry also liked classic cars, buying a beautiful red Jaguar E-type Roadster that he would use to navigate his way around London. One of his first cars was the ultimate boy racer automobile, a white Ford Capri that was all the rage back in 1970. His vintage model of choice in LA was a white Mercedes.

He was behind the wheel of a Porsche when he drove up to the disused aircraft hangars in Cardington, Bedfordshire, where One Direction was rehearsing. He would be back on 'official duties' when the South American leg of the *Where We Are* tour began in the Colombian capital of Bogotá at the end of April 2014.

To prove his legal point about not seeking to stop fans approaching him, he was all smiles and posed for selfies when he was seen by some teenage girls. As soon as word got out the band was there it became the biggest local event for years, with hundreds gathering, hoping to catch a glimpse of one of the boys. The police were needed to keep a watchful eye on things. Harry cryptically tweeted that he was 'just hanging around today', which was the signal for the fans that he would be at the sheds.

This wasn't a repeat of the old-style bedlam when One Direction arrived at Heathrow. Mums turned it into a three-day social event, bringing their daughters, many of whom were under ten, to meet up with friends as if they were waiting for a glimpse of a member of the Royal Family.

The children would sing all the songs while they waited patiently. One mum, Dannii Ruff, who had brought her three children, observed, 'I am here because the kids wanted to come along – honestly! They spent two hours making all their posters. Everyone has been in a really good mood and when they've been driving off there's been no pushing or shoving from the crowd.' There was lots of screaming, though.

Harry always appreciated support from parents, who were, after all, bankrolling the tickets, the merchandise and everything connected with the group. At the press conference before the first show at the El Campin Stadium in the

Colombian capital, he said: 'I think with parents when they grow up they probably have a thing they were a fan of. I think they can relate to how their children feel. They get to relive it through their kids, which is quite nice.

'I think we put on a show where the parents come and enjoy it and they might not even be a fan of the music but they would say they've seen a good show.' They had their money's worth on the *Where We Are* tour. The band performed twenty-three songs, beginning with 'Midnight Memories' and ending with 'Best Song Ever'.

They had already played in front of more than 400,000 South American fans before the show moved to Europe, beginning with three nights at Croke Park in Dublin where Niall had first auditioned for *The X Factor*. The *Irish Independent* noted two strands to the band's audience – teenage girls and those still at primary school. The review was not exactly full of praise: 'While there's no shortage of energy – as you would expect from young men aged twenty and twenty-one – there just isn't the sort of U2-like showmanship that is necessary to make such a huge setting work.'

Was One Direction about to enter a phase of negative publicity? For once it wasn't Harry who hogged the headlines but Zayn and Louis. Footage emerged of them apparently smoking a rolled-up joint while in a car in Peru. A video was posted by the *Mail Online*, in which Louis is heard to say, 'So here we are, leaving Peru. Joint lit. Happy days,' before passing the suspicious cigarette to Zayn.

Liam, still the group's dad, issued an apology via Twitter: 'I love my boys and maybe things have gone a little sideways; I apologise for that. We are only in our twenties, we all do stupid things at this age. We all have a lot of growing up to do in extreme circumstance. I'm not making excuses but it's fact we are gunna fall short somewhere.'

Even Simon Cowell felt the need to give the band a positive comment: 'They're really respectful of their fans and they're a great British export … they've been a joy to work with … I've worked with lots of artists in the past who do lose the plot, who do lose respect for their fans, they've never done that.'

Harry said nothing about it but *The Sun* carried a story claiming that he was angry at the 'stupid and reckless' behaviour of his bandmates. Smoking a little weed was hardly grounds for being upset, although filming it might be thought to be stupid and reckless.

Perhaps more shocking to the Directioners was the strong rumour that Harry wanted to leave the band and strike out on his own. The dynamic within the group had subtly changed. Louis and Harry, for instance, didn't seem as close as they once were.

Louis would later explain that things became awkward between the two friends because of the constant rumours about the nature of their relationship. Conspiracy theorists online invented the name Larry Stylinson, an unwelcome variation on the Haylor label that had been given to Harry and Taylor Swift. Louis found it disrespectful to his girlfriend Eleanor Calder.

The fear that fans might question and analyse every minor interaction between him and Harry caused them to stay away from one another to a certain extent: 'It created this atmosphere between the two of us where everyone was looking into everything we did. It took away the vibe you get off anyone.'

Zayn confirmed that the constant scrutiny made it hard for Harry and Louis: 'They won't naturally go put their arm around each other because they're conscious of this thing that's going on, which is not even true. They won't do their natural behaviour.'

All the boys were far too professional for fans to notice any tension between them. They played three summer nights at Wembley Stadium. A crowd of 80,000 each night spent two hours queuing to get in. The London *Evening Standard* identified the band as Britain's most successful pop act of the twenty-first century. Tellingly, though, the headline in the newspaper referred to One Direction as 'Harry Styles and Co.'.

The band was filmed when they played the San Siro Stadium in Milan at the end of June. This time the director was Paul Dugdale, well regarded in the industry for his work with Adele, Coldplay and The Prodigy. Ben Winston and his partner at Fulwell 73, Leo Pearlman, were involved as executive producers. It wouldn't be the last time they would all work with Harry.

Subsequently, *Where We Are: The Concert Film* was shown in cinemas over a weekend in October when the American dates were completed. Over two days, it took an estimated $15 million worldwide, becoming the best-selling ever event cinema movie. The film was also the top trending topic on global Twitter, a further illustration that One Direction had no equals when it came to dominating the internet.

In her *Guardian* review, Leslie Felperin had an interesting view of Harry: complimenting him on his hair, she thought he had grown more handsome but 'he also looks like he can barely conceal his boredom. He's literally just going through the motions.' She added that it was surely only a matter of time before he went off to make that first solo album. Would she and many others who thought the same be proved correct?

The band was still on an annual conveyor belt: they needed to produce their fourth album during 2014 on the same shattering schedule as previous years. Julian Bunetta and John Ryan were heavily involved again but this time Liam and Louis were the most active songwriting members of the band and there was no blanket credit for all five on every track.

Harry's most memorable contribution was as co-writer of a track called 'Stockholm Syndrome'. He was the principal lyricist on a song that referenced the psychological attachment some captives experience towards their captors. Every song seems to have to be about a specific person or event and Harry said this was about a 'nympho' he had once known. Lyrically, it was an interesting song although the chorus 'Oh baby, look what you've done to me' was more boy band than Bowie.

The co-writers were Julian, John and the Swedish songwriter and producer Johan Carlsson, who had already worked with Harry. Together they had composed 'Just a Little Bit of Your Heart' for Ariana Grande. She recalled how it came about: 'I was at the studio one day and he was there, and literally, Johan and Savan [Kotecha] were like, "Hey, do you want to write something for Ariana?" And Harry was like "Sure, mate". And he just did.

'It's a beautiful song. He's an amazing writer. It's really beautiful. He's amazingly talented.'

The wistful ballad featured on her second album, *My Everything*, which was a US number one while One Direction's *Where We Are* tour was playing to packed stadiums around the States in the late summer of 2014. Intriguingly, Jeffrey Azoff and his partner, Glenne Christiaansen, went to several concerts on the tour. Glenne was also well known in the pop world as Snap Inc's Global Head of Music Partnerships.

Harry meanwhile had more than music on his mind, revealing the type of thoughtful individual he was becoming. When the band arrived in New Orleans in the last week of September 2014 to perform in front of 50,000 people at the Mercedes-Benz Superdome, he took the time to post on Twitter his support of the actor Emma Watson. Earlier in the week she had given the keynote address at the launch of UN Women's HeForShe initiative at the Museum of Modern Art (MoMA) in New York.

In front of an audience that included the then-UN Secretary General, Ban Ki-moon, the first female president of Finland, Tarja Halonen, and Meghan Markle before she met Prince Harry, Emma gave a rousing speech, pressing the point that gender equality was not just a 'woman's issue' but 'everyone's issue'.

Emma forcefully explained that in order for gender equality to be achieved, harmful and destructive stereotypes of masculinity and behavioural expectations for boys and men had to change. She urged, 'Both men and women should feel free to be sensitive. Both men and women should feel free to be strong.'

Her words inspired Harry, encapsulating the essence of non-toxic masculinity that he would come to embrace. He posted a picture of himself holding a handmade sign that declared 'HEFORSHE'. Underneath he wrote, 'I'm support-ing @UN Women and @EmWatson in HeForShe. As should you.'

It was a simple, unexpected gesture. Harry's post was retweeted 300,000 times and liked by nearly half a million users. He had a powerful global presence.

HeForShe was new and exciting. A much older and more familiar cause was Band Aid and One Direction took part in the 2014 version to raise money to combat the Ebola crisis in West Africa. The format hadn't changed since the original recording thirty years earlier. Some of the biggest names in music took part, including Chris Martin, Sam Smith and Ed Sheeran. One Direction was handed the Paul Young role of singing the first verse.

Harry was sporting his rock-star hair and a white shirt with racing cars dotted all over it, but he seemed subdued and out of sorts during the day at the Sarm Studios in Notting Hill. At the 'post-match' interview the band were not their old exuberant selves, giving rise to rumours that all was not well within the group and they might be on the verge of splitting or, at the very least, going on hiatus.

The new release was expertly sung by all, if perhaps, a little more downbeat than the original. The song reached number one in the UK, the only time One Direction topped the singles chart that year. The album, *FOUR*, however, reached the pinnacle on both sides of the Atlantic. This time round, they became the first band to have their first four albums debut at number one in the US.

As ever the reviews were mixed. *Time* magazine was very positive, highlighting further evidence of the boys' 'maturation into men'. It noted Harry's 'raspy swagger' and the 'spunky Styles-penned "Stockholm Syndrome"'. *Rolling Stone*, always big supporters of the group, was equally enthusiastic, declaring that One Direction had 'mastered the ancient boy-band art of whispering directly into listeners' ears'. Harry was described as a 'weapons grade hottie' but best of all, from his point of view, 'Stockholm Syndrome' was nominated as the album's brightest song: 'a slick, body-moving R&B ditty'.

Although *FOUR* didn't quite match the success of *Midnight Memories* it was still the sixth best-selling album of the year worldwide, with sales of 3.2 million. The tour, however, was a phenomenal success, with breathtaking figures. *Where We Are* was seen by nearly three and a half million people, generating gross receipts of more than $290 million.

But there would be very little time to bask in that success. Next year's stadium tour, called – accurately – *On the Road Again*, had already been announced with a fifth album needing to be written while on the road. Zayn, perhaps most of all, struggled with the rapid turnaround. He wanted a proper studio, not a makeshift one in a hotel room. He wanted to take his time.

The game was up as far as he was concerned when he completed some songs, including one called 'Pillowtalk', that were for him alone. It was thought that he wrote the song after the 'break' but that wasn't the case. A few years later Julian Bunetta would recall that Zayn played him the track in a smoky hotel room in Saitama, Japan. His verdict says it all: 'Fucking amazing!'

Three weeks later, Zayn was gone. The announcement came after the concert on 18 March 2015 at the AsiaWorld-

Arena in Hong Kong. His departure was brought on by stress and anxiety and he flew back to the UK to recover. In the official statement put out by the band on Facebook, he said, 'I want to be a normal 22-year-old who is able to relax and have some private time out of the spotlight. I know I have four friends for life in Louis, Liam, Harry and Niall. I know they will continue to be the best band in the world.'

That all sounded very reasonable but gradually that carefully constructed publicity line unravelled. In his very first interview after the split, he told *Fader* magazine that One Direction's music was as 'generic as fuck'. Two years later he admitted that he and Harry were not close while they were in the band. He revealed he 'never really spoke to Harry' and that he had never been under the impression they would keep in touch.

Harry has said very little about it, although he did say he thought it a shame that Zayn felt that way about One Direction's music. He wished him good luck in doing what he was doing. He did make one amusing reference to his now ex-bandmate when he guest-hosted *Saturday Night Live* in 2019. Recalling those boy-band days, he said, 'I love those guys, they're my brothers: Niall, Liam, Louis and, uh, Ringo, yeah, that's it.' People often forget that Ringo Starr was the first member of The Beatles to leave the group, if only for a short time.

Zayn's departure was actually perfect for Harry. While it had been widely assumed that he would be the first to leave, he would now not have that label on his back. He would not have to answer interminable questions about why he left. He would not face the natural disappointment of the millions of

The four faces of a budding superstar:

Top Left Cool: Harry does his best Bryan Adams impersonation as lead singer of his school band, White Eskimo.

Top Right Apprehensive: Harry wonders if Simon Cowell thinks he has the X Factor after he sings 'Isn't She Lovely' at his first televised audition in 2010.

Left Charismatic: The smile that melts a million hearts is already in place when Harry arrives at the BBC Radio 1 studios in Central London.

Below Excited: After singing Rihanna's 'Only Girl (In the World)', One Direction were within touching distance of the *X Factor* final.

The Harry hug: Throughout the UK promotional tour of 'What Makes You Beautiful', Harry showed he had a genuine connection with his fans.

In the modern world, every fan has a phone to capture a golden moment – Harry arrives at BBC Radio 1's Teen Awards at Wembley Arena in October 2012.

What Gareth Southgate missed – Harry shows off his skills at the Newcastle United training pitch in April 2013.

Harry looks as if he's strayed in from a different band when the remaining four members of One Direction attend the American Music Awards in Los Angeles in November 2015.

Harry has an inner circle of his closest friends: he greets James Corden at the Aquascutum show during London Fashion Week in February 2012.

Harry was often seen out and about in London with DJ Nick Grimshaw during the early years of One Direction.

Spot the celebrity: Harry fits right in among the front-row stars at the Burberry Prorsum show during London Fashion Week, September 2013, when supermodel Cara Delevingne has all his attention.

Growing up, Harry owed much of his enlightenment and empathy to the two most important women in his life. He clearly also inherited his winning smile from his mum, Anne, pictured with her son at the Sony Music BRITs afterparty in February 2013.

Harry has always praised his sister Gemma's intelligence, but she shares his eye for a fashionable outfit – looking elegant with him during the launch party of *Another Man* magazine at Albert's Club, London, in October 2016.

Harry jumped at the opportunity to introduce his hero, Stevie Nicks, when she was inducted into the Rock and Roll Hall of Fame for the second time in New York, March 2019. One day it might be the other way round.

In good spirits getting ready to play Spill Your Guts, Fill Your Guts with Kendall Jenner on *The Late Late Show* in December that year: his great pal Ben Winston, now the show's producer, is next to Kendall.

The Harry hug again. This time he joyfully embraces his manager Jeffrey Azoff after winning the Best Solo Performance Grammy for 'Watermelon Sugar' in March 2021.

The fashion icon: Harry models Gucci as co-host of the Met Gala in New York, May 2019.

He wore three outfits to the 2020 BRIT Awards, finishing the evening in a vibrant yellow Marc Jacobs suit.

This fabulous green feather boa makes the perfect accessory at the 2021 Grammys.

Perhaps the ultimate Gucci suit for the Red Carpet: at the BRIT Awards in May 2021 when he collected the Mastercard British Single award for 'Watermelon Sugar'.

Left: Director Christopher Nolan said Harry had 'an old-fashioned face', when he cast him as a beleaguered young soldier in the acclaimed war drama *Dunkirk*.

Below: Another period piece, this time set in the 1950s – playing Florence Pugh's husband in the psychological thriller *Don't Worry Darling*, in which he had the added bonus of indulging his passion for vintage luxury cars.

His hair was still the right length for *My Policeman,* starring alongside Emma Corrin.

Nothing about Harry Styles is uniform, except when filming his latest movie, *My Policeman*, in Brighton.

Harry cools off in beautiful Tuscany after finishing filming *My Policeman* in June 2021. At least he no longer had to spend an hour in make-up every morning covering his tattoos!

There's nothing better than a stroll after Sunday lunch, especially in the LA sunshine. Harry puts his arm around a happy Olivia Wilde after a meal with friends in their home neighbourhood of Los Feliz, in August 2021.

Directioners. Instead, he could knuckle down and put the fans first; there was a tour to finish and an album to make. And while all that was going on, he could quietly continue to plan for life after 1D.

PART THREE

A MODERN MAN

14

HISTORY

Los Angeles was becoming a home from home for Harry. His twenty-first birthday party in Hollywood was like an after-show night at the Oscars – there were so many stars who he could call friends. Kendall was there; and Cara; and Alexa; and Becks; and James; and the Azoffs.

Harry looked like a rock star, more heavy metal than boy band. He wore a black military-style jacket with a matching unbuttoned shirt. His hair was long, curly and casually messy. He couldn't stop smiling at Lola's Bar as he greeted guests who also included Chris Martin and Jennifer Lawrence, Kelly Osbourne and Rita Ora. His mum was back in the UK but Harry made sure they shared FaceTime from the party so that she could see what was going on and that he was enjoying himself on his birthday.

Adele, who had settled happily in Los Angeles, dropped by and gave him a signed copy of her iconic album *21* with a note just for him that said, 'I did some pretty cool stuff when I was twenty-one. Good luck!' Harry, who thought Adele was amazing, was understandably thrilled.

None of One Direction attended, unless they managed to sneak in and out and avoid any cameras. Niall, at least, had the excuse of being in Melbourne watching the Australian Open tennis. The supermodel Gigi Hadid, a great friend of Kendall and Cara, was there demonstrating again the small celebrity circles in which Harry moved. A few months later she would embark on a serious relationship with Zayn.

Harry was involved briefly with the Austrian model Nadine Leopold and she was at Lola's, although she didn't pose with him. Geographically the relationship was a non-starter, with Nadine based in New York, but they were seen by paparazzi shopping together in Beverly Hills and getting into his black Range Rover.

He wasn't back in Los Angeles again until May, after the Asian leg of the *On the Road Again* tour, when all anyone wanted to talk about was the Zayn drama. The now-four members of One Direction were booked to appear on *The Late Late Show with James Corden*, who had just taken over presenting the long-running late-night talk show from Craig Ferguson.

Harry's small world in London had now become his small world in Los Angeles. James had moved to California with his wife Julia and their young children. Ben Winston had moved too, becoming the executive producer on his show. The two old friends would become astonishingly successful in Hollywood in a very short space of time.

Harry was understandably delighted to have them close by in LA. There would always be somewhere to stay! When One Direction first appeared on *The Late Late Show*, it was too soon for Harry to make everything about him. Instead, he made sure he was very much part of the group, although he wasn't seated next to Louis. Instead, he was between Liam and Niall.

The rapport between Harry and James, who calls him Harold, was clear, especially when the host was trying to suggest he would have been the perfect replacement for Zayn. Harry was having none of it. Diplomatically, Liam said there were no hard feelings against their old bandmate. They had been a bit angry before experiencing a feeling of disappointment.

They had a laugh with James about the things that were thrown at them on stage, including the obligatory bra and pants, a hamburger and a dildo that almost hit Harry in the face. Louis admitted he preferred to sleep in the familiar surroundings of the tour bus rather than in an anonymous hotel room.

Perhaps of most interest was the news that Harry had been on a juice cleanse since they had arrived in LA. He admitted that he had been feeling 'gross' after flying so much while on tour. Although wellness was obviously not exclusively a California pursuit, Harry was embracing some of the aspects into his lifestyle.

He had taken up yoga and Pilates to help with a bad back. He had struggled with it for many years and hurling himself around a stage night after night didn't help. Sometimes he said the cause was his paper round back in Holmes Chapel when the bag was so heavy he would be lopsided on his bike. Other times he thought it was due to having one leg shorter than the other.

Yoga helped, particularly when they were on tour. He even tried Bikram Yoga, during which the room temperature is turned up very high to encourage the class to sweat. While in the Far East, he had started to meditate twice a day to properly rest his body and mind to cope with a schedule that was as demanding as ever.

Harry liked to party but readily understood that it was a one-way ticket to disaster if that's all you did on tour. He didn't sample the fleshpots of Bangkok, for instance, preferring to wander around some local markets and visit a Buddhist temple. There was more to his life than tequila.

The purpose of the break in LA was to promote the DVD of their concert film and to spend some studio time fulfilling their contract for a fifth album. For a change they had a few weeks to just write songs. 'It was just the coolest time to sit and think,' reflected Harry. 'It gave us the chance to focus on writing good songs that we like and we wanted to listen to.'

Harry's most memorable contribution was a wistful ballad called 'If I Could Fly', which became a big favourite among Directioners and one he would play live in the future when he began touring as a solo artist. As always, the fans wanted to know who Harry was missing in the melancholic lyric. He didn't say.

Instead, he explained that love songs did not have to be about one specific person. They should not always be taken too literally: 'They can be about a time or a place and you kind of personify it and stick a name on it and then everyone thinks it's about a certain person but I don't think it's always so black and white.'

Sometimes Harry was merely the observer. He explained, 'You can write a great love song about two people you're not.' He wrote or co-wrote two other songs, 'Perfect' and 'Olivia'. Again, he declined to say who, if anyone, the songs were about.

The principal difference between *Made in the AM*, as it would be titled, and the previous album was that the band knew it would be the last – at least for a very long time. Julian Bunetta, who again was very involved in writing and producing the album with John Ryan and fellow LA-based songwriter and producer Jamie Scott, confirmed that the vibe was different this time round. But he did notice how much they had all grown as songwriters and musicians.

One Direction soon had to leave Los Angeles for Cardiff when the *On the Road Again* tour resumed at the Millennium Stadium, as the Principality Stadium was then called. This was the first time the UK had seen them perform as a four-piece. While Zayn's easy high notes might have been missed by connoisseurs, the fans were as excited as ever, responding enthusiastically when the band instituted a screaming contest. The boys chatted to each other about the time they had first played the Welsh capital as part of the *X Factor* tour four years earlier – time really had flown by.

The *Daily Telegraph* thought their charm and personality was arguably their greatest asset, maintaining a 'kind of shambling boy-next-door amateurism at the heart of a slick, stadium-scale production'. But a more passionate review came from a devoted fan in her online blog. She burst into tears before they came on stage and spent the whole concert 'bawling her eyes out'. She concluded: 'I'm still wishing I could go back to that day and relive it.' As Harry said, 'We're not us if you're not you.'

They were back in the US at the end of August, performing at Soldier Field in Chicago when news leaked that they would be taking a break when the current tour finished.

Harry unofficially became a muse when he stepped out for a party during the second London Fashion Week in late September 2015. He looked very different as he arrived for *Love* magazine's Miu Miu brand event at Loulou's private members club in Mayfair. He was seen out for the first time in an eye-catching Gucci suit.

Quietly, he had been adopted by Italian-born Alessandro Michele, the game-changing creative director of the legendary label. A graduate of Rome's Academy of Fashion and Costume, he grew up with a love and appreciation for museums, art, antiquity and the romance of classic cinema.

Alessandro, who looks like a cross between Jesus and a member of the Grateful Dead, had set the fashion world buzzing at the first London Fashion Week that year in February when, at five days' notice, he produced the Gucci runway show. Originally, he had been hired to design handbags, before progressing to be the accessories designer, and then was called up to take charge of the prestigious London show.

Vogue Runway noted the collection's androgynous languor and, more relevantly as far as Harry would be concerned, its 'blurred gender divide'. At the time Gucci badly needed a boost amid reports of plunging sales. Alessandro was tasked with turning its fortunes around and nothing would benefit that ambition more than an association with one of the most popular pop stars in the world. Alison Jane Reid observed, 'Harry's partnership with Gucci is a marriage of celebrity and heritage. He is one of the biggest artists on the planet and when he wears Gucci that generates a huge amount of press, interest and cachet in the brand which directly leads to sales.'

His first public Gucci was a bold geometric-designed suit worn over an Yves Saint-Laurent black shirt. Alison Jane thought it a visual masterpiece: 'It's the look of the dandy rock star who likes to take a trip back to the sixties and seventies.' If it was a trial run then the public reaction was very encouraging. The floral suit he wore to the 2015 American Music Awards – the AMAs – was even bolder. While his bandmates looked sombre in dark well-tailored suits, Harry literally stole the red carpet. His suit, again worn over a black shirt and, this time, a black bolo (shoestring) tie was all anyone was talking about the next day, which was job done.

Alison Jane Reid was impressed: 'He looks extraordinary. Flamboyance and flower power suits him. It's about showmanship, whimsy and fantasy. The rest of the band appear so dull in comparison.' Not everyone took his new look seriously, some suggesting that it resembled some curtains or a bedspread you could pick up from Ikea.

Few people realised at the time that Harry now had a personal stylist. Harry had his own ideas and Alessandro produced the eye-catching wardrobe, but it was a young British stylist, Harry Lambert, who was responsible for the whole 'look' – from the way he wore his hair to the shiny black boots on his feet. Without any fanfare, the other Harry is arguably the most important figure in his client's journey to genuine fashion icon.

Lambert was the man who thought it was time for something new. He wanted the boy band pop star to be bold and be noticed more. Harry Styles was the first famous celebrity to wear one of Alessandro's catwalk creations on the red carpet. Lambert believed this was a turning point for Harry. He observed, 'It was very exciting to see everyone's responses, but also how great he looked in it.'

Lambert is very much a behind-the-scenes figure. He had been working with Harry since 2013 when they met during London Fashion Week. Just as the young Harry Styles had done in Holmes Chapel, Lambert grew up in his home town of Norwich with a love of clothes. He was the teenager dressing the mannequins in his local charity shop and who marvelled at the provocative costumes of Madonna.

His first thought was to be behind the camera, and he achieved First Class Honours in photography at the University College for the Creative Arts (UCCA) in Rochester, Kent. He realised, though, that it was styling the subjects for photographs that he preferred, so he did an internship with British *Vogue* before working directly as an assistant to one of the magazine's stylists.

There, Harry worked closely with a flotilla of young, go-ahead photographers, gaining a reputation that led to him being one of the judges at the Elite Model UK competition. He also worked for leading brands including Topman and Tommy Hilfiger. He was recognised within the industry but didn't have any celebrity clients until he met Harry Styles, a blank canvas who seemed willing to try anything. They shared the same relaxed outlook about fashion, which is why they both found the criticism of his AMA suit so funny.

His outfit almost overshadowed the band's second consecutive victory in the premier award category, Artist of the

Year. They were also named favourite group in the pop/rock category. It was old friends' night, with Ed Sheeran picking up favourite male artist and Ariana Grande winning favourite female artist. Taylor Swift won album of the year for *1989* – widely believed to have been mostly about Harry – but she wasn't at the Microsoft Theater on the night.

One Direction performed 'Perfect' on stage, which was very much an archetypal One Direction song – beautifully sung verses followed by an anthemic chorus that everyone in the audience could sing along to, whether in tune or not. At the time it was their latest release, the second single from *Made in the AM* after 'Drag Me Down'. The video for 'Perfect', directed by the renowned Sophie Muller, was a diverting snapshot of their life on the road. Beautifully shot in black and white at the InterContinental Hotel in New York, it showed them passing the time – Niall practised his golf-putting; they kicked a ball around; they looked at the skyline; ran down the corridors with their security or just sat about. Mostly, Harry wore a killer patterned shirt, but there's one quick scene where his stylist, Harry Lambert, is helping him put on a jacket.

'Perfect' was part of the publicity drive to coincide with the release of *Made in the AM*. For the first time a One Direction album did not debut at number one in the US, beaten to the top spot by Justin Bieber's *Purpose*. That scenario was reversed in the UK. Worldwide, *Made in the AM* sold more than 2.4 million copies and was the sixth best-selling album of the year.

Harry was determinedly upbeat, describing it as 'the best album we feel we've done'. Zayn said he didn't buy it. *NME* were unimpressed, describing the album as 'pretty silly' and suggesting that the band had 'shown their age'. (Harry was twenty-one.) The review concluded, tongue-in-cheek, 'Now they can get on with the fall-outs, drug binges, bankruptcy and podginess.'

More positively, *Rolling Stone*, always great supporters of the band, commended the album as 'the kind of record the world's biggest pop group makes when it's time to say thanks for the memories'. *USA Today* singled out 'Perfect' as an 'exemplary pop song' and praised the band's defiance and maturity; but the writer, Patrick Ryan, also made the point: 'It's tough to promote a new album when everyone's marked your gravestone.'

They had to soldier on for a little longer. They were back with James Corden for Tattoo Roulette, in which either Niall, who didn't have one, or Harry, who was covered in them, were going to lose. Harry lost and during a commercial break had 'Late Late' tattooed on his left arm. James referred to Harry as a good sport and he was a natural for what makes good TV. During the 'Never Have I Ever' game on *Ellen*, the question was 'Never have I ever made out with someone double my age'. He responded with good humour, 'What is this game?!'

The very last concert, if you can call it that, was when they were the guests on James Corden's popular Carpool Karaoke in December. Harry was wedged in the back seat of a Range Rover between Liam and Louis. There was no knock-about banter between them. With James, who has a good voice, they sang 'What Makes You Beautiful', 'Story of My Life', 'No Control', 'Perfect' and 'Drag Me Down'. The video has been watched nearly 184 million times on YouTube.

Just before that was broadcast in the US, they had jetted over to London to appear, fittingly, as the special guests on the live final of Season 12 of *The X Factor*. It was old pals' day for Harry. Simon Cowell and Cheryl were there as usual but they were joined by new judges Rita Ora and Nick Grimshaw. Olly Murs, who had been a support act for them on tour, presented alongside Caroline Flack.

Harry stood centre stage, in a red floral Gucci suit that had already become a trademark look for him. Five years after their own final on the show, they sang 'History' from the new album: 'We got a whole lot of history' … and they had.

15

AN OLD-FASHIONED FACE

The first thing that had to go was the hair. Harry needed a military clip for his role as Alex in the epic World War II drama *Dunkirk*. He couldn't look like a rock star if he was meant to be a soldier crawling along a beach in Northern France. At least any decision about a new look as a solo artist was taken out of his hands. He was philosophical about the short back and sides: 'We had to make the chop,' he said. 'I felt very naked but it was good! It's very breezy.'

He first auditioned for the film in February 2016. It wasn't just a whim, waking up one morning and deciding to try out for one of the biggest movies of the year. Behind the scenes Business Team Harry had been assembled to take over formally as soon as the final commitments to One Direction had been fulfilled. The announcement that he was leaving Modest Management and joining Jeffrey Azoff at CAA was made just six weeks after Simon Cowell had wished the band a fond farewell on *The X Factor*.

Modest, run by music stalwarts Richard Griffiths and Harry Magee, were gracious about the train of events and said, 'We wish Harry the very best. It has been a real pleasure working with him. Harry is a total gentleman and we know our good friend Jeffrey Azoff will look after him. We look forward to sharing some great wine with them next time we are in LA.'

The next step was Jeffrey Azoff's departure from CAA a couple of weeks later to set up his own company, Full Stop Management. Harry was his star first client. The Creative Artists Agency remained his agents and it was through them that he was sent along to his first audition for the new Christopher Nolan blockbuster. He has kept very quiet about any coaching in Hollywood he may have received. His agents sent a tape of Harry acting to the casting director and he was invited along to a workshop audition.

All any of the hopefuls knew was that the movie would be about the evacuation from Dunkirk in 1940, one of the most famous events of World War II. Nobody was concerned about the lack of information, because London-born Nolan was one of the biggest name directors in Hollywood, famed the world over for his three Batman films, *The Dark Knight Trilogy*.

Harry was already a fan of Chris, as he called the director, because he had loved *Memento*, his acclaimed breakthrough thriller starring Guy Pearce as an amnesiac victim. Harry observed, 'I think I always found his structure so interesting and in terms of the way he keeps stuff from the audience when the characters don't know about it and it hits you so much harder.'

He also appreciated the director's ability to involve the audience in what is happening: 'You always feel you're right alongside the character, rather than watching a film of stuff happening to them.' That would be of particular significance in his new movie that transported us to the beaches alongside the desperate soldiers.

Harry didn't even know what part he was up for when he arrived for his first audition since his *X Factor* journey began back in 2010. He was in a group of other young actors who were making their way in their profession by more traditional methods.

One of them, Olivier Award winner Jack Lowden, remembers the day when Harry joined them at the workshop: 'Of course I knew who he was. When he walked into the audition, I was like "Whoa, that's Harry".'

The process that day was best described as a round robin, with the actors reading for different parts so that Nolan could see who was best suited to certain roles. Harry recalled chatting to another hopeful, Fionn Whitehead, who would end up being cast as the everyman soldier, Tommy, whose story starts and ends the film.

Fionn and Harry would become great friends. The film was a breakthrough for Fionn, who had been working in a coffee shop while Harry was touring the world. At nineteen, he was even younger than Harry, but like the pop star, his hair was much too long and curly for the part and needed to be sorted out.

While the young actors all knew of Harry Styles, the director himself said he hadn't realised just how famous his new cast member was. Christopher admitted, 'I mean, my daughter had talked about him but I wasn't really that aware of it. I cast Harry because he fit the part wonderfully and truly earned a seat at the table.'

One of the qualities that Harry possessed that raised him above most of the other actors at the workshop was his old-fashioned face. 'He has the kind of face that makes you believe he could have been alive in that period,' observed Christopher.

The excitement of the younger generation at the prospect of Harry Styles the film star was echoed by the eleven-year-old niece of the theatrical heavyweight Mark Rylance, who had a major role in the film. He remarked, 'She was just more excited than anything I've ever done because I was going to be acting with Harry Styles. I went up in her estimation.'

Mark was just one of many well-known actors in a cast that included Kenneth Branagh, Tom Hardy and Cillian Murphy. The prospect of working alongside such luminaries was daunting even for a man who had performed in front of millions.

Harry started training for his part of young soldier Alex. The movie would primarily be made in Northern France between July and September 2016, so he had some time to prepare. He had always enjoyed swimming in the Hampstead ponds near his North London home, but this was entirely different.

Harry was sent to Dunkirk two weeks early to train as a soldier alongside Fionn and the Welsh actor Aneurin Barnard. Surprisingly, he wasn't actually asked if he could swim until the day before they set off. This was a proper bootcamp, not one where they hung out rehearsing songs. Now he had to swim in the sea wearing an overcoat and carrying a pack.

Understandably, Harry was nervous, at least when filming began. He was in awe of a director of Christopher's reputation: 'You definitely feel like you don't want to let him down.

It's a big part of the nerves.' Harry was frank about how he felt in an interview with *The Big Issue*. He recalled that he was surprised by the sheer scale of the production: 'You walk on set the first day and get taken aback by everything.'

Christopher deliberately chose young, inexperienced actors such as Harry and Fionn so that everything they said and did would appear fresh and a new experience for them. At the end of one scene on his first day, the director turned to Harry and said, 'Congrats on your first close-up.' He gave him confidence in what he was doing. 'He never makes you feel like you have to try too hard.'

Harry plays one of the young soldiers desperately trying to reach England from Dunkirk by boat. It was an unglamorous role in an unglamorous film that reflected the sombre enormity of what actually took place in 1940, when more than 338,000 allied troops were rescued by an assembled potpourri of 800 boats.

Harry's opening line in a film was delivered with a mouthful of toast and jam : 'What's wrong with your friend?' He has quite a few lines but they are mostly short sentences, although he delivers 'For fuck's sake!' with vigour and manages to get his tongue around, 'If he does, it's in an accent thicker than sauerkraut sauce.'

Sometimes Harry happily admits he didn't really know what was going on. One day his character was in the water near a boat when all hell was let loose: 'There was a boat blowing up as you were swimming, there were bullet noises everywhere, there was fire, people screaming … There was a lot going on. There was a bit where you're like, are we filming? What just happened?'

That wasn't the scariest part of filming. He discovered being under water, especially for a long scene, created a natural sense of panic. He explained, 'While you're down there filming and acting out the scene, you're also thinking, "I cannot breathe for much longer".'

Harry put any hardship he and his fellow actors may have faced into perspective, comparing it to the soldiers' ordeal. He observed, 'When you watch the film, it puts it in context what these guys might have actually gone through. It was so real. And it makes it very difficult to complain about what we might have gone through for a few hours.'

Harry endeared himself to the cast and crew by not playing the 'big I am' on set. He may have had security discreetly on hand to make sure no fans turned up to disrupt filming but that was as far as he took his star status. His modesty is almost as much of a trademark as his fashion choices. Christopher noted that Harry just enjoyed being part of the ensemble: 'Like the soldiers they played, the actors were all in it together and supported each other very well.'

This is not a film in which the heroes bask in triumph and are welcomed home with a tickertape parade. There were no winners at Dunkirk – only survivors. It's a film that almost exclusively features male characters. Only two women have brief speaking parts – one a nurse and the other waving at Kenneth Branagh from a rescue boat. Having Harry Styles in the film ensured that thousands of young women who might have given a grim war movie a miss would be queuing up to see it at their local cinema.

Unsurprisingly, most of the publicity surrounding the film centred on Harry, but the hype was controlled and he made sure he didn't overplay his role, keeping his interview responses quite bland: 'I feel incredibly lucky to have been a part of such an amazing story. I really enjoyed it. It was a good experience.'

The reviews for the film were exceptional and Harry was mentioned favourably in most of them. The *Independent* said, 'Styles is very competent and his performance does not stick out like a sore thumb as many feared.' *Rolling Stone* observed that he played a small role with 'subtle grace and zero pop star showboating'. *Glamour* magazine thought he was 'too darn handsome to play an undernourished, exhausted soldier'. NPR (National Public Radio) meant it as praise when pointing out that he didn't stand out in the part 'except for being a little handsomer than anyone else'.

One thoughtful point made by *Insider* online was that you could appreciate the movie without thinking, 'Hey, that's Harry Styles.' To achieve that, it was very important that Harry didn't sing. Ed Sheeran, for instance, did not receive universal applause after he sang during an episode of *Game of Thrones*. He looked and sounded exactly like Ed Sheeran. Fortunately, Harry did not lead his stricken comrades in a beach chorus of 'Kumbaya'.

His co-stars answered questions about Harry with good grace, recognising that he didn't ask for any of it. Jack Lowden observed, 'I feel like if he wants to act, then why shouldn't he! It's a very brave thing to just jump straight in like he has.' Fionn summed it up, 'The media have put too much emphasis on this one guy instead of the piece as a whole and the ensemble as a whole.'

Just how much Harry Styles added to the film's box office is impossible to guess. The film was the most successful World

War II movie of all time, grossing worldwide $522 million on an estimate budget of $100 million. More importantly perhaps, it was widely regarded as a masterly film, although it lost out on the Best Picture award at the Oscars to *The Shape of Water*.

Christopher Nolan said he thought Harry was a natural actor and would work with him again in the future. Harry commented drily that he definitely improved his swimming while shooting the film but would not commit to any future acting, declaring that he was 'one and done'. That, of course, stopped any speculation.

The beauty of making a film was that it could fuel interest in Harry's solo musical career, too. The public and media interest could all tie in together, presenting him in a completely different light from his image as one member of a boy band – make the film, record the album, release the album, release the film. Harry's next job was to actually write the album.

16

THE PINK ALBUM

After spending what seemed like years up to his neck in the English Channel, Harry chose the ideal spot to recharge the batteries and get away from it all – the sun-kissed Caribbean island of Jamaica. It wasn't all play, however; there was the serious business of writing songs and, just as importantly, finding the right tone and direction for the first solo album.

Harry took with him the recently assembled Team Styles – the group of super-talented musicians, writers and producers who had been working with him on his solo music project in Los Angeles before he set out on his filming adventure. He had made a clean break from everyone connected with One Direction.

The only throwback to the old days when he checked in to the Geejam writing and recording retreat in Port Antonio on the north-eastern coast of the island was a song called 'Two Ghosts'. He had written the track with Julian Bunetta and John Ryan in 2013 but had kept it in his back pocket, believing it would need some extra attention in the future.

'Two Ghosts' is a break-up song and at the time One Direction had another Harry slice of melancholia, the plaintive 'If I Could Fly', so it made extra sense to hang on to this one, especially as amateur sleuths reasoned it was about Taylor Swift and that debate would have been a distraction when *Made in the AM* was released.

The song begins 'same lips red, same eyes blue', which many assumed was a reference to her. Harry never said, and when pressed about it by Nick Grimshaw on Radio 1, let out a little scream and called for Jeffrey Azoff to help him out. 'I think it's pretty self-explanatory' was all he would say.

Such speculation always attracts interest in a song. It's a tried-and-tested publicity device that Taylor herself has used many times. Much of the album *1989* was said to be about Harry, including one track entitled 'Style'.

'Two Ghosts', as Harry explained, explores a universal theme about two people changing and growing apart. Musically the track represented a more mature sound for Harry, in line with his desire to hark back to the classic eras of the past where Joni Mitchell, Fleetwood Mac and Pink Floyd would jostle for favouritism in vinyl record collections.

But it was only one song and enjoying the peace and tranquillity of the Caribbean was not getting the other nine he needed for the album written. Harry's Jamaican entourage was led by the Grammy Award-winning producer Jeff Bhasker, a well-respected figure in LA music circles.

Jeff was a very accomplished musician, having studied at the Berklee College of Music in Boston. His entrance into the music business came as the keyboardist with Kanye West and, subsequently, as his musical director. He was far from being just a hip-hop specialist, however, and won Grammys for his work with Fun on the number one 'We Are Young' and on the equally successful 'Uptown Funk' by Mark Ronson.

He was a big name for Harry to have in his corner, but Jeff was initially unsure if the association was right for him. He asked Harry round for an initial chat and to give him the sniff test. His dog was notorious for biting people but Harry seemed completely unfazed when given the wary eye by the pet. He pointed his finger at him and the dog walked over and started licking it. Jeff recalled, 'That was when I was like, "This guy has something special".'

Harry already had a good idea of the direction he wanted his solo music to take. He brought round some examples, or 'references' as he called them, so that Jeff could hear the type of music that inspired him – there were no big Swedish anthems. Instead, he played him The White Stripes, the peerless American rock duo. At first Jeff thought Harry was playing his own actual demos and was mightily impressed until he realised it was the genuine article. He was still excited with the direction Harry wanted to take with his music.

Jeff was in his early forties with a young family, so he was keen to share the load. He brought in Alex Salibian and Tyler Johnson, both of whom had originally been his assistant before moving on to producing roles within his company, Kravenworks. The idea was to form a band around Harry that would become a creative unit.

Jeff wasn't there at the first day, which had been back in Venice, Los Angeles, before Harry's *Dunkirk* commitment. A new studio engineer, Ryan Nasci, joined Alex and Tyler to welcome Harry. They had arranged for a guitar player to join them but he failed to show. Ryan piped up that his roommate was a guitarist and he could give him a call. The man in question, Mitch Rowland, was working as a dishwasher in a pizza restaurant but could come in the next day. Mitch was in a local band and Tyler had already seen him play a kind of seventies rock guitar that would fit perfectly with what Harry wanted.

Mitch, who had recently moved to LA from his native Ohio, had never been in a recording studio before. He'd never heard of Harry Styles. Jeff recalled, 'Mitch comes down and the second he plugged in his guitar and started playing, Harry's eyes just lit up and he was like, "This is the guy".' Mitch would become Harry's new best friend in California.

Harry's admiration for Mitch increased when he discovered he was an accomplished drummer as well. Everyone, it seemed, could play, so Harry had an instant band with whom he could write and record his first album. After a couple of days, Mitch said he couldn't come in tomorrow because he had a shift at the pizza parlour. 'Well, you might not need to do that anymore,' said Harry.

Alex, a classically trained musician, acted as musical director, but Harry had taken the lead on the first morning and was the boss. During his time with One Direction he had improved his musical skills, playing guitar with Niall and practising on any piano he came across. As a result he could make far more of a contribution to songwriting than just a smart line to start things off. He was creative and involved every step of the way.

While there was a flurry of songwriting at the outset of the Instant Harry Band, he felt they needed to have some weeks with no other distractions, which is why he suggested Jamaica. Artists including Drake, Florence and the Machine, Katy Perry and Lily Allen have all found Geejam an idyllic place to work and play. Even the legendary artist Banksy was a guest one year.

Harry and the gang were there to work 90 per cent of the time and play was limited to watching rom-coms on Netflix in the evening. Then it was back to the studio, even if it was two o'clock in the morning. Jeff Bhasker, who had pretty much seen it all, was energised by the informality and immediacy of the way they were working.

Jeff was particularly impressed with Harry's clever wit and how well-read he was. Harry has been modest about his intelligence, preferring to applaud his sister for her academic achievements, but brains and the ability to absorb cultural influences was something he brought to the table – whether discussing philosophy with Alain de Botton or poetry with his producer.

Harry was appreciative of the work of the renowned Los Angeles poet and novelist Charles Bukowski, who was born in Germany but grew up in the US. He chronicled the tribulations of the less-advantaged in LA, where he spent most of his life. In the land of Hollywood, he described the ordinary lives of poor Americans.

A fan once threw a copy of *You Get So Alone at Times That It Just Makes Sense* for Harry on stage at the Gillette Stadium near Boston during One Direction's *Where We Are* tour. Harry picked up the book, stopped the concert – in front of 80,000 people – for a moment or two and quietly read a passage from the book of poetry that Bukowski wrote in later life. It contained observations that could resonate across the generations. 'Regret is mostly caused by not having done anything.'

Harry and Jeff would talk of Bukowski's gritty realism and his ability to speak from the heart. That was the direction they both wanted for the album. During one session after lunch, Harry started playing them a melody on the piano. He already had a lyric. Mitch and Ryan jumped all over it to flesh out the sound and, with Jeff now on the piano, Harry started singing. Mitch played guitar and drums, Ryan took the bass and three hours later they had made the first cut of 'Sign of the Times'.

The lyric was not a slice of whimsy but a thoughtful commentary on the things that matter in the world, especially equal rights for all, written by a man with a developing social conscience. The basis for the song was the story of a mother giving birth to a child and being told that she only has five minutes to live: she has to tell her child to stop crying and have the time of their life. The final song was an epic six minutes of sensitivity including the memorable line: 'You can't bribe the door on your way to the sky.'

His original version of the song contained the words 'Why are we always fucking running from the bullets?' One of the team suggested ditching the f-word in favour of 'stuck with' which sounded just as good and reduced the risk of anyone being offended by the song.

Jamaica wasn't all work. The team's two-storey hilltop villa was luxurious and Harry could begin his working day by going for a swim in a quiet, out-of-the-way cove where he was unbothered by anyone or anything – exactly what he wanted from this island interlude.

A film, *Behind the Music*, showing the making of the album revealed Harry to be quite drunk on one occasion after he enjoyed a few cocktails at the local Bush Bar after recording. He jumped over a bridge and landed in the water fully clothed.

Most of the album was written in Jamaica, but back in Los Angeles, Harry was still one song short. For a complete change, he went on a blind date with a student from Greenwood, South Carolina, called Townes Adair Jones. She had moved to California to study French and philosophy at UCLA. Apparently her sister, the actress Gilland Jones, made the arrangement.

Harry enjoyed the evening and next morning, seeking inspiration for one last song, decided to write about the experience. The clues that this was a girl from out of town were clear from the lyrics. She was also a big reader who had a book for every situation – though he didn't say if they talked about Bukowski or Alain de Botton.

As usual, Harry refused to be drawn on her identity but he did admit that her name, 'Townes', was in the song, which rather gave the game away. Harry had created a little piece of mystery which acted as publicity catnip for the media when he was promoting the record. Townes herself, who is named after her father, has never spoken about Harry, although a 'friend' was quoted as saying she loved the song but didn't want any attention.

Now the album was finished other than the all-important final mix, the title had to be finalised as well as the choice of first single. Provisionally the first Harry Styles album was going to be called *Pink*. He often quoted the observation from the artist Paul Simonon, bass player with The Clash, that, 'Pink is the only true rock and roll colour.' One major drawback was that one of the biggest artists in the world was called Pink so it might be confusing, and the superstar didn't need any free advertising. *Sign of the Times* was also a non-starter because it was already the title of a classic album by Prince.

So they went with *Harry Styles* as the title, which was obvious, accurate and left no doubt that this was the first solo album. He decided to take it with him on a trip back to the UK so he could play it to his family. His mum liked it and cried happily at her son's achievement. Unfortunately, there was some sad news. Louis Tomlinson's mother Jay had died from leukaemia at the age of forty-three. Jay had become a great friend of Harry's mum in particular, but he too had always enjoyed her company. Privately, there were also concerns regarding the failing health of his much-loved step-father Robin.

Having chosen the album title, the next job was selecting the first single, which would act as the most important tool in the promotion of the album. There was little argument where Harry was concerned – it was always going to be 'Sign of the Times'. The only dilemma was whether to edit a radio version of the six-minute song.

Fortunately, the boss of Columbia Records, Rob Stringer, decided they should definitely go with the long cut. He was a great supporter of Harry, in much the same way as he had nurtured Adele through the early days of her first album, *19*. Harry was rumoured to have signed with the One Direction label, a subsidiary of Sony, back in the summer of 2016, but it wasn't until the following February that Rob confirmed that his company would be releasing *Harry Styles*.

Following the end of their contracts as 1D, Harry was the only member of the band that signed with their existing label.

Harry, who was always aware of a business opportunity, started his own record label, Erskine Records, which would release his output under the Columbia umbrella. His personal assistant, Emma Spring, who kept well away from the limelight, was named as the company director. He called it Erskine after Erskine House, a large property next to Hampstead Heath and the sixteenth-century Spaniards Inn. Harry already had two companies in his name – HSA Publishing and Rollcall Touring.

While the whole world seemed to know 'Sign of the Times' was coming, the first time it was heard in full was on its day of release in the UK at the beginning of April 2017. Nick Grimshaw played it on his Radio 1 breakfast show when Harry was his special guest. The release coincided with Rob Stringer being appointed as chief executive of Sony Records, the parent company of Columbia, making him an even more powerful ally.

Harry performed the song for the first time for a television audience on *Saturday Night Live*, the long-running late-night US show. He had a very good relationship with *SNL*. One Direction had appeared on the show three times but this was his first time as a guest without the band. It was a tour de force and he showed he had comedic flair and didn't mind sending himself up. He started off by dancing and singing his way through 'Let's Dance' by David Bowie during host Jimmy Fallon's opening monologue.

The highlight was his hilarious impression of Mick Jagger as a contestant on *Celebrity Family Feud*, dressed in a white suit and employing all the over-the-top mannerisms of the Rolling Stone. 'Why would anyone in a successful band go solo? That is insane!' said Harry in his best Mick voice. Lastly, he was in a Civil War sketch as a Confederate soldier when a downbeat Civil War song turned into a boy-band number. He even dealt with his stick-on beard becoming unstuck in a slapstick way.

The serious point of the show was to showcase two new songs. He began with 'Sign of the Times', negotiating his way past some very high notes, dressed in a Gucci patterned suit. His band had now changed to the musicians who would play live with him. Mitch was still there, laidback as ever, but he couldn't play drums as well as lead guitar, so fortunately his girlfriend Sarah Jones was a superb drummer and was able to take over the sticks.

Mitch and Sarah had met in the pizza parlour where he worked and hit it off discussing music. Sarah, originally from Hereford, was an experienced touring drummer, playing with Bat for Lashes, Bloc Party and the synth pop band Hot Chip. She had also released her own records as Pillow Person. They would have to get used to Harry sleeping over at their house.

This particular episode of *Saturday Night Live* was the first to go live coast to coast, so it was the best possible showcase for the new material. Harry played guitar for the second song, 'Ever Since New York', which was an interesting choice as it's a downbeat, world-weary reflection on love and loss and a throwback to the seventies folk rock of the Eagles. He didn't choose to play his favourite track from the album, 'From the Dining Table', which he liked because, he said, it was the most personal.

Harry sang 'Sign of the Times' for the first time in the UK on *The Graham Norton Show*. It was a powerful and confident performance – a step up from the initial outing on *SNL*, with more smiles and less grimaces. The audience shrieked.

On the couch afterwards he sat next to Rob Brydon and was a good sport when Graham played a game of Warren Beatty Deadpan – a sort of true or false depending on the guest's ability to keep a straight face. Taking a slice of carrot cake along to present to Stevie Nicks on her birthday in 2015 when he took Gemma to a Fleetwood Mac concert at the O2 turned out to be true; catching chlamydia from a koala was definitely not true; and auditioning for the role of the next Hans Solo was a maybe.

'Sign of the Times' went to number one in the UK charts on its release, knocking Ed Sheeran's 'Shape of You' off the top after thirteen weeks. Ed was back at number one the following week. Harry had played his friend the tracks from the album before it was released and ignored the fact that he had liked one particular song – it didn't make the final selection and Harry has never said what song it was. Ed had also offered him one of his own songs in the early days of writing the album – that wasn't chosen either.

Unusually, 'Sign of the Times' made number one before the video was released. In this case, it was used as another promotional tool for the album. Harry was featured on a blustery day on the scenic Isle of Skye, singing and soaring as a spirit on his way to heaven. He even walked on water. It's just Harry in the video and we don't realise he is suspended from a helicopter the whole time. The effect was immensely atmospheric and won many plaudits for the French director, Woodkid (Yoann Lemoine), including winning the BRIT Award for Best Video.

Harry flew back to Los Angeles for the launch of *Harry Styles*. The name did not feature on the front cover; instead, we see Harry's bare back and the back of his head as he splashes himself with water. The artwork was shot by the much sought-after, award-winning London-born photographer Harley Weir. She infused her work with a dream-like, erotic quality that perfectly suited Harry, who was styled for the pictures by Harry Lambert. This was photography as high art not jumping out of the bushes hoping to catch an unguarded moment.

Harley graduated from Central Saint Martins School of Art and Design with a BA in Fine Art in 2010. She taught herself photography with the goal of moving people with her images. She was soon in demand with magazines and leading fashion brands including Stella McCartney, Calvin Klein and Topshop. She has also been constant in using her work to support charities that mattered to her – something that Harry was about to do.

A second single, 'Sweet Creature', was made available for streaming and downloads. Again, he declined to say who it was about, although he did admit the ballad was specifically about one person. *Teen Vogue* observed that it might ruin the listening experience if we actually knew, although it was widely speculated that Kendall Jenner was his muse on this occasion. The magazine also described Harry as the 'king of the vague answers'.

The final push for the album was a week-long residency on *The Late Late Show* when he appeared every day with James Corden, culminating in his own Carpool Karaoke. They sang 'Sign of the Times', 'Sweet Creature', 'Hey Ya!' (the Outkast hip-hop party favourite) and 'Kiwi', a rock track from the album. The banter between the two friends was fun and natural, particularly when they sang 'Endless Love', the Diana Ross and Lionel Ritchie classic that Harry used to sing on his karaoke machine back in Holmes Chapel.

The highlight, though, was probably not the singing but Harry acting scenes from *Titanic* and *Notting Hill*, from which he delivered the famous Julia Roberts line, 'I'm just a girl, standing in front of a boy asking him to love her.'

Harry Styles debuted at number one on both sides of the Atlantic. The first-week sales in the US of 230,000 were the highest by a British male artist on debut. Globally it sold more than a million copies before the end of the year.

Generally, the critics were kind. They took the album seriously and not one to dismiss as a boy-band vanity project. The *NME* noted the debt to seventies and eighties classic rock, fusing together the Eagles, Elton John, Warren Zevon and Mötley Crüe. The Laurel Canyon sound of 'Sweet Creature' contrasted sharply with the 'Aerosmith stomp' of 'Kiwi'.

Variety observed that few people could have predicted that Harry would 'drop the kind of album that makes your uncle or mum perk up and say, "what's that?"'. The review also assessed the three defining themes of the record to be: 'Romance', 'lost love' and 'sex' – stating that even the 'sex is laced with sadness'.

Harry's use of dinosaur-rock lyrics to describe women was noticed. Roisin O'Connor, in the *Independent*, drew attention to lines such as she's a 'devil in between the sheets' and 'she's a good girl, such a good girl'. Giving Harry credit for his enlightened views on women she said, 'it's a shame he hasn't tried to break away from some of the more fatigued gender archetypes that dominate the rock music he clearly loves'.

He barely had time to enjoy his new house in Beverly Hills before he was flying back across the Atlantic for the premiere of *Dunkirk* but, first, the sad news that had been expected was announced. Robin Twist had died aged fifty-seven. Harry was very fond of his stepdad and the family asked for privacy as they grieved. Liam Payne tweeted, 'Harry my heart really goes out to you – such an extremely sad day for us all who knew Robin. What a kind, gentle and beautiful soul, a true rarity in today's world. Sometimes they really do take the best of us far too soon.'

Although Harry was now properly settled in Los Angeles, his family still came first. He dedicated *Harry Styles* in a simple, sweet way that said it all:

'To my family, I thank you every day for supporting me
And for loving me, H.'

17

RAINBOW

———

Six months before she met Harry, the chic and ultra-cool French-American model Camille Rowe was asked by a fashion magazine to name some of her favourite books. She suggested *The Master and Margarita* by the Russian novelist Mikhail Bulgakov, practically anything by Richard Brodhagen, author of *Finding God in Sin City*, and … *In Watermelon Sugar* by Richard Brautigan.

Camille was a passionate reader whose ambition away from the catwalk was to open a rare bookstore in Los Angeles that would be more like a community club where like-minded people could meet to chat and discuss literature. She would certainly have a willing participant in Harry Styles.

They were introduced at a fashion party in New York by mutual friend Alexa Chung, who seemed to know everyone. They were seen together for the first time having a dance at the Classic East Festival, at the Citi Field baseball stadium in Queens, when Fleetwood Mac was the headline act.

Camille was brought up mainly in Paris where her father, René Pourcheresse, owned a restaurant. Her mother, Darilyn

Rowe-Pourcheresse, was a model and dancer at the Cabaret Le Lido in the Champs Elysées. Their daughter came to modelling quite late, especially in comparison to Cara Delevingne and Kendall Jenner. She was already at university studying film when she was 'discovered' seated outside a café in the Le Marais district.

Her rise to prominence was rapid, fronting campaigns for Louis Vuitton, Chloé, Abercrombie & Fitch, and in particular Dior, for whom she was the face of new fragrance Poison Girl.

In 2016 she modelled in a Victoria's Secret show, as many of the women linked to Harry seemed to have done.

The same year, she was the Miss April cover girl in *Playboy*, six months after the magazine had announced it would no longer be publishing nude pictures. Camille styled herself for a series of photographs across fourteen pages wearing a combination of lingerie and her own clothes. *Highsnobiety*, the online lifestyle magazine, described the images as 'classy and sensual in equal measure', pointing out that they had a retro feel.

Camille was an enthusiastic advocate of feminism, participating in The Women's March through downtown LA the day after Donald Trump's inauguration. Across the country, millions of women and men took to the streets to protest against the values he represented. Harry was moved to tweet his support the following day: 'Yesterday was amazing. Unity and love. Always equal. H.' Camille had strong political views to impress upon Harry. When she was asked by *Elle* what she would do if she was invisible for the day, she replied, 'I'd go to the White House and punch President Trump.'

It's not surprising that she and Harry got along so well right from the start. They had so much to talk about: books and fashion, naturally, but also equal rights for everyone. Harry had already given his support for the HeForShe campaign. They also shared a devotion to yoga, both finding the time each day for a session of exercise and reflection that Camille said made her feel sane.

And they both had acting ambitions. Harry had just finished his first film while Camille, who had already appeared in a number of short films and videos, saw acting as a career path after her modelling days were over. They could swap stories about their first roles – Harry as Buzz Lightyear in *Chitty Chitty Bang Bang* in Holmes Chapel. Camille, aged twelve, was in a school production of Edmond Rostand's verse play *Chantecler*, in which all the characters are farmyard animals. She played a nasty hen.

The only less-desirable thing they had in common was no time. Harry was about to embark on his first solo tour. He warmed up for the year-long global marathon with a small gig at the world-famous Troubadour club on Santa Monica Boulevard in West Hollywood. Many of the greats had played there over the years, including Elton John, Bruce Springsteen, Joni Mitchell, Carole King and James Taylor.

Harry's gig was an unadvertised surprise only announced on the day, but he did manage to organise a special guest to join him on stage. He described it as one of the best nights ever when he told the crowd, 'In my entire life, I never thought I'd be able to say this. Please welcome to the stage, Stevie Nicks.' He had forged a great friendship with the iconic Fleetwood Mac singer since his gift of carrot cake two years earlier. He called her his 'queen of everything'.

Together they sang 'Two Ghosts' – described by Stevie as a

great song – the Fleetwood Mac seventies classic 'Landslide' and her song 'Leather and Lace', which she originally performed with the Eagles singer Don Henley. A welcome legacy from his One Direction days was that Harry was excellent at harmonies. Stevie had a commanding presence at the age of sixty-eight. Harry was so overcome with emotion at singing with his idol that he had to pause midway through the performance to take a moment to compose himself. When she left the stage, Harry slapped his face and declared, 'I am losing my shit in a cool way.'

The gig was an ideal start to his solo performing career. *Variety* found his melodies 'irresistible'. During the punchier numbers from the album, including 'Only Angel' and 'Kiwi', Harry was described as embodying the 'swagger of Jagger', which was not the first or last time he was compared to the Rolling Stone.

Harry gave the proceeds from the ticket sales to the charity Safe Place for Youth that had started up in Venice Beach in 2011 to provide food and shelter for homeless young people. He would go on to support a whole raft of good causes throughout his tour.

Live on Tour began in San Francisco in September 2017, then the following day continued down the coast to Los Angeles. Harry had deliberately chosen small venues to start with, moving on to larger arena dates in 2018. The eighty-nine concerts sold out in minutes or, in some cases, seconds. The final concert would be at the Forum in Inglewood the following July.

His musical director on tour was his friend Tom Hull, known professionally as Kid Harpoon. Tom, who was from

Chatham, in Kent, was a singer-songwriter in his own right but was best known for his work with Florence and the Machine, Jessie Ware and Calvin Harris. He had first met Harry in London but started working with him in Los Angeles, where he had set up his own studio, Harpoon House, in West Hollywood at the beginning of 2016.

Harry brought him in to help with two tracks on the first album, 'Sweet Creature' and 'Carolina', and was keen for them to work more closely together going forward. They had musical chemistry. They also shared the same management at Full Stop, where Jeffrey Azoff was now guiding Tom.

Although Tom was more than eleven years older, it was Harry who introduced his friend to the sounds of the seventies that so influenced him. For his part, Tom helped Harry put the set for the tour into a cohesive shape, encouraging him not to completely ignore One Direction as that was part of his musical heritage and the starting point for many of the fans who had bought tickets.

At his very first *Live on Tour* concert in the Masonic Auditorium, San Francisco, he picked up a gigantic rainbow flag that a fan had thrown on stage. The universal symbol of LGBTQ+ Pride would become a fixture on tour. Harry wrapped it around the microphone, then around himself and waved it constantly. He encouraged his spellbound audience to wave their own flags back at him. It became as much a part of his performance as the hand-crafted Gucci suit and Gibson electric guitar.

His support for all things Pride was neither something he had just thought of nor an affectation. In January 2015 he wrote, 'I study rainbows.' These three words were retweeted more than 350,000 times. During One Direction's concerts later that year in Vancouver and in Buffalo, New York, he wore the flag as a cape when the band sang 'Act My Age' from the *Four* album.

A year earlier, when they performed at the then-named Edward Jones Dome in St Louis, Missouri, during the *Where We Are* tour, he wore a jersey with the American footballer Michael Sam's number '96' on it. Harry was showing his support for Michael, who had made headlines for being the first openly gay athlete to be drafted in the NFL.

His opening act in San Francisco, throughout North America and onto Europe was the Californian electronic pop band Muna, a trio of women who identify as queer. Harry had invited them to tour with him after he fell in love with their acclaimed first album, *About U*, a thought-provoking and empowering work that dealt with issues including sexual assault and the emotional abuse of women.

One of the trio, Naomi McPherson, explained that they felt protected as a group of three, a 'little army', and as a result she didn't feel afraid to be herself: 'That makes me proud to be queer. That's the whole point of why we do this. We want a safe haven.' Camille Rowe would have approved of the t-shirts they were prone to wear on stage, declaring simply, 'Fuck Trump'.

They were stunned when Harry asked them to tour with him and they were totally unprepared for the experience and the visceral passion of his fans. Muna singer Katie Gavin observed, 'They pass out, overwhelmed by being in the same room as him.' Katie had graciously referred to Harry on stage during the first concert: 'Harry has built his career, his essence, on kindness,' she told the crowd. The mere mention of his name launched a thousand and more screams.

A fire alarm, triggered by theatrical smoke in Muna's act, threatened to cut short the evening before the man himself appeared to start the concert in quietish mood with 'Ever Since New York'. His debut album had just ten tracks on it so he needed to include some extra numbers, choosing his own compositions, 'Stockholm Syndrome' and 'Just a Little Bit of Your Heart', the song he wrote for Ariana Grande and one made more poignant after the bomb attack at her concert in Manchester just four months earlier. His choice of 'What Makes You Beautiful', arguably the most famous One Direction song, was bold but he made it more of a stomping anthem, described by one critic as an 'empowering, inclusive sing-along'. One of the encores was 'The Chain', a signature Fleetwood Mac song that often opened their gigs. 'Sign of the Times' was a fitting finale.

Right from the start, the mantra for the tour was 'Treat People with Kindness'. He had picked up a pin for his guitar strap that had the slogan written on it. The sentiment resonated with Harry, who had it emblazoned on t-shirts that fans could buy at this and subsequent concerts. He explained, 'I saw a lot of t-shirts around. I'd be driving or something and see someone in one and I started feeling like, "Oh, this is a bit of a thing."' It was more than just a thing. It was the basis for a huge charitable drive throughout the tour that raised more than $1.2 million for his chosen good causes.

Camille was in the audience the next night when the tour moved down the coast to the Greek Theatre in Griffith Park,

LA. She was dancing and laughing happily with a friend. Other old friends were in the audience as well, including Niall Horan, Oscar-winner Emma Stone – a great buddy of Taylor Swift – and Mick Fleetwood, who according to his band mate Stevie Nicks had 'kind of adopted Harry'. They had met during One Direction days when the drummer had taken his two thirteen-year-old girls to see the group in concert. He was under strict instructions from his daughters: 'Don't embarrass us. No dad dancing!' His stock rose, however, when he did a meet and greet with Harry and they realised their dad was a superstar as well. Mick and Harry would keep in touch, writing to each other from all corners of the world. Harry, it seemed, could make a friend in any situation and it didn't matter what age or gender they were.

Backstage, he also met one of his childhood heroes for the first time. He loved the country legend Shania Twain for her fashion and her music. He and his mum would sing along to her CD as Anne drove around the quiet lanes of Cheshire. Shania was impressed by Harry, too, particularly his breathtaking blue floral suit.

At the start of his set, Harry told the crowd, 'My job is to entertain you. Your job is to have as much fun as you possibly can.' The *LA Times* was appreciative: 'Styles' charm offensive could settle wars. He was made to be the frontman.'

After the concert, Camille and Harry went out for sushi – one of the advantages of playing a concert in your adopted home town was winding down in a favourite restaurant. Camille was now living in the trendy Beachwood Canyon suburb of LA but still hankered after the small out-of-the-way bistros that she had loved so much in Paris.

They had another relaxed dinner out at the weekend before he left for Nashville. This time they were photographed and the newspapers couldn't help notice that Harry was carrying her handbag. He was certainly carrying a bag that might have been hers, or might have been his, or might have been one they were sharing. The media hadn't quite caught on yet to Harry's relaxed approach to breaking masculine stereotypes.

He had some time in Nashville so he went to The Cave studios where Tyler Johnson was working. Mitch and Tom joined them to kill time and kick around some ideas. They spent all day working on the song that would become 'Watermelon Sugar'. It's not about or inspired by *In Watermelon Sugar*, but the title of Camille's favourite book was inside Harry's head. Perhaps she slipped a copy into his suitcase. She wasn't there with him because she was modelling at Paris Fashion Week.

The book itself is an account of life in a commune in the aftermath of the fall of a civilisation. Harry's song was about the start of a relationship: 'That initial euphoria of when you start seeing someone, or sleeping with someone, or being around someone and you have that excitement.'

The song took ages to come together – probably the longest time he had ever spent on the initial writing of a song, even though the chorus chant of 'watermelon sugar high' had the gang throwing their arms aloft in the studio all afternoon. Harry was quite pleased with their efforts at the time but, as he once admitted on the radio, he grew to hate it. There was no way that particular song was ever going to see the light of day.

After a flurry of American dates, the tour moved on to Europe in late October. One of the principal sports of fans seemed to be reporting sightings of Camille. She was everywhere. She was even seen in Cheshire before the two of them flew back to Los Angeles to celebrate New Year. He had a break between a concert in Tokyo at the beginning of December and resuming in Europe in March, when he would be playing bigger arena venues including the O2 in London.

His first official job of 2018 was mixing business with pleasure when he went to Radio City Music Hall for the annual pre-Grammys MusiCares Person of the Year night that recognised the philanthropic endeavours of famous musicians.

For the first time it was given to a group – his great friends, Fleetwood Mac. Harry and Stevie Nicks chatted backstage and he asked her if she was nervous. She was but she told him that 'those butterflies' are what make the magic on stage. Harry's job was to introduce them for their mini-concert that closed the evening. He joined them to sing harmonies on 'The Chain', naturally.

Live on Tour resumed at the St Jakobshalle in Basel, Switzerland. Harry had made the decision to support a local charity in most of the venues as he toured around Europe and, subsequently, the rest of the world. Part of the proceeds from ticket sales and the Treat People with Kindness merchandise would go to a carefully selected chosen cause.

In Basel, Copenhagen and Oslo, for instance, he supported organisations improving the lives of children with cancer. In Amsterdam, Madrid and Milan, projects involving the provision of food for the poorest members of society was the priority, while in Munich he backed an association that offered support for refugees. And in Los Angeles, he chose the TIME'S UP Legal Defense Fund that provided subsidised legal support for anyone who had suffered sexual harassment, assault or abuse in the workplace.

One of the charities to benefit in the UK was the We Love Manchester Emergency Fund, which was set up to assist those bereaved, injured or traumatised by the Manchester Arena bombing in 2017. Harry was still including 'Just a Little Bit of Your Heart' in the show, but elsewhere he had freshened up things. He now began with the powerful crowd pleaser 'Only Angel' and had added two songs that were written for the album but didn't make the final ten. 'Oh Anna' rocked along with a supremely catchy chorus and a homage midway to the iconic 'Faith' by George Michael. The second, 'Medicine', had a similar musical tone but an explicit lyric that prompted discussion about its bisexual links: 'The boys and the girls are here, I mess around with them and I'm OK with it.'

Camille-spotting continued around Europe. She was seen applauding next to Harry's mum at the Paris show at the AccorHotels Arena. A few days later, during his concert at the Ericsson Globe in Stockholm, Harry took a moment to address the fans: 'I love every single one of you: If you are black, if you are white, if you are gay, if you are straight, if you are transgender — whoever you are, whoever you want to be — I support you. I love every single one of you.' He was creating that safe place for everyone in the arena that night. His message to the fans as the tour had progressed had become more focused, much more than a pop star invitation to have fun.

That message of safety and kindness filtered through his performances, concert to concert. Back in the US, at the SAP Center in San Jose, California, he stopped the concert when one of the audience held up a sign that read, 'I'm gonna come out to my parents because of you.' Harry asked the young woman, who was called Grace, if he could read it out and asked her the name of her mother. It was Tina. He persuaded the entire crowd to shout out, 'Tina, she's gay!'

Grace, who identified as bisexual, agreed that Harry had created a caring environment for his fans: 'He is a proud supporter of the LGBTQ+ community and he's made a lot of fans feel comfortable and proud to be who they are and I'm just one example of that.'

His support for the community was evident in Philadelphia at the Wells Fargo Center when he noticed a fan, Karla, holding up a flag that declared 'Make America Gay Again', a riposte to President Trump's slogan 'Make America Great Again'. It was handed to Harry, who held it aloft to wild cheering.

Harry had been keen to emphasise that he was not a star making political statements but someone supporting what he called the 'fundamentals' of decent human behaviour. That philosophy did not stop him signing the petition supporting the March for Our Lives, the youth-led protest in Washington, DC and beyond demanding stricter gun control after the notorious Valentine's Day mass shooting at the Marjory Stoneman Douglas High School in Parkland, Florida in 2018. He tweeted that he had signed the petition and encouraged others to do the same.

He waved a Black Lives Matter flag in one hand and the rainbow flag in the other when he was on stage at the United

Center in Chicago. He did the same at Madison Square Garden in New York when he sang 'What Makes You Beautiful'.

The concerts took place during Pride month. He had started the month, June 2018, by announcing special limited editions of his 'Treat People with Kindness' t-shirts on which the words were spelled out in the rainbow colours. They would be available to buy online throughout the month with all the proceeds going to the educational charity GLSEN, which stood for Gay, Lesbian and Straight Education Network. The organisation championed inclusive and safe school environments.

Harry's support act for the second round of North American dates on *Live on Tour* was Kacey Musgraves, one of the foremost gay icons in modern country music. She was promoting her latest release, the critically acclaimed *Golden Hour*, which would go on to win the Grammy for Album of the Year.

One of the tracks on this album was called 'Rainbow', which she hoped would be an anthem for those facing adversity, particularly in the LGBTQ+ community. She dedicated the song to them, although it was a 'song for anybody with any kind of weight on their shoulders'.

At Madison Square Garden in New York, she came on stage in a stunning metallic rainbow-patterned dress for a duet with Harry of 'You're Still the One'. Harry confided to the audience that the song was a personal favourite. *US* magazine described his duet with Kacey as 'one of the biggest treats of the night'.

Live on Tour ended back in California where it had begun. On the last evening at The Forum, he stopped to chat with the audience. One girl from Rhode Island had been to see the show seven times from New York to LA. He then read out a sign that said 'I'm gay and I love you.' Harry said, 'I love you too,' before adding to huge cheers, 'We're all a little bit gay, aren't we?'

In ten months, he had performed in front of more than 800,000 fans, grossing more than $62 million dollars. He had told 20,000 of them in New York: 'There is just pure joy in this room.' That had been true of eighty-nine evenings and would be hard to top.

18

FEELING BLUE

Harry was in the shower when Tom Hull popped round, so his friend and collaborator sat down at the piano and started tinkering with a few melodies. Harry heard him, came out dressed in a towel, grabbed a pen and notebook and started to sing along. They were supposed to be heading out, but this was more important. An hour later they had written the bones of 'Falling', one of the most moving songs on Harry's second album.

It was about Camille. Her relationship with Harry had not survived the end of *Live on Tour*. He was distressed about it, unused to a painful break-up that left him unhappy.

When the media realised that he and Camille had split, the lyrics of his new album were studied for any references to their relationship. 'Falling', it was thought, was a half-hidden reference to Harry being unfaithful. The most obvious link to Camille was in the mention of the coffee being out at the Beachwood café, the local eatery that was one of her favourite breakfast and brunch places.

The most obvious song about Camille is 'Cherry', which has nothing whatsoever to do with fruit. She is heard speaking on the track, which gives the game away. Cherry is probably a playful corruption of *cherie*, the affectionate French word for darling. The song is about jealousy and hurt. In the past Harry had spoken of his songs not being aimed at specific people but this one clearly is, especially apparent in the line, 'Does he take you walking round his parents' gallery?', which seems to be a reference to Camille's new boyfriend Theo Niarchos, one of the most prominent members of the art scene in Los Angeles.

Theo is a member of the famous Niarchos Greek shipping family and the son of billionaire Philip Niarchos, one of the most prominent collectors of art in the world. Theo owns the prestigious gallery 6817 Melrose in West Hollywood, and he and Camille have continued their relationship, described by *Tatler* as the art world's latest 'It-couple'.

'Cherry' was another song that grew from some dabbling around in the studio – on this occasion the famous Shangri-La studios in Malibu, owned by the famed record producer Rick Rubin. Both Adele and Ed Sheeran are among the artists who have recorded there. One evening, everyone had gone home except Tyler Johnson and Harry's chief engineer for the new album, Sammy Witte. Tyler had already given Harry the good advice of not forcing himself to compose big songs: 'You just have to make the record that you want to make right now. That's it.'

Sammy was toying with some riffs on the guitar and, as was the case with 'Falling', the song just grew from a simple beginning. The finishing touch was the sound of Camille's voice.

The lyrics very much reflect a bitter moment in time but Harry had recovered enough to ask Camille if it was alright to use a recorded message that she had left on his answer phone. She agreed and was happy with the result. Luckily, she had said 'Coucou', her familiar French hello greeting, in the perfect key.

Her words are just snatches of conversation spliced together and don't make any proper sense but they gave the melancholic song an atmosphere, especially as Harry had sung that he 'missed her accent'. The third mournful song on the new album was 'To Be So Lonely', in which he gives himself a hard time for being an arrogant man who finds it impossible to say sorry.

He had to move on. Camille had left a distinct impression on him; she had a sense of style he embraced, often wearing each other's clothes, and from being an occasional reader, he became an enthusiastic one. To begin with, he had followed her reading lead so as not to appear a 'dummy' but now he might spend a whole day devouring one book. That was the case with *Norwegian Wood*, the 1987 novel by the much-admired Japanese author Haruki Murakami. The sensitive and nostalgic tale of passion, sex and loss is triggered when the narrator hears a version of the famous Beatles song. It became a favourite book for Harry. When he was asked by *Rolling Stone* what his new album was about he replied, 'It's all about having sex and feeling sad.'

He had to get on and write the rest of the album. His Camille trilogy – 'Cherry', 'Falling' and 'To Be So Lonely' – would eventually be placed consecutively on the album and would have qualified Harry as an old-style singer-songwriter, but he had other plans for his new music. He was determined the album was not going to be a one-dimensional wail into his hankie.

Fortunately, there was no rush with the new material. He didn't have to record in his hotel bedroom while on tour. He spent two years writing and recording *Fine Line*. The idea for the title track was one that came very early on. During the break midway through *Live on Tour* he and Tom started out just strumming on a guitar and gradually the song took enough shape for him to take an early demo on tour with him. He was so pleased with it that every night he would listen to the song before bed. Harry always planned for it to close the album, as well as be the title track. He observed, 'It's one of those songs that I've always wanted to make.'

He only took two weeks off after the tour ended before he was immersed in the album. Any fans who were hoping that 'Medicine' or 'Oh Anna' would be included would be disappointed. 'Watermelon Sugar' returned, however. Harry had warmed to the song again, although it still wasn't his favourite – the two he liked most were 'Cherry' and 'Fine Line'.

The first of the new tracks was 'Golden', a perfect soft-rock car song for driving on a summer's day with the hood down. He was thinking of a trip along the Pacific Coast Highway in California. 'It feels so Malibu to me,' he said. The video filmed on the beautiful Amalfi coast in Italy featured Harry running, swimming and sitting behind the wheel of a vintage Alfa Romeo car.

While he was writing and recording *Fine Line*, two of the great classic albums were on his mind – *Astral Weeks* by Van Morrison and Joni Mitchell's *Blue*. Harry had written a song called 'Canyon Moon', which many fans thought referred to Beachwood Canyon where Camille lived. The song had a folk-rock theme and Harry decided to track down the dulcimer that featured on several of the tracks from *Blue*. That album, which also has a melancholic feel, included many songs that were inspired by a doomed relationship – this time between Joni and Graham Nash of Crosby, Stills and Nash. They had lived together in the Laurel Canyon area of LA for three years.

Harry found the maker of Joni's dulcimer, Joellen Lapidus, in Culver City just north of the city and bought one just like the instrument she had sold to Joni at the Big Sur Folk Festival in 1969. The ancient stringed instrument, akin to a zither, subsequently featured on this new track.

Eventually, Harry just needed one track to finish the album. He had been reluctant to write a song called 'Treat People with Kindness' in case it looked as if he was cashing in on a message that he believed in. He had mentioned the possibility to Jeff Bhasker, who encouraged him to just go ahead and get on with it. The result was like no other track on the album.

'TPWK', as it was often shortened to, was not a break-up song or a navel-gazer but an uplifting slice of choral musical theatre that might have featured in one of the popular stage shows of the sixties or early seventies – perhaps *Hair*, *Godspell* or *Jesus Christ Superstar*. Once again, he wasn't sure if he actually liked the song but he grew to embrace it.

It contained a simple but strong message. He explained, 'It's about being a lot nicer to each other than, "Don't do this, or don't do that, not this yes that." It's just saying "treat people with kindness".' He always felt it would be a showstopper when he toured *Fine Line*.

* * *

Harry cited Joni Mitchell when he spoke in honour of Stevie Nicks at the Barclays Center, in Brooklyn, in March 2019. Harry was the perfect choice to give the presentation speech when she became the first woman to be inducted twice into the Rock and Roll Hall of Fame. His speech was a tour de force: he was full of praise for her but was able to mix in some personal details at the same time.

He recalled how the classic 'Dreams' was the first song he knew all the words to before he knew what they meant. He thought the song was about the weather – 'Thunder only happens when it's raining' – and not about the agony of a relationship in turmoil, which was rather an apt subject for a song considering what he had gone through the previous year.

He told his audience that Stevie walked a path created by Joni and Janis Joplin – 'visionary women who had to throw a couple of elbows to create their own space'. He continued, 'If you're lucky enough to know her, she's always there for you,' and added, 'Her songs make you ache, feel on top of the world, make you want to dance, and usually all three at the same time. She's responsible for more running mascara – including my own – than all the bad dates in history combined.'

He then sang another duet with the star he idolised. This time it was her 1981 hit 'Stop Draggin' My Heart Around', which she originally sang with the late Tom Petty. Backstage, Stevie amusingly referred to Harry as a member of NSYNC – Justin Timberlake's boy band – although she quickly corrected herself. She was very complimentary and said, 'This beautiful child should've been born in 1948 too, because he just fits in with all of us.'

He was back in New York in May 2019 for one of the biggest events in his career to date. He attended the world-famous Met Gala – also known as the Met Ball – for the first time but he wasn't a guest, he was a co-chair. In just a few years he had progressed from sitting in the front row watching Cara Delevingne walk the runway to being the centre of attention himself at one of the fashion fundraising events of the year.

Celebrities and the leading names of fashion literally queue up at the Metropolitan Museum of Art (the Met) on Fifth Avenue to be seen. The permanent host each year is *Vogue*'s Anna Wintour, who had been a great supporter of Harry since his earlier days at London Fashion Week. Alongside her are guest co-chairs that in the past had included such superstars as Rihanna, George Clooney and Justin Timberlake.

In 2019 her co-chairs were Lady Gaga, Serena Williams, Alessandro Michele and Harry, who would be the youngest ever star to accept her invitation. The theme for the evening was 'Camp: Notes on Fashion', inspired by the American writer Susan Sontag's groundbreaking 1964 essay of that name, which explored the history and connotations of 'camp' in culture through the ages.

This was camp as art, not as a saucy seaside postcard. Its importance as a genre was highlighted by Max Hollein, the Met's director, who explained that while it has often been trivialised, the exhibition 'will reveal its profound influence on both high art and popular culture'.

The theme was perfect for Harry, pushing back the boundaries of contemporary taste by blurring the traditional lines of gender. Anna said she was hoping that he would wear something that was 'daring and fearless and colourful and different'. He wore Gucci, of course, but his outfit turned out to be not at all colourful – he left that to Alessandro, who was in bright red.

Instead, Harry was dressed in a sheer black ruffled top with a lace bib, very high-waisted black trousers, patent leather boots and a single pearl-drop earring in his right ear. He also wore a number of Gucci rings on his fingers, including one that was the letter H and another a large S.

After the extravagant stage wear of *Live on Tour*, the look was a complete surprise – not a sequin in sight. Harry Lambert explained that they had decided to take traditionally feminine elements of fashion – the frills, the sheer fabric and the pearl earring – 'rephrasing' them as masculine pieces with high-waisted tailored trousers and the striking tattoos. He described the effect as 'elegant', adding, 'It's camp but still Harry.' Afterwards the fashion commentators concluded that Harry had 'won the night'.

For the Gucci after party, he changed into a white, billowing top with a large red bow tie that Harry Lambert said was homage to the New Romantic movement of the 1980s when Duran Duran and Spandau Ballet ruled the charts. Harry didn't wear Alessandro's designs exclusively but it seemed everyone thought he did, so it was a win–win arrangement for the fashion house.

Kendall Jenner was at the event, looking the epitome of glamorous fun as she paraded in a scarlet Versace creation of feathers that represented fire. Understandably, pictures of them happily chatting away went round the world. They were clearly still the best of friends. Like Harry, Kendall had a wonderful smile for the cameras when working but preferred to keep pictures of her with a significant other to a minimum. Since she was first linked to Harry, she has had a number of boyfriends, most of whom seemed to be very tall basketball players. She has been dating NBA star Devin Booker of the Phoenix Suns since early 2020. Devin, who won a gold medal with the USA team at the 2021 Tokyo Olympics, has a perfect middle name for dating a supermodel – it's Armani.

Kendall would be seeing more of Harry in Los Angeles later in the year when they were set to appear on *The Late Late Show*. Before that, he flew to London to take his mum and sister to the Fleetwood Mac concert at Wembley Stadium. They all posed with the band backstage.

Stevie addressed the crowd: 'I'd like to dedicate this to my little muse, Harry Styles, who brought his mother tonight. Her name is Anne; and I think you did a really good job of raising Harry, Anne, because he's really a gentleman, sweet and talented, and boy, that appeals to me.' Anne put her arms around the son she loved so much while Stevie sang 'Landslide'.

Behind closed doors, Harry and Jeffrey Azoff were having meetings with Rob Stringer to plan the strategy for turning *Fine Line* into the massive commercial success they felt it deserved to be. Rob doesn't have to take a personal interest in every artist but he had detected a 'uniqueness' in Harry and believed that he had an exciting musical future in front of him.

The attraction of Harry as a long-term star was that he wasn't constrained by the expected. Rob observed, 'There is nothing formulaic about him whatsoever.' Jeffrey echoed that view, praising Harry for delivering music that people didn't see coming. He famously described his client and friend as a 'unicorn', the legendary mythological creature that symbolises something rare, unique and precious.

In these meetings Harry was not some vague pop star nipping to the toilets for a line of coke – although he is happy to admit that magic mushrooms at the Shangri-La studios added enjoyably to the creative process of *Fine Line*. Instead, he is focused, business-like and brimming with ideas. He insisted, for instance, that 'Lights Up' should be the first single from the album.

The song could scarcely have been more different from 'Sign of the Times'. Instead of a six-minute musical odyssey, this was a throwback to more succinct pop times, when after a couple of minutes the DJ was lining up another track. 'Lights Up' was two minutes and fifty-two seconds.

The track was advertised mysteriously on billboards that declared simply, 'Do You Know Who You Are?' using the same teasing tactic that had worked so well for Adele with 'Hello'. The words were the last line of the song. In one tweet he even shortened it to just 'Do'.

Harry was quite enigmatic when he talked about the song, telling Roman Kemp on Capital Radio's breakfast show that it was about freedom: 'It's about self-reflection and self-discovery. It feels very free to me – a couple of things that I've thought about and I guess wrestled with a little bit over the last couple of years. It's kind of like accepting all of those things. It's a very positive song to me.'

In another interview, he told Hits Radio that the track was 'very liberating'. His words were seized upon as an indication that it was a bisexual anthem, especially as it was released on 11 October 2019 – National Coming Out Day. Harry didn't address the date specifically or in any personal way but it reflected his ongoing support for the LGBTQ+ community and the right to celebrate one's sexuality openly and safely.

Harry was expanding on the culture of acceptance that he promoted so strongly during the concerts of *Live on Tour* and with his mantra 'Treat People with Kindness'. He even started up a website called 'Do You Know Who You Are', in which a visitor could enter their name and receive a personal compliment from Harry to give them a boost. It was signed H and TPWK and was created for World Mental Health Day – another cause that Harry strongly supported. He even responded personally to a post from a fan who said she would skip therapy to come to his next tour. He told her: 'Go to therapy, it's important. I'll wait for you.' He had started counselling in Los Angeles while working on his first album and had found it to be of enormous help in addressing some personal issues. He was sceptical at first but subsequently advised his friends to go.

The video for 'Lights Up' also premiered on the day of its release. Harry had travelled to Cancun, Mexico, back in August for filming. The director was Californian, Vincent Haycock, who had made videos for Florence and the Machine, Calvin Harris and Lana Del Rey. He shot Harry bare-chested amongst a group of young men and women gently caressing each other and him. His torso was glistening, which he later revealed was down to liberal use of aloe vera.

In other shots, styled by Harry Lambert, he was riding on the back of a motorcycle and wearing some custom-made

Gucci as well as a design by a recent addition to his fashion circle, Harris Reed. The outfits caught the eye of the Harry Styles Fashion Archive, which ran a poll among its online followers to discover Harry's Best Look of the Year. The winner was the Met Gala ensemble but the Mexican designs were a close second.

Harris was at the forefront of gender-fluid culture. Originally from California, he was a student at Central Saint Martins when he met Harry through an introduction from Harry Lambert, who was the first person he had worked with in fashion and had acted as a mentor. It was Lambert who suggested he meet 'a person', without disclosing the star's identity.

The young designer made up a small portfolio of references – the modern way of describing examples – that revealed the influence of Bowie, Jagger and Jimi Hendrix in his early work. He went along to a *Live on Tour* concert at the Eventim Apollo in Hammersmith in late October 2017 to meet Harry Styles for the first time, battling his way through the horde of fainting fans at the stage door.

He found Harry very receptive to new ideas and someone who wanted to be involved throughout the process. While Harry loved his Gucci suits, he didn't want to be tied down to one look and would commission Harris to devise more informal, flowing outfits. All he had to work with for the 'Lights Up' video was a couple of swatches that showed the shade of blue Harry wanted. He had just three days to come up with the finished article, which in the old days might have been described as a sleeveless pant or trouser suit. Harry loved it.

Musically, 'Lights Up' was a perfect appetiser for the new album because it was authentically Harry and not so easily compared to Bowie, Jagger or Pink Floyd – as critics liked to do with his music. *NME* made one comparison, though, saying the track was less Fleetwood Mac and more Justin Timberlake. The *Guardian* suggested he had left behind the seventies' rock influence for 'more soulful territory'. The *Vulture* column in *New York* magazine called it 'well-tailored pop' and a 'breezy tune' but also discussed the lyrics: 'Styles doesn't owe us more than he wants to tell us, and it's not wise to assume that pop lyrics come from personal experience.'

Surprisingly, the track did not go to number one in the UK or the US, where it only reached number seventeen on the *Billboard* Hot 100. The video, however, has been viewed on YouTube more than 95 million times, so it was a job well done.

When 'Lights Up' was released, Harry received a text from his mum saying that she had played it to her dad, his beloved grandfather Brian, who had always been such a support. 'He likes it,' said Anne. 'He's just happy you're still working.'

19

THE PRICE OF FAME

Not everything was sweetness and light in Harry's world. He locked his bedroom door at night and made sure he had round-the-clock security. He had a stalker camped outside his Hampstead home for several months, a distressing situation that left him feeling 'scared' and 'very uncomfortable'.

Three days after celebrating the release of 'Lights Up', Harry was seated behind a screen at Hendon Magistrates Court in North London telling a district judge what had happened after he first saw a homeless man near his house earlier in the year.

Harry recalled, 'I thought it was sad that someone so young was sleeping rough at a bus stop when it was cold.' That evening, he stopped his car outside the bench, wound down his window and offered the man some money for a hotel room or some food at least.

Declining the money for religious reasons, the man, Pablo Tarazaga-Orero, asked for some edamame beans, which Harry thought an odd request, but he popped to a local vegan café to buy some sandwiches, a salad and muffins, and handed them to him on his return. It was the start of a nightmare three months that led to him eventually contacting the police.

His security team advised him not to interact with the man but the situation became worse. The court heard that Tarazaga-Orero would show up at Harry's local pub up to four times a week 'anywhere between a minute and two minutes after I arrived'. Harry said that he started to feel as though he was being followed.

During a run in Regent's Park, the man blocked his path and asked him for the money Harry had previously offered. When he was at his house in London, Harry would see his stalker nearly every day and receive notes from him. He even pushed almost £50 in coins through Harry's letterbox for some unexplained reason.

One local resident gave evidence of a conversation he had with the defendant: 'He said he is a soulmate of my neighbour, Harry Styles.' Tarazaga-Orero pleaded not guilty to the charge of harassment and claimed that Harry had propositioned him, offering him money to go to a hotel with him for 'some fun' – a version of events that Harry had to deny in court. The district judge Nigel Dean found the suggestion to be 'completely incredible'.

Judge Dean found Harry to be a 'reliable and credible' witness. He described Harry's actions: 'These were honest, well-intended, good intentions from somebody who was trying to help another for whom he felt sorry and who he thought was down on his luck.'

Sentencing the defendant the following week, he banned him from going within 250 metres of Harry, his home or business addresses or attending any concert or event where he was due to appear. He was ordered not to contact the singer directly or indirectly, or post about him on social media; he was also handed a twelve-month community order and told to complete a thirty-day rehabilitation requirement.

It was a very unfortunate sequence of events in Harry's life. He was an ardent campaigner for causes that would benefit society and here he was involved in a court case against a homeless man. Harry has made no comment about the matter but he asked the prosecutor, Katy Weiss, to make a statement in court. She said, 'I spoke to Mr Styles yesterday and he is adamant he wants the defendant to get help, although he doesn't want to see him again.'

Within Harry's own showbusiness circle, stalking was a widespread problem: Taylor Swift, Ariana Grande and Cara Delevingne having all faced this unpleasant side-effect of fame. The worst affected was Kendall Jenner, who has endured several stalkers including one who was deported back to Canada and another who was jailed. Harry remained highly sensitive and cautious about revealing exactly where he was living at any one time.

Harry had not invited any glossy magazine to photograph his New York home, for instance. He had bought a luxury apartment in Manhattan for more than £6 million in 2017 – another highly desirable property investment.

He was there in November to host an episode of *Saturday Night Live*, a testament to his growing status. He was able to sing 'Lights Up' as well as newly released promotional single 'Watermelon Sugar', but it was his appearance in a wide variety of sketches that signalled his arrival as an all-round star talent. He was very funny.

His appearance was a good way of promoting *Love on Tour*, which he announced would start at the Birmingham Arena on 15 April 2020. Initially he would play sixty-three dates but he planned to add shows in Australasia, Asia and South America.

Harry was the host of *SNL* two days before the tickets to his tour went on sale to the general public, so the timing was perfect. In the show, he acted in one rapid sketch after another, including playing an airline pilot, a Chihuahua, an over-the-hill vaudeville act and one half of an Icelandic couple at a childbirth class. He had some fun in the regular monologue spot, declaring that he was grown in a test tube by Simon Cowell.

The regular cast were very appreciative. Chris Redd said Harry had been 'dope all week'.

In Stevie Nicks fashion, comedian Cecily Strong did not hold back: 'Harry Styles is from another planet where the most beautiful and talented beings exist. He is magical and I think it's safe to say we were all enchanted and delighted.'

An intriguing side bar was the response to his performance of 'Watermelon Sugar', which on the night received more than a million online views. Perhaps the song deserved more intensive exposure than being used just as a promotional single.

Reviewing the show, pop culture site the A.V. Club observed, 'Styles was into it all night, clearly invested in furthering his fledgling acting career, while getting to showcase some above-average sketch comedy chops.'

The acting career would have to remain 'fledgling' for the foreseeable future. There was no time. He was in the running to play Prince Eric in the live-action version of Disney's *The Little Mermaid* and met with the director Rob Marshall, who he described as 'the most wonderful man'. Disappointingly, his tour commitments in 2020 meant that he could not commit to the long production schedule. He had also turned down the pop-star role in *Yesterday*, the Danny Boyle comedy written by Richard Curtis that was inspired by the music of The Beatles. Chris Martin also said no before Ed Sheeran was cast.

Harry did have the chance to show more of his comic touch when he stepped in to host *The Late Late Show* when James Corden left abruptly to be with his wife, Julia, who was about to give birth to their third child, Charlotte. Harry had little more than two hours to make a dash to the studio, but at least Ben Winston was there in his role of executive producer to make sure it all went smoothly.

The highlight was a game of 'Spill Your Guts or Fill Your Guts', which he played with Kendall Jenner. Harry could either answer an embarrassing question or eat a piece of disgusting food that would have left the contestants of *I'm a Celebrity ... Get Me Out of Here!* gagging.

Kendall asked him which songs on his first album were about her. Just when you thought Harry was going to tell everyone, he popped a piece of cod sperm in his mouth. He also didn't want to be drawn on ranking the solo careers of his former One Direction band mates, opting instead for a delicious mouthful of water scorpion.

Such exposure was great promotion for *Fine Line*. The artwork for the new album was revealed five weeks ahead of the official release. This really was a work of art and not just a few matinee-idol pictures of Harry smiling winningly. The cover was unmistakably the work of acclaimed fashion photographer and filmmaker Tim Walker, especially his signature use of a fish-eye lens.

Tim is one of the artistic pioneers with whom Harry has always aspired to collaborate. His photography for *Vogue*, *W* magazine, *Another Man* and *Love* captures the essence of the model or performer. He doesn't just roll up, shoot a few reels and go to lunch. He carefully researches the passions of the artist, which explains why some of his best-known work has been with two of the most fascinating and innovative stars of modern popular culture, Kate Bush and Björk.

Brought up in rural Dorset, Tim had decided to follow a career in photography in the early nineties after spending a year as an intern in the archive of the legendary Cecil Beaton at the Condé Nast library in central London. His job, stuck in the basement day after day, was to catalogue the collection. Now, he too is featured in the permanent displays of the National Portrait Gallery and the Victoria & Albert Museum.

The *Guardian* described Tim's work as 'dreamily surreal', a fitting description of his photographs for *Fine Line* in which Harry was dressed in Gucci – bold pink trousers, white braces and a black hat, styled as usual by Harry Lambert – in a set designed by Tim's long-time collaborator Shona Heath. One shot received the most attention – 'the lone nude', as Harry described it. He wasn't dressed in Gucci but lying naked on a yellow floor, his legs across a giant model of a real heart with his right hand placed across his crotch.

He told Ellen DeGeneres how Tim had persuaded him to strip for just one frame: 'It was like, "those trousers aren't really working so let's try it without the trousers." And then he looked at me and I was like, "These pants aren't really working are they?" So that was how it worked out.' Unsurprisingly the nude picture became a media story everywhere, which only added to the hype surrounding the album.

Behind the scenes, helping to guide the whole process was Harry's creative director, Molly Hawkins – an unsung hero but a vital component of his success. Harry had a stylist, a designer or two, various photographers, but Molly was a constant, orchestrating the visual image he was seeking.

She had first become involved in the Harry Styles machine after she heard some of the then-unreleased tracks from his first album. Impressed, she simply texted his manager, Jeffrey Azoff, who she already knew. She recalled, 'I was like "Dude, let me meet Harry. I think we could do something really special."'

Molly was far from just starting out. Her father was the celebrated bass guitarist George Hawkins, Jr, who died in 2018. He had played on many of Fleetwood Mac's projects as well as the duet between Kenny Loggins and Stevie Nicks, 'Whenever I Call You "Friend"'.

Molly had been in the music business for ten years, first as a DJ, then as manager of American synth group Chairlift, before being based in London as creative director for the Young label (formerly Young Turks) where she met and subsequently married its founder, Caius Pawson. While there she worked with Mercury Prize winners the xx, and, according to her future husband, took the label's 'game to a whole new level'. In Harry's artistic small world, Tom Hull released his solo records on Young Turks, so Molly already knew him.

Working with Harry Styles would give her the chance to bring her ideas to a much bigger global audience. She would be unobtrusively at his side if he was making a video or on a fashion shoot. Ten years older than Harry, she was attracted to the romanticism he brought to modern culture: 'When I think about seeing Harry live as a fan, I try to remember how I felt about Leonardo DiCaprio when I was thirteen; And how as a young woman it was fucking awesome to see a man that was so romantic and unabashed.' They have become great friends. It was Molly who gave Harry a copy of Murakami's *Norwegian Wood*, because she thought every man should read it.

Molly was heavily involved in the promotional campaign for the second official single from the album, 'Adore You', which involved creating the fictional island of Eroda. It wasn't too difficult to work out that this was 'adore' spelled backwards. Critics described the slightly surreal video as whimsical. Filmed in atmospheric locations around Scotland, it featured Harry caring for a small fish that he found flapping helplessly on some rocks. One of Harry's co-writers on 'Adore You', Amy Allen, described it as 'totally a love song.'

All the publicity and meticulous planning that had preceded the release of *Fine Line* paid off in spectacular fashion when the album was a huge and immediate success, particularly in the US. For starters, its debut sales week of 393,000 was the largest by a solo UK male artist since Nielsen Music started tracking the data in 1991. It was sixth biggest-selling album of the year in the States after just seven days. Perhaps most impressively, Harry became the first UK male artist to debut at number one with his opening two albums.

The critics were generally positive about what they heard. The influential online music site *Pitchfork* said, 'The actual sound of *Fine Line* is incredible, and most songs have at least one great moment to grab hold of.' The upbeat review was slightly spoiled by the observation, 'Styles doesn't have the imagination of Bowie.'

Variety noticed the influence of Paul McCartney but also the Californian sound of Crosby, Stills & Nash. Commonly, most reviews looked to cite possible influence and comparable sounds from Pink Floyd to Frank Zappa, from Motown to Mark Ronson, and from Lorde to Bon Iver.

In the first week of release, Harry played the whole album in order from 'Golden' to 'Fine Line' at a one-off gig at The Forum, in Los Angeles. It was yet more publicity and an early run-through for the tour. He performed five songs in an extended encore that included just 'Sign of the Times' and 'Kiwi' from the first album. He also kept 'What Makes You Beautiful', was joined on stage by Stevie Nicks for 'Landslide' and, eccentrically, chose to sing McCartney's slightly cheesy 'Wonderful Christmastime' as his seasonal offering.

During Christmas week he slipped over to London for a secret gig at the Electric Ballroom in Camden Town. For once Stevie wasn't the guest. Instead, during the encore Harry introduced the multi-BRIT Award-winning artist Stormzy for a rendition of his rap 'Vossi Bop', in which Harry joined in from time to time, including on the line, 'Fuck the Government and fuck Boris (yeah)'. Stormzy called Harry 'a legend'.

It was an uplifting end to the year and, for Harry, 2020 promised to be even better. What could possibly go wrong?

* * *

On Valentine's Day, of all days, Harry was robbed at knifepoint by a group of men wearing hoodies who followed him while he was walking home down a quiet Hampstead street. He told the US radio host Howard Stern that he knew he was in trouble when he twice crossed the street to avoid them and they were still behind him.

They surrounded him. One asked him if he smoked weed and Harry said no. Then the man asked, 'What have you got on you?', so he handed over a wad of cash he had in his pocket. One of the men lifted his shirt to reveal a knife when Harry refused to give them his phone. He told Howard that his first thought was how 'annoying' it would be to lose everything on his phone – all the contacts, photos, videos and snatches of new songs. He even considered hurling it into the pond behind them, but instead he ran into the middle of the road when two cars approached with their headlights on. Then he sprinted back towards Hampstead Village, cursing the fact that he wasn't wearing trainers. Fortunately, the men didn't pursue him. Howard observed, 'You could have been stabbed.'

Harry reported the mugging to the police but the men were not found. The next evening he went for a walk locally, accompanied by friends, just to make sure the unpleasant incident wasn't going to ruin life in his home neighbourhood by making him feel unsafe – although he still had the night guard at his house.

There had been the grimmest news that day. The body of Caroline Flack had been discovered in her Stoke Newington flat. She had hanged herself. Harry didn't mention her at the BRITS three days later. He didn't have to. Instead, when he arrived on the red carpet at the O2 Arena he was wearing a discreet black ribbon in the lapel of his maroon Gucci suit. That was enough.

Caroline's career had soared since her romantic interlude with Harry back in 2011. She had been perfection when winning *Strictly Come Dancing* in 2014 and helped to turn *Love Island* into the most-watched programme on ITV2.

That all came tumbling down when the police were called to her home in December 2019 after her boyfriend, Lewis Burton, phoned 999 and reported that she had struck him while he slept. Despite the tennis player not wishing to pursue the matter, she was charged with assault. *Love Island* dropped her as presenter for the upcoming series. Although ITV always insisted the door was left open for her return, her career, she thought, was finished.

In an Instagram post that was published after her death, Caroline said, 'Within twenty-four hours my whole world and future was swept from under my feet and all the walls that I had taken so long to build around me, collapsed.' She added, 'I'm not thinking about how I'm going to get my career back. I'm thinking about how I'm going to get mine and my family's life back.'

An analysis by the *Guardian* revealed that there had been 387 stories about Caroline in the UK's national newspapers in the previous six months: 18 per cent were positive while a quarter of them were negative in tone. In the month she was charged, however, there were twice as many negative stories as positive ones.

Caroline took her own life the day after she learned the case against her was going ahead and that she would stand trial on 4 March. At the inquest into her death, the coroner Mary

Hassell concluded, 'I find the reason for her taking her own life was she now knew she was being prosecuted for sure and she knew she would face the media, press, publicity – it would all come down upon her.'

She added, 'Caroline had fluctuating mental ill health, she had struggles in the past. In spite of the fact she may have led – to some – a charmed life, actually the more famous she got, the more some of these difficulties increased – she had to deal with the media in a way most of us don't.'

Harry was never going to make a spontaneous comment about Caroline for use in the tabloid press. He might have something to say in the future to one of his trusted magazines but for the moment he kept his thoughts to himself.

Harry's mum Anne had tweeted that it was 'heartbreaking' when she learned of Caroline's death and posted a profoundly moving poem about the woman she had always liked:

> 'How must your heart ache
> To feel so all alone …'

She signed off her message to her 2.5 million followers, 'May you have found your peace @Caroline Flack.'

At the BRITs, Harry had added a badge to his suit during the evening that declared 'Treat People with Kindness'. Although it had been his mantra for quite a time, it was even more appropriate and touching now as it mirrored one of Caroline's final Instagram posts that read simply, 'In a world where you can be anything, be kind.'

Harry sang a moving version of 'Falling' at the award ceremony, sat next to his sister Gemma and, ever the professional, appeared in cheerful good humour when the host, Jack Whitehall, came over for a chat. The R&B star Lizzo was conveniently placed at the next table so that she and Harry could exchange some banter before she downed his glass of tequila in one. He had already performed a version of her song 'Juice' at the Electric Ballroom and on Radio 1's *Live Lounge*. He had also joined her on stage for a pre-Superbowl duet in Miami.

Any future collaboration would have to be put on hold, however. On 19 March 2020, California became the first US state to issue a stay-at-home order to combat the spread of Covid-19. Just a few days later Harry made the inevitable announcement that he was postponing *Love on Tour* until 2021. The big question now was one that all performers were facing at a difficult time: What on earth was he going to do for the rest of the year and beyond?

20

IN VOGUE

Five days after the shocking killing of George Floyd in May 2020, Harry posted a heartfelt message on Twitter that revealed his true feelings about the scourge of racism and his support of the subsequent Black Lives Matter protests sweeping across the United States and around the globe.

He kept it short but immensely powerful: 'I do things every day without fear because I am privileged and I am privileged every day because I am white.

'Being not racist is not enough, we must be anti-racist. Social change is enacted when a society mobilizes in solidarity with all of those protesting.'

More than 820,000 people liked his post, an indication of the reach of genuine superstars if they choose to address things that matter to them and the world. He had already shared a petition calling for the resignation and arrest of the Minneapolis police office Derek Chauvin, who suffocated George Floyd with his knee and was subsequently jailed for his murder. Harry also donated to funds set up to help post bail for organisers arrested during the nationwide protests and urged supporters to do the same.

Harry's anti-racist sentiments echoed those of his new friend Lizzo, who had moved to Minneapolis in 2011 and began her recording career there. She posted a video in which she said it was not the job of black people to educate white people about racism.

She urged white men and women to speak up: 'This is your daily reminder that as long as you stay silent, you are part of the problem. I know you're not racist but you have to be more than that, you have to be anti-racist.'

And Harry did actually stand 'in solidarity'. A few days later he took part in a peaceful Black Lives Matter protest through the streets of Hollywood, barely recognisable in a bandana mask, sunglasses and a dark hoodie. He also knelt with others who felt as he did while listening to a rousing speech and he was thoughtfully attentive when a black fan told him of her experiences being surrounded by a sea of white faces at One Direction concerts and his own solo shows. This was a weightier commitment than waving a flag around on stage.

In London his sister Gemma stressed in a post to her nearly four million followers that Black Lives Matter was not an issue or topic that went away just because it wasn't trending on Twitter.

These were sobering times. As well as the hurt and outrage triggered by the killing in Minnesota – and the belated recognition of other black citizens who had died in police custody – the death toll from Covid-19 in the US passed 100,000 the same week.

In the middle of such stressful news, 'Watermelon Sugar' was released at last as an official single – the fourth from *Fine Line*. At first, there was no indication that this was going to become his most famous song to date. The video, though, reminded everyone of sunnier days at just the right time. It had been filmed back in January on the beach in Malibu – close to where One Direction had shot 'What Makes You Beautiful'. Because it was made at the beginning of the year, the effect of social distancing had yet to come into play and the advertising slogan declared, 'this video is dedicated to touching'.

Perhaps it would have been more accurately dedicated to 'slurping', as various male and female models tucked into numerous slices of melon. They were totally full up and fed up with melon as they cavorted around the beach. One model remarked, 'I was just praying it didn't come across but I just felt so uncomfortable.'

For once Harry seemed overdressed as everyone else was semi-naked. He endeared himself by being courteous and thoughtful to the girls, respectful of the #MeToo and TIME'S UP sentiments that had swept through Hollywood. When one of the directors told him to play with the hair of American model Ephrata, he paused and asked her, 'Are you even cool with that? Is that okay? Are you comfortable with that?' Ephrata was bowled over by his consideration and called him the 'consent king'.

The directors were Bradley and Pablo, part of the London art scene so appreciated by Harry, who were carving out a reputation in Los Angeles. Bradley Bell and Pablo Jones-Soler met while studying graphic design at Chelsea College of Arts and Central Saint Martins in 2010, the same year that Harley Weir graduated. The start of the decade had been a golden period for innovative thinking in modern culture in London.

Bradley and Pablo quickly established themselves when they moved to Los Angeles and had already worked with Dua Lipa, Cardi B and Kanye West. They had been hoping to collaborate with Harry for some time and grabbed their chance, although to begin with they hadn't realised the song's sexual connotations.

They met with Harry and Molly Hawkins, who suggested two images they should have in their minds. The first was the actor Jack Nicholson eating a watermelon with one of his devilish grins and the second a photograph of Paul McCartney at a beach party in the sixties. Harry and Molly wanted a video that represented 'boys and girls and sexual pleasure'.

Bradley and Pablo discovered that Harry actually owned a watermelon farm in a secret location near Los Angeles and so, on the day before shooting, the two directors and other members of the crew, including make-up artists and set designers, met up to harvest wheelbarrows of melons.

The following day's filming was a great success but as the time neared to release the video they grew worried that the record company might not go ahead, fearing that it would be seen as insensitive in Covid times. The opposite seemed to be true, as the public warmed to a reminder of better days. Bradley and Pablo observed, 'It speaks to what everybody is missing right now – physical human touch and connection.'

Since *Fine Line*'s release there had been much speculation as to whether 'Watermelon Sugar' was about giving women oral sex. The video settled any doubts.

The track didn't race up the charts, but in August it finally became Harry's first number one single in the US. From now on he would be referred to as the 'Watermelon High' singer and not the 'Sign of the Times' or 'Adore You' singer. The video has been watched online more than 256 million times.

By the time the song reached the top Harry had decided that he should spend at least part of the rest of the year making a film; that would still be possible even if a concert was off the agenda. He had taken time to think during a summer road trip through France and Italy with his friend the artist Tomo Campbell.

Harry was a keen collector of the fashionable London-based artist, who was another member of his circle that was shaping modern culture in the capital. Tomo was also an alumnus of Central Saint Martins who secured his big break at his degree show in 2010 when the famous photographer Mario Testino bought one of his vivid canvases. Alexa Chung was a collector too.

Tomo was introduced to Harry by his wife Sam, who is the sister of the former One Direction make-up artist Lou Teasdale and founder of the trendy hair and beauty business BLEACH London. They are part of a Stoke Newington set that had included Caroline Flack.

Harry returned to Los Angeles and was staying as the temporary house guest of Mitch Rowland and Sarah Jones. He was looking for a movie role that would be completely different to *Dunkirk*. He found it when he was cast in the psychological thriller *Don't Worry Darling*, the second film directed by the actor Olivia Wilde, who was also represented by the Creative Artists Agency. Harry was brought in to replace the original star, Shia LaBeouf.

At the time it was reported that the controversial LaBeouf had dropped out due to 'scheduling difficulties' but it was later alleged that he had been fired by Olivia for his poor behaviour on set. Olivia did a 'little victory dance' when Harry agreed to step up.

She had quickly become one of the most sought-after directors in Hollywood after the success of her first feature, the 2019 multi-award-winning high school comedy *Booksmart*, which President Obama included in his list of movies of the year. Olivia originally gained attention as an actor for her role as Dr Remy 'Thirteen' Hadley in the hugely successful drama *House*, which starred Hugh Laurie as an unconventional medical genius.

Olivia is a prominent activist and feminist. She was born in New York and comes from an illustrious literary and artistic family. Her grandfather was the renowned communist journalist and writer Claud Cockburn; her father Alexander was the Washington, DC editor of *Harper's Bazaar*; while her mother, Leslie Cockburn, is an Emmy Award-winning investigative journalist and filmmaker. Together Olivia's parents produced the 1997 movie *The Peacemaker*, starring George Clooney and Nicole Kidman.

They lived in the well-to-do Georgetown district of Washington and she attended the Phillips Academy in Andover, Massachusetts, where Presidents George Bush Sr. and Jr. went to school – as well as Hollywood stars Jack Lemmon and Humphrey Bogart. Olivia studied acting at the prestigious Gaiety School of Acting in Dublin, which boasts Colin Farrell and Aidan Turner among its alumni. She has dual American and Irish nationality and, growing up, had spent many summers at the family home in County Waterford. She changed her professional name to Olivia Wilde in honour of the great Irish writer Oscar Wilde.

At the age of nineteen, she eloped with the photographer and filmmaker Tao Ruspoli, a member of an aristocratic Italian family, who was eight years her senior. They married on a school bus in Virginia with a couple of random witnesses and were together for eight years until divorcing in 2011.

By then, Olivia had become one of the best-known faces on American television, firstly through *The O.C.*, in which she played bisexual bad girl Alex Kelly, and then featuring in eighty-one episodes of *House*. After she finally left the show in 2012, she appeared in several films but, more importantly perhaps, she branched out into production, taking on some serious subjects including *Baseball in the Time of Cholera*, about an epidemic of the disease in Haiti, and the Emmy Award-winning *Body Team 12*, which told the stories of those responsible for collecting the dead bodies during the Ebola outbreak in Africa.

For her directorial breakthrough in *Booksmart* she called all the cast together for a read-through and encouraged each of them to raise their hand if they thought anything sounded inauthentic. She wanted that collective experience. She also had one unbreakable rule on set: 'No assholes allowed.' She mentioned no names when she expanded on her thoughts to *Variety*: 'It puts everybody on the same level,' she explained. 'I also noticed as an actress for years how the hierarchy of the set separated the actors from the crew in this strange way that serves no one.'

One of the actors who benefited from this approach on *Booksmart* was Jason Sudeikis, who played the school principal.

He had become a household name as part of the regular cast of *Saturday Night Live* before becoming an in-demand movie star through films including *Horrible Bosses* and *We're the Millers*. He featured in a comedy drama called *Drinking Buddies* in which Olivia had a starring role. They were an engaged couple by the time the film was released in 2013, and subsequently had two children together, Otis and Daisy.

Olivia was determined to bring up her children in a modern, caring way, speaking openly about her desire for her son to understand feminism: 'I want to promote the idea that the definition of feminism is equality and it is not difficult to teach children because they are born with that sensibility.' It's easy to see that she might find a kindred spirit in Harry Styles – and vice versa.

Her second directorial project, *Don't Worry Darling*, was going to be supremely stylistic and she and her Oscar-nominated costume designer Arianne Phillips were well aware of Harry's appreciation of fashion and style. A film set in the 1950s exhibiting all the retro glamour of an old Cary Grant movie was perfect for Harry, although he did have to start the day of each shoot with a tedious hour in make-up covering his tattoos. Nobody had mentioned that future treat when he was a regular at the Shamrock Social Club.

In the film, Harry plays the husband of British actor Florence Pugh, star of *Little Women* and *Black Widow*. She is a fifties housewife whose life begins to unravel as she suspects all is not as it seems in her utopian world. Harry was cast as her 'picture-perfect husband Jack, who loves her dearly but is hiding a dark secret from her'.

Harry was happy this time round to see a familiar face on set, the actor and former model Gemma Chan. She was a good friend of Cara Delevingne and had gone out with Jack Whitehall for several years. She was one of Harry's circle who would enjoy nights out in Soho House or the Groucho Club back in London. Her career had moved forward quickly since she had appeared in the hit comedy *Crazy Rich Asians*, although her starring role in the Marvel Studios' blockbuster *Eternals* was yet to be seen, the release having been postponed owing to Covid-19.

The set for *Don't Worry Darling* was a happy one, partly due to the atmosphere of mutual respect cultivated by Olivia. She praised Harry, in particular, for allowing a woman – Florence – to hold the spotlight. She explained, 'Most male actors don't want to play supporting roles in female-led films.'

The popular actor Chris Pine, who had the other important male role in the film, said of Harry, 'He is an absolute delight. He's one of the most professional people I've ever met: Couldn't be kinder, more gracious. I mean, really, I was stunned by this kid. He's off the charts cool.'

Filming for *Don't Worry Darling* took place in Los Angeles and Palm Springs and coincided with the demise of Olivia's relationship with Jason after eight years together. They never married.

A crew member tested positive for Covid-19 in November, which resulted in Harry, Florence, Olivia and the rest of the cast going into isolation for two weeks. By the time it was over, all anyone could talk about was Harry's sensational cover for *Vogue*. It was instantly iconic. Anna Wintour had personally asked Harry if he might like to be the first solo male featured on the front. He did not need to be asked twice.

The front cover courted both controversy and praise because he was wearing a sky-blue lace Gucci ballgown that reached to the floor and was matched with a black Gucci tuxedo jacket. He broke the internet. Victoria Famele in the American lifestyle and fashion magazine *HOLR* picked up the positive; she called being on the front cover of *Vogue* a 'lifetime achievement'. She said it was 'an honour that tells the world that you are the real deal, it helps show the world what you stand for and helps the world realize how beautiful it can be'.

Harry went on a six-day juice cleanse to be in the best possible shape for the images. He was pictured by the acclaimed Brooklyn-born photographer Tyler Mitchell, who had taken the portrait of Beyoncé the previous year, which had become one of the most famous *Vogue* covers of all time.

Tyler, who was brought up in Atlanta, was just twenty-three at the time and was the first African-American to shoot the front of *Vogue*. Tyler describes himself as a 'concerned' photographer embracing all forms of popular culture, much as Harry crosses the boundaries of many art forms. He would have approved of Tyler's sentiment that he wanted to show a younger generation that they can climb the ladder and do what he was doing as well.

All the usual gang seemed to be involved: Alessandro Michele, obviously, was one – although Harry was by no means wearing Gucci exclusively. He now had a more formal arrangement with the company. The previous year, for instance, he had become the face of Gucci's first unisex scent,

Mémoire d'une Odeur, which was designed to transcend both gender and time. Harry explained how perfume triggered memories – his mum had always worn one that smelled of jasmine and Roman candles: 'Anytime I smell it, I feel like a kid.'

Harry Lambert was on hand to assist *Vogue*'s esteemed fashion editor Camille Nickerson in styling Harry for the day's shoot at the picturesque Seven Sisters chalk cliffs on the East Sussex coast. Harry's sister Gemma joined them for the day and featured in a criss-crossed Chopova Lowena dress, sitting on a bench next to her brother in one of Tyler's photographs.

One of the most striking outfits was designed and made in six days by Harris Reed. He produced a hooped skirt on top of a well-tailored suit. Some commentators weren't sure whether it was technically a dress or a suit, which was exactly the point of a fluid design and reinforced Harry's position as a face of gender neutrality. Harris observed, 'Harry just really understands the way gender can be restrictive.'

Harry explained his philosophy in a fascinating read by Hamish Bowles that accompanied the fashion pictures. He explained to the writer the importance of breaking down the barriers in fashion between men and women because then you open the 'arena in which you can play'.

Probably the most enduring quote in *Vogue*, however, was not one made by his close circle of friends, fashionistas or style generals. It came from Olivia, before anyone realised there was a spark between the two. She said, 'To me, he's very modern and I hope that this brand of confidence that Harry has – truly devoid of any traces of toxic masculinity – is indicative of his generation and therefore the future of the world.'

Her quote went round the globe and back again. Unsurprisingly, not everyone online was supportive of Harry breaking boundaries, with one commentator insisting we needed to bring back manly men. Olivia responded, 'You're pathetic.'

Olivia had very strong views that connected with Harry's – particularly where feminism was concerned. She and Jason took part in the 2017 Women's March in Washington, DC after Trump's election, declaring afterwards, 'that was the most incredible crowd I've ever been lucky enough to be part of. WOW.' A year later she carried her little daughter in her arms at the Women's March in Los Angeles.

Like Harry, she would demonstrate her support for a cause by wearing a pin at an occasion where she knew she would be photographed. She had attached a small gold one supporting Planned Parenthood to the red floor-length Michael Kors dress she wore on the red carpet at the Radio City Music Hall in New York where the 2017 Tony Awards were being held.

Harry also actively supported Planned Parenthood, a non-profit organisation that provided important sexual and reproductive health care, sex education and information to millions of men and women around the world – including advice and counselling about abortion. He wore a t-shirt that declared 'Women Are Smarter', inspired by the Women's March, which could be purchased through a site that donated part of the proceeds to Planned Parenthood.

Olivia encouraged people to support the TIME'S UP Legal Fund at the beginning of 2018, declaring, 'Time's up on silence. Time's up on waiting. Time's up on tolerating discrimination, harassment and ambush.' Later in the year, Harry donated $42,000 to the fund from his *Live on Tour* profits.

They clearly thought alike on many issues and, after a day's filming in Palm Springs, they could discuss them over seafood. They are both pescatarian. Harry had given up meat altogether during his tour, inspired by some of the musicians who were vegan. Olivia had moved between a vegetarian and vegan diet for several years before deciding that eating fish had added health benefits.

During filming they had been able to keep their blossoming relationship secret by meeting up at either Jeffrey Azoff's house in the Hollywood Hills or at James Corden's luxurious home near Palm Springs. There were the occasional paparazzi shots that hinted they might be more than work friends but the question remained: when, if ever, would they go public?

21

LOVE ON TOUR

New Year's Day 2021 began with the release of a new video that was practically guaranteed to put a smile on your face, especially as it featured Phoebe Waller-Bridge and Harry, doing more choreographed dancing than he ever did in One Direction.

The black-and-white video to 'Treat People with Kindness' was three minutes of undiluted joy. The directors this time were Harry's great friends Ben and Gabe Turner, two of the partners of Fulwell 73.

Harry and Gabe had been to see Phoebe's famous show *Fleabag* at Wyndham's Theatre in the West End and thought it would be wonderful if she worked with them on a Harry Styles video. The next day Gabe was watching old dance videos from the twenties and thirties and texted Harry to suggest it. He texted back simply, 'Treat People with Kindness'.

He phoned up Phoebe to ask her, which you can do if you are Harry Styles, and she readily agreed. They had to put in the hours with renowned choreographer Paul Roberts, with whom Harry had worked many times. The idea was a dance sequence in the style of old musical stars such as Danny Kaye or Fred Astaire and Ginger Rogers, with just a hint of Busby Berkeley.

It was as if Harry and Phoebe had been dancing together for years. Dressed in vintage Hollywood-style matching white outfits, they literally put on a show and was no surprise when their performance won Best Choreography at the 2021 MTV Video Music Awards. There had already been so many singles released from *Fine Line*, but it kept Harry's name in the spotlight.

A few days later, he was the centre of attention again when he was photographed for the first time with Olivia. They arrived together holding hands and wearing black masks at Jeffrey Azoff's wedding to his long-term partner Glenne Christiaansen at the San Ysidro ranch in the celebrity paradise of Montecito near Santa Barbara. Inevitably the gossip columns were fired up by a new celebrity couple. This time, the ten-year age gap was not a dominant issue.

Olivia didn't accompany him to the Grammys in mid-March, which avoided them being the story of the night. He began the entertainment with a performance of 'Watermelon Sugar' dressed in a leather suit and no shirt, accessorised by a green feather boa. He had been nominated for three awards: Best Music Video for 'Adore You', Best Pop Vocal Album for *Fine Line*; and the one he won – Best Pop Solo Performance for 'Watermelon Sugar'. It was his first Grammy.

His acceptance speech was gracious, thanking everyone including Jeffrey, Rob Stringer and his three co-writers – Tom, Tyler and Mitch, from the first session in Nashville when they wrote the song. Part of his speech had to be bleeped out when he spoke of the other nominees: 'All these songs are fucking massive,' he said without thinking.

After the ceremony he flew back to London where Olivia was staying with her children. Circumstances had worked out well. Jason was in the capital filming the second series of his hit comedy *Ted Lasso*, so it was timely that Harry had signed up to star in his third movie, *My Policeman*, which would also be set in the UK.

Again, this film was set in the 1950s, which at least meant he had a retro look already in place. The film is an adaptation of the 2012 novel by the Brighton-based author Bethan Roberts. She had been inspired by the real-life love affair between the iconic novelist E.M. Forster, author of *A Passage to India* and *Howards End*, and a young policeman.

Bethan explained, 'They were in love for thirty years, during a time when homosexuality was illegal, but they managed to negotiate a shared relationship with his wife. I took some of their stories and built *My Policeman* on that.'

The screenplay was adapted by the gay activist Ron Nyswaner, who has been responsible for bringing some compelling stories to the cinema, including the legal drama *Philadelphia* that starred Tom Hanks, who won an Oscar for his portrayal of a gay man living and dying with AIDS.

The director of *My Policeman*, Michael Grandage, is one of the best-known figures in UK theatre, acclaimed for his early work as artistic director of the Donmar Warehouse and more recently as head of the Michael Grandage Company, which has branched out into film.

Harry was cast as the policeman. The names are different from the real-life story and in the film his character is called

PC Tom Burgess. His wife, Marion, is played by Emma Corrin, who won a Golden Globe Award for her portrayal of Princess Diana in the Netflix classic *The Crown*.

Emma and Harry were already good friends, having met after one of his gigs. She tells the story of one evening when he agreed to look after her sweet cockapoo, Spencer, at his Hampstead house. She was having dinner at a local restaurant and halfway through the meal received a text from her distraught dog sitter: 'He won't stop farting. Is this normal?' Laughing, he told her later that he would not be helping out again.

Emma is another big celebrity client of Harry Lambert. She too is a wonderful blank canvas for a fashion designer, always bold enough to try something new. Her floor-length Pierrot-style Miu Miu gown with a frilled ruff was the fashion high-light of the Golden Globes at the Beverly Hilton in Los Angeles in March 2021. Lambert had devised a stunning series of red-carpet outfits for a promotional tour of *The Crown* but they were all put back in the wardrobe when Covid-19 caused a postponement.

After the filming of *My Policeman* had finished, Emma came out as queer and said she would now be using the she/they pronouns. Her co-star, meanwhile, had been keeping a very low profile with Olivia in London. They were seen having lunch together and once in a pub but that was about it. They were certainly not pictured with her children. As was usual with Harry, no one knew for sure where everyone was living – although he was in the habit of visiting a boutique coffee house in Hampstead.

Towards the end of filming, he slipped away from the set of *My Policeman* to go the BRITs at the O2. He seemed to pop up from nowhere to collect his award for British Single for 'Watermelon Sugar', having arrived too late to show off his eye-catching seventies-style Gucci suit with brown leather bag on the red carpet beforehand.

He managed to avoid using the F word in his acceptance speech, in which he thanked everyone politely, but he was a 'talking point'afterwards in that he had a decidedly American twang to his voice, which became the subject of many articles and online comments after the show. Harry attracted the most post-show publicity without doing anything much more than saying thank you. He even managed to eclipse Taylor Swift winning Global Icon.

Coincidentally, Jason Sudeikis finished filming *Ted Lasso* shortly afterwards, at the beginning of June, and flew with Otis and Daisy back to New York to his home in Brooklyn – one he no longer shared with Olivia. She was free, therefore, to join Harry on a trip to Italy, where he was shooting the final scenes of *My Policeman* in Venice.

After that wrapped, they moved on to an idyllic romantic break on a yacht in Monte Argentario, in Tuscany. It would be the last chance for the two of them to get away before *Love on Tour* resumed in September at the MGM Grand Garden Arena in Las Vegas. This time round he would be spending the first three months of the tour in the US. Hopefully that would mean he would see something of Olivia, although she, too, was very busy professionally preparing for her next big director project, a film called *Perfect* about an Olympic gymnast. She has also been cast for an acting role in the upcoming new Brad Pitt movie *Babylon*, set in 1920s Hollywood.

They returned to Los Angeles, renting a smart home in the very fashionable Los Feliz area of the city while Harry began rehearsals again for the tour. Their blossoming relationship is complicated by Olivia's commitment to her children and any future arrangements are quite rightly kept private behind closed doors. In reality, it was quite early days and Harry has remained completely discreet about his relationship with Olivia.

Just two weeks before the tour began in Las Vegas, Harry received some very sad news from England. His beloved grandfather, Brian, had died. His heartbroken mum, Anne, wrote a moving message on Instagram about her 'brave and courageous' dad: 'We love you totally and forever. Sleep sweetly, you beautiful man. Go be with Mum.' Harry said nothing publicly about the man who had been such a fixture in his life.

Love on Tour finally began on 4 September, seventeen months after the intended first night in Birmingham. It had been such a long time since the postponement that the concert seemed more like a greatest hits event than one supporting a newly released album. He began with 'Golden', the first track on *Fine Line*, and ended two hours later with 'Watermelon Sugar' and 'Kiwi'. He didn't disappoint fans hoping to hear his version of 'What Makes You Beautiful', nor those waiting to see him dance with a Pride flag.

Harry had already announced that audiences at his concerts should have proof of double vaccination. On the night he said on stage: 'I want to thank you guys for getting vaccinated or tested to be able to come here tonight. The staff on the entire *Love on Tour* team has done the same and we are all taking the precautions we can to make sure these shows happen safely.

'I know things are a bit different, but in order to protect each other, I also ask that you do your part by keeping your masks on while in the building and during the shows. I've always found that you can tell the most about a person from their eyes anyway. Treat people with kindness. I love you all and I'll see you very very soon.'

Two questions needed answering. Would he be wearing something fabulous, and would Olivia be there? The answer to both was yes. Harry wore an all-Gucci ensemble of an open vest covered in a pink-sequinned fringe, matching pink wide-leg trousers, and no shirt, revealing his famous butterfly tattoo looking as good as ever. The Harry Styles Fashion Archive online described it as a 'banger of an outfit'.

Olivia, who looked elegant in a powder-blue pantsuit, was accompanied by Jeffrey Azoff. They stood to the side and she waved at fans who called out her name when they recognised her, even though she was wearing a mask. And she danced along with the rest of the crowd. It was a happy night, although it was disappointing that neither Gemma nor Anne could make the concert because of pandemic travel restrictions from the UK.

The tour was a blockbuster success. *Forbes* magazine wrote of his three nights at the Forum in Los Angeles: 'Harry Styles showed he has all the traits needed to become the next great arena rock star in music.'

Arguably, he was already there. His tour was officially number one in 2021 for number of tickets sold. And his gross receipts of $94.7 million were second only to the mighty Rolling Stones who charged considerably more for a ticket. Harry also raised an estimated $1 million for charitable causes.

Despite Covid-19 disrupting so many hopes and expectations, Harry had managed to win his first Grammy, his second BRIT, had his first US number 1 single, been on the front cover of *Vogue*, made two feature films that will hopefully come to our screens later in 2022 and popped up unexpectedly in the Marvel adventure, *Eternals*. He played Eros in a post-credits scene that traditionally acts as an appetiser for a future story, although how he's going to find the time to make another movie is anyone's guess.

The Harry Styles juggernaut showed no signs of slowing down as 2022 began. In January there was such a demand for tickets to the long-anticipated UK leg of *Love on Tour* that the Ticketmaster site immediately crashed in the scramble. He announced two dates at Wembley Stadium, already perhaps endorsing the opinion of *Forbes* as to his future stature. The entire world tour sold out in minutes.

He wasn't taking it easy before six months of touring, however. He was seen filming a new video in The Mall outside Buckingham Palace. He was posing on a giant bed in a pair of brown and blue polka dot pyjamas. The media referred to it as secret, which, of course, it wasn't because the whole world seemed to know what was going on. That was also true a couple of weeks later when he was pictured filming around the Barbican estate in Central London wearing an eye-catching bright red coat and a pair of sequinned trousers.

The set was a happy one but, inadvertently, tinged with sadness. In charge was the multi-talented and much in demand Ukrainian-born director Tanu Muino. She admits that Harry is her favourite performer and directing the video was 'a bucket list dream come true.' But she explained, 'Shooting him was bittersweet as it was one of the happiest days of my life, but on the second day of the shoot, my country Ukraine was invaded, so you can imagine the insane emotions we had while shooting.'

Tanu had risen rapidly to the top thanks to her work with Katy Perry, Cardi B and the controversial 2021 video for Lil Nas X's 'Montero (Call Me By Your Name)', in which the rapper pole-dances for the Devil before killing him. She was a perfect choice for Harry, embracing the world of fashion and film in equal measure. Originally a model, then a stylist and a photographer, she had branched out into video because she wished her photos would move.

The world would not have long to wait to see the result of her days with Harry. His loyal fans seemed to know that the third Harry Styles album would soon be announced and that proved to be the case in March with the briefest of tweets on his little-used Twitter account, '@Harry_Styles'. It stated simply: Harry's House. May 20th.

Nothing more was disclosed, other than the cover art that featured Harry scratching his chin while standing on the ceiling of an upside-down living room. The tweet was liked more than a million times. Music aficionados quickly pointed out that this was a discreet nod to Joni Mitchell, whose song of that name featured in her 1975 album *The Hissing of Summer Lawns*. Joni retweeted Harry's post adding that she 'loved the title.'

The Barbican filming proved to be a rapid turnaround for the release on 1st April of 'As It Was', the lead single from the new album. His co-writing crew of Kid Harpoon and Tyler Johnson had helped produce an instantly catchy throwback to the synth sounds of the eighties, an era to revisit musically with a smile on your face.

'As It Was' could not have been more different from the epic six minutes of 'Sign of the Times'. The *Evening Standard* described it as a 'sub three-minute rush of indie pop with a fizzing bassline, loopy guitars and crashing bells.' The *Guardian* could not have been more enthusiastic, awarding it five stars and declaring, 'It is music to skip down the street to on a spring day, clicking your heels and picking up passing cocka-poos for a cuddly spin.' The lyrics were self-reflective, as Harry's songs always seem to be, perhaps with an added touch of melancholy. The line, 'Leave America, two kids follow her; I don't wanna talk about who's doin' it first:' seemed an obvious reference to Olivia. She had kept a low profile during their London stay, although occasionally a new photograph would surface of them out and about near his North London home.

A week after release, 'As it Was' went to number one in the UK chart. More impressively, it earned a place in the Guinness World Records as the most-streamed track on Spotify in twenty-four hours by a male artist. The final figure was more than 16 million streams in its first day. By the time it reached number one in the charts, Tanu's video had been watched nearly 50 million times on YouTube.

The pitch-perfect promotion of Harry's new music is an indication of an artist in charge of his own destiny. The world, it seems, is no longer watching vulture-like to see if his solo career is going to fail. Those days have long gone and Harry Styles has become a true global icon. Instead, we wait to see what this gifted and very modern man will do next. And we wait with a smile on our face.

LAST THOUGHTS

On 1 February 2019 a quiet, unassuming character sat reading and drinking tea in a Tokyo café. It was his twenty-fifth birthday and Harry Styles was relishing the opportunity to enjoy his own company.

He read unbothered for five hours, engrossed in *The Wind-Up Bird Chronicle* by Haruki Murakami, an author he loved and arguably the most famous modern-day Japanese novelist. The *Daily Telegraph* described it as 'labyrinthine and hallucinogenic' and listed the 1994 work as one of the ten best Asian novels of all time.

The teeming streets of Tokyo were the perfect place for Harry to be alone. He walked back to where he was staying, listening to music on his AirPods, absorbed in his own thoughts. He chose tracks by the late, great Bill Evans, one of the most influential of all jazz pianists and composers.

Evans died in 1980 aged just fifty-one, after too short a life that was blighted by cocaine and heroin abuse. His 'Peace Piece' (1959) is a supreme example of musical tranquillity and Harry had chosen it as the ringtone on his phone.

The world is a better place with the Evans piano soothing your ear. His light and lyrical touch was once described as the music that would be playing at the gates of Heaven. Media organisation NPR described him simply as 'a genius'.

So there you have the perfect recipe for a Harry Styles birthday – the words of Murakami and the chords of Bill Evans. It's not exactly rock and roll, is it? But then this is a complex, intelligent and empathetic man who critics and so-called experts are forever trying to categorise.

Harry spent five weeks in Japan at the start of 2019, creating memories and thoughts to take with him. He explained, 'I never travelled alone. I wanted to spend some time on my own. It was a quiet time for me, a time to reflect on things.'

He had much to reflect on, since, in effect, he had left home at the age of sixteen, never to return to live there. He was very young and potentially vulnerable in the celebrity world of partying, but instead of going off the rails in a mad whirl of sex, drugs and rock and roll, Harry forged long-standing friendships with a mainly older group of people who loved his company and in return would be loyal and supportive.

Musically, it was a slow start for the boys in One Direction. Niall Horan always had a guitar with him but that was about it. Everything was done for them under the guidance of the leading Swedish producers of the day. They were worked very hard by a series of Svengali businessmen who successfully plotted their world domination.

Gradually their individual talents and forceful personalities came to the fore. They were five very different men. Harry, as this book has suggested, was always destined to be a frontman but he took a little time to be confident in his own abilities. His songwriting contributions in the early days were relatively scarce, but in 'Stockholm Syndrome' and 'If I Could Fly' he wrote two of the most enduringly popular of the band's songs. He also composed 'Just a Little Bit of Your Heart' for Ariana Grande and joined forces with Meghan Trainor to write 'Someday', which she sang as a duet with Michael Bublé – not exactly as prolific as Ed Sheeran but a more than promising start.

By the time he became a solo artist, Harry was ready to take centre stage with a small band of producers and musicians who would become loyal friends as well as workmates. That's one of the positive things about Harry – he works best and most creatively with those he trusts and actively likes, such as Tom Hull and Mitch Rowland, his rock-geek guitarist who knew next to nothing about One Direction before they met.

Harry's musical ability took shape as his own experience of life developed. A sixteen-year-old boy from rural Cheshire can write about his first kiss or his maths homework but not so much about life, love and loss.

These three key components of a songwriter's staple subjects – not forgetting sex – affected Harry as he forged new relationships and friendships. It's no secret that he has written songs about Kendall Jenner or his ill-fated relationship with Camille Rowe. They ignited his lyrical creativity.

Music is just one aspect of Harry Styles, the artist. He now has fully justified his status as a fashion icon for the modern generation – blurring the lines of gender and just loving 'dressing up', as he used to call it as a boy when playing games with his mum and sister back home in Holmes Chapel.

When Harry released the video for his single 'As It Was', almost as much attention was given to what he was wearing as it was to his singing. In particular, fashion writers noted the tight-fitting crimson jumpsuit created by the Spanish designer Arturo Obegero. He had worked closely with Harry and Harry Lambert to create a look that was inspired by the tour outfits worn by Mick Jagger and David Bowie in the late sixties and seventies – both artists who were in touch with their feminine side.

Critics, including fashion experts, like to compare and contrast influences and styles. I asked fashion commentator Alison Jane Reed if Harry Styles was a leader of fashion or a follower of fashion. She replied neatly, 'That is a very interesting question.'

Great rock and pop stars of the past have paraded on stage in the most eye-catching and flamboyant costumes. It is entirely justified to look at David Bowie, Mick Jagger, Prince, Marc Bolan or Freddie Mercury and decide that Harry is following their example. It's easy to imagine him coming on stage at Hyde Park in 1969 – as Mick did – wearing his famous white dress over white flared trousers and white boots.

But, quite frankly, what these greatest of stars wore fifty years ago is of no consequence to a generation born since the turn of the century. Yes, fashion trends come and go, but for anyone under twenty, under thirty – or maybe even under forty – Harry is a trendsetter and a breath of fresh air. It's all new to this current young generation; it's exciting and relevant to who they are and aspire to be now – blurring the lines of gender and breaking down the barriers of toxic masculinity. Alison Jane adds, 'Harry is using fashion to say whoever you want to be is fine. He is the poster boy for gender equality, the idea that boys can show a feminine side, and that is great.'

Harry keeps and cares for all his amazing outfits and it can only be a matter of time before there is a major retrospective of his fashion at the V&A Museum in London. The JW Anderson patchwork cardigan he wore to a rehearsal in February 2020 is already there.

As a brand, Harry continues to grow his business empire. In the autumn of 2021 he launched his own vegan and cruelty-free beauty line called Pleasing. His nail polishes and skin products have proved an instant hit and the endeavour is already expanding successfully. His ad campaign for the brand featured his old friend and mentor Mick Fleetwood, a sixties survivor who would not be everyone's idea of a supermodel but was perfect for showcasing the product.

Olivia Wilde did her bit too by sporting a sky blue crew neck on a walk in North London. The one hundred per cent cotton sweatshirt that cost £100 featured a picture of a reclining frog with the word Pleasing emblazoned in red across the front. And then there is acting, which as yet does not rival the heights of music and fashion on Harry's CV. He will make more films, as he seems to have a serious talent and others seem to enjoy working with him on set. He may bring a large entourage with him, but he doesn't bring a big ego.

In each of the three main areas of his creative world, Harry has joined forces with a select few people that he can trust and whose opinion he values. In the introduction to this book, 'First Impressions', I posed the question: who are the people that have helped Harry on the journey to become the man he is today?

The making of Harry as a modern man starts at home, where his mum Anne and his sister Gemma were a constant female presence in his life. He may not always have seen eye to eye with his elder sibling, but there was a mutual respect which still exists.

Anne and Gemma are compassionate women whose outlook on life hugely influenced Harry as he grew up. He may be modest about his academic achievements in comparison to Gemma, but he has a natural intelligence and inquisitiveness that has allowed him to absorb and respond to different aspects of culture as he has come across them – whether it's art, fashion, photography, literature, film or, of course, music.

Gemma is a gifted writer, a talent she uses to highlight the causes she believes in online and through social media. It is an ambition she shares with her brother. During Mental Health Awareness Month in June 2021, she wrote on her blog: 'Something I can do with my platform is to help amplify the voices of others.'

Harry embraces that ethic. Clearly they think as one on many issues.

Gemma has more than 8 million followers on Instagram and nearly 4 million on Twitter, so she really can influence online. Anne has 2.6 million on Instagram and in recent years has used her voice to tirelessly fundraise for Parkinson's UK, inspired by her dad Brian's illness. In October 2020, she raised more than £10,000 by undertaking a wing walk. She was strapped to the top of a biplane flying the Gloucestershire skies. 'It was a terrifying experience,' she said afterwards.

When Brian died in August 2021 the family asked for donations to the charity to honour his memory.

Through the early female influence of his mother and sister, Harry learned to mix easily with an older generation without ever becoming old before his time. He also appeared to have a sixth sense in choosing his friends wisely, favouring those who value their own privacy and are never likely to shout, 'Look at me; I'm a friend of Harry Styles.'

He is surrounded by a small circle of extraordinarily talented friends and influences that are at the coalface of popular culture, shaping the style and thinking of a new generation. Hopefully Harry can remember them all should he ever receive a lifetime achievement award, for he has quite ruthlessly ditched anyone who has spoken out of turn about him to the tabloid media.

He doesn't give interviews to the popular press, preferring to speak to trusted writers on *Rolling Stone*, *Vogue*, *GQ*, *Another Man* or a very few other publications who will produce a biographical feature that will be read and enjoyed for many years and not be tomorrow's fish-and-chip wrapper.

One of his go-to writers is the American journalist Rob Sheffield, a contributing editor for *Rolling Stone* whose 2007 autobiographical memoir *Love Is a Mix Tape: Life and Loss, One Song at a Time* remains a favourite book of Harry's. In it, Rob uses music to tell the story of his love for his wife, the writer Renee Crist, and how it helped him cope with her sudden death from a pulmonary embolism after six years of marriage.

The *Los Angeles Times* wrote, 'Sheffield is mourning another death as well – of the 90s, a decade of "peace, prosperity and freedom" when smart, creative musicians found a wide audience and women were encouraged to be visible and vocal.'

One can appreciate that an enlightened man such as Harry Styles would respond positively to such a lament. What makes him more interesting than the average run-of-the-mill icon is that he shares his private views – which have developed within his close circle of friends and loved ones – with a wider audience.

While his talents in all three key areas of his life have also matured – he is now a true Renaissance man – so have his views on the things that matter to his generation. They are not recent eureka moments. He supported HeForShe when he was twenty. At twenty-one he danced on stage with a rainbow flag during a One Direction concert, and at the age of twenty-four he backed the March for Our Lives. He was twenty-six when he took part in a peaceful Black Lives Matter protest in Los Angeles. And at the Ball Arena, Denver, on the second night of *Love on Tour* in September, he held a bisexual Pride flag that a fan had thrown on stage while he performed 'Treat People with Kindness'. He is still just twenty-eight.

So, I asked in the introduction what it actually means to be modern. For me, it is to represent the values that matter for a modern generation, not constricted by the 'good old days' and 'the way we were'. The modern generation thinks millennials are middle-aged!

The new generation – Generation Z, if you like – is sincere about racism, mental health, feminism and gender equality. This group responds positively to the genuine concerns of Harry Styles as he articulates his support in a way that isn't patronising.

His famous defence of his young girl fans perfectly encapsulates his absence of toxic masculinity: 'How can you say young girls don't get it?' he argued. 'They're our future. Our future doctors, lawyers, mothers, presidents, they kind of keep the world going.'

A Modern Man, indeed.

HARRY'S STARS

In Harry's birth chart, the Sun – symbol of identity and direction in life – is in the progressive, humanitarian sign of Aquarius. One expects a strong social conscience with this placement, along with independent thinking, a marked interest in the collective, and honesty. Harry's Sun ruler, Uranus, planet of originality, is joined to creative, visionary Neptune, which is the first of many indicators of Harry's gifts as a highly imaginative artist and star performer.

Mars and Venus, traditional symbols for masculinity and femininity, flank Harry's Sun, in a beguiling combination that gifts him with hypnotic attraction and universal appeal. This planetary combination suggests how important popularity is for Harry but, equally, that he is very courageous and that he can, albeit with enormous grace, resolutely push an agenda – one that at its core will be about embracing individuality, difference and the rebel.

It is impossible to ignore the sheer love of life that the tight link between Harry's Sun and Venus suggests. He values and deeply enjoys existence, is accepting and good at making

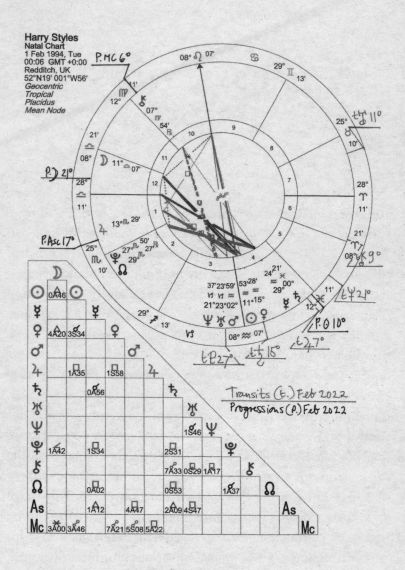

Harry Styles
Natal Chart
1 Feb 1994, Tue
00:06 GMT +0:00
Redditch, UK
52°N19' 001°W56'
Geocentric
Tropical
Placidus
Mean Node

allowances, is instinctively diplomatic – with so much affection to give, has refinement and appreciation of beauty, and more. Does it matter then, if, thanks to competitive Mars, he always wants to come first?

There is a sense with this chart that the gifts Harry brings to the uncertainties and needs of our present times go beyond those of a shining entertainer. Here is someone who, through his craft, has gained a platform and has such enormous potential for contributing positively towards the balance of generational good. With his Sun and three other planets in revolutionary, egalitarian Aquarius, Harry will very consciously feel obligations to his world tribe and peer group.

He will also instinctively have the faith and vision that can move mountains. A strong link from the Sun to unbounded Jupiter hints at magnetic success and control over his destiny, but with a caveat: there may be times when his goals could run away from him. His sense of identity, then, could suffer – from unrestrained optimism and limitless agendas either of his own making or the design of others. And of this he must be careful. Like many of our leaders and idols, Harry will carry the projection of our hopes and expectations and, knowing this, he may feel harder hit by any failure to deliver. But deliver he will, giving back and paying forward, helping in the moment, because he can, with his Aquarian Sun being so at ease with the issues and zeitgeist of our times.

There is just a hint that when very young Harry may have been a shy communicator, finding it hard to express opinions, sometimes struggling to think positively and clearly – perhaps an older sibling expressed what he thought for him? However, as an adult – and partly because he will feel driven by just causes – Harry will become an assured, charismatic and genuine voice of authority.

Expansive, restless Jupiter, ruler of adventurers and seekers, is the planet that reveals much about Harry's initial education. It suggests that from early years he needed to test his faith and confidence in life and the classroom would sometimes have felt too small. Jupiter's urge for growth is amplified by the influence of obsessive Pluto, a sure sign that Harry would have strong instincts to evolve, to be rid of his old self and experience renewal. This is an ambitious signature, one of someone who needs a bigger stage, far away from the comfort zone of immediate community, neighbours and siblings.

These groups *are* important to him – he will feel the debt of brotherhood and positive experiences but he will want to respect this by following his destiny and then returning with the trophies of wisdom. There is, in the chart, a slightly Promethean feel, revealed by the melding of the energies of Uranus, Neptune and Saturn. Harry may bring a rebellious creativity and innovative mindset to issues of spirituality and our common values. There will be an instinct for finding peace and peaceful solutions, driven by appreciation of the sheer value of living in harmony and fear of the wasteland of negativity and hate. Few mediums are more suited to endorsing the concept that we are all part of one world than music, but Harry will be a role model in bringing that notion home, in making an abstract concept feel more real and attainable.

Despite the stellar trajectory of Harry's career – the glamour, the spotlights, the wealth, the recognition and the leadership credentials this provides – Harry's Sun position, at the bottom of his chart, tell us that home life and family will always be of fundamental importance to him. His background and his family circle are what provide both his confidence and sense of self, and he will need the security of a base far more than most.

Harry's love of his parents is a given – no matter if they disappoint – together with respect for his upbringing, the traditions and his personal history that have made him the man he is. He will spend a lifetime working through the issues that were created and thrown up in his early developmental years. These issues include fairness – whose voice gets heard, the rights of the individual over the needs of the group, who leads and how to manage the emotional fallout from members who no longer fit the team and his ability to move on from them.

For Harry, the Sun in progressive air sign Aquarius indicates a modern, collective family structure within which everyone pulled together but that also places a high value on each individual's freedom. There would have been unpredictability built into the very foundation of this unit because rationality, honesty and ambition would have prevailed as standard over the need for emotional passion or intimacy. The very close and very positive link between the luminaries the Sun and the Moon – representing father and mother – indicate parents who could easily express their feelings in a logical and tolerant manner and act considerately both to each other and their children. Thus when the group was placed under pressure, the default would be a civilised and intelligent split, with minimal conflict between the past, symbolised by the Moon, and the future, embodied by the Sun.

But such changes will have come at a cost to sensitive Harry – his conciliatory Libran Moon revealing through its position the pain of trying to keep his loved ones together.

A link between Harry's Libra Moon and dynamic Mars highlights the protective nature of his mother. She is somebody with an instinctive need to help others and will enjoy a challenge, quickly recognising opportunity when it comes. With her grace, ability to motivate and highly developed social skills, she will be more comfortable within a partnership than living on her own, and she has the skills to constructively turn around difficult situations. Mother may have side-stepped facing awkward emotional demands in favour of a placatory smoothing of the waters.

The father in Harry's chart is shown by the independent Aquarian Sun and Saturn in escapist, idealistic Pisces. Both placements signal absence but also duty and sensitivity. The father perhaps struggled with the commitment to satisfy other people's needs before his own but may have ultimately accepted responsibility and was supportive, embodying authority and vulnerability at the same time. A tight link between Saturn and intense Pluto hints at a degree of defensiveness and inflexibility that could be a block to emotional closeness.

No matter the fairness and kindness modelled by parents at challenging times, no matter the consistent loyalty and affection, there are indications in Harry's chart that it is hard for him to reveal his feelings and articulate his emotional needs. Harry has learnt that charm will take him a long way; his identity is very strongly tied up with being liked – he is compassionate and a people-pleaser and thus may shy away from revealing any emotions that seem ugly. As a result, anger and discord will be repressed or projected.

A great deal of Harry's determined and ambitious character can be traced back to his sibling connections. The linking of competitive Mars and rebellious Uranus shows how from his earliest days he would learn how to retain his individuality within the group. He would do this partly by fighting (probably with charm) for access to the parent, which is excellent training for navigating group workplace situations where he needs to lead and come out on top. A combination of authoritative Saturn and the youth symbol Mercury suggests a sibling filling the void for an absent parent and reinforces that sense of his need to push for recognition as the best. Often, these drives lessen the sense of connectedness to brothers and sisters, but they are beneficial for becoming self-reliant in adult relationships – sometimes too much so. Harry is highly focused and self-contained and may find it hard to depend upon others.

Harry's need for security will make it very important to found a home base or family group at some point because it is really only when he feels safe and able to express his deeper emotions that he functions at his best. Then there will be some sort of re-balancing towards a different ideal, one where he can live with a foundation of openly expressed emotional truth. The challenging connection between Saturn and Pluto suggests this will always feel dangerous until he has learnt how to be comfortable with acknowledging and stating what he really wants rather than what he feels others want him to be.

As far as relationships go, much of his life's purpose will centre upon his links with others – whether personal or professional – learning how he uses his considerable power and the journey of working out his own values for intimacy. In one-to-one partnerships Harry enjoys the fun, excitement, the glamour and unpredictability of romance, but the shadow of Saturn colours his Mars, suggesting his ability to trust others will be hard-won. He may be cautious about initiating flings and happier if others come to him. Then he might experience a clash between enjoying his relationships and pursuing his goals. Harry has very strong personal defences and part of him will remain alone in the midst of the crowd. He has enormous empathy, but in order for this to flow he needs to feel safe and able to withdraw, to be confident he will not feel trapped and that the privacy he needs to be creative will not be invaded.

In the run-up to Harry's Saturn Return, which occurs in March 2023, he will experience significant changes in his relationships. Pluto, symbol of death, resurrection and irrevocable change, first links positively to his natal Pluto and then contacts his Ascendant in a more challenging manner. Initially he will be drawn towards a greater understanding of his own psychology, the strengths and impediments of character. This may be prompted through a profoundly stabilising appreciation that his self-made resources are more than adequate to provide for his own needs and any important projects to which he would like to commit. His sense of identity will be supported by this to the extent that he will be prepared to take more risks. He will probe his values, able to prioritise the altruistic and intimacy goals that he can see will promote his own creative and spiritual growth.

Harry has reached a point where he is ready for change, allowing certain aspects of himself – perhaps illusions of control – to die. One of the spiritual laws that he will encounter is the Law of Abundance, which dictates that we must not hold on to things – he must willingly let things go, to let energy flow and trust this process of release and return. It is a period in which he must fearlessly confront the possibility of crisis and change. Relationships that have outlived their usefulness will go, and new ones, which have a more constructive purpose, will form. Harry can expect power struggles now and must be careful not to act ruthlessly or feel his ends justify any means. Challenges will uncover his weaknesses, but he will learn how to deal with them.

This clearing out precedes the return of Saturn to the place it occupied at Harry's birth twenty-eight years previously. Where he has undertaken the burdens and restrictions that life has imposed upon him responsibly and well, there will be evidence of gratifying, solid success. In the areas he may have neglected or from which he sought to escape, he may have some regrets. Aspects of life that have been tolerated, but are not truly where his energies need to be, will probably fall away. This sounds a little bleak, except that Harry's natal Saturn positively links to his Ascendant and Descendant – the relationship axis. Thus we may predict that Harry will find himself in the company of a group of people, or a significant person, or experience events that will play a profoundly important and positive role in shaping his destiny.

Madeleine Moore
September 2021

LIFE AND TIMES

1 Feb 1994: Harry Edward Styles is born in the Alexandra Hospital, Redditch. He has a sister, Gemma, who is three, and they live with their mum Anne and dad Des, a financial consultant, in Evesham, Worcestershire.

March 1996: The Styles family move to the Cheshire village of Holmes Chapel, twenty miles south of Manchester. Harry would go to school in this rural setting until he is sixteen.

Sept 1998: Moves from nursery, Happy Days, to the Hermitage Primary School. He is a boisterous little boy who makes friends easily – with both boys and girls. 'I wasn't one of those boys who thought girls were smelly,' he said.

Dec 2000: In the school's Christmas musical, he plays the title character of Barney, a church mouse. He recalls, 'I like to think I was a good church mouse.' He would also appear in productions of *Chitty Chitty Bang Bang*, playing Buzz Lightyear, and *Joseph and the Amazing Technicolor Dreamcoat*, as the Pharoah who performed a song in the style of Elvis.

Nov 2002: Harry and Gemma move to the Antrobus Arms near Northwich when Anne and her new partner, a publican called John Cox, take over the popular pub. She and Des had split when Harry was seven.

April 2003: Anne and John marry at a local golf and country club. She is still Anne Cox when Harry becomes famous, even though she and John are divorced and she and the children have moved back to Holmes Chapel.

Sept 2005: Starts at Holmes Chapel Comprehensive where one of his best buddies is Will Sweeny, son of Yvette Fielding, the host of TV's *Most Haunted*, which also featured her second husband, Karl Beattie. Harry is a regular visitor after school, scoffing pizza and chips in the kitchen with her son.

June 2009: Will persuades Harry to join his band White Eskimo with other friends Nick Clough and Haydn Morris. At the end of Year 10 they win Holmes Chapel Comprehensive's first Battle of the Bands. They perform 'Summer of '69' and 'Are You Gonna Be My Girl'. Adult tickets are £5 each.

April 2010: Skives off school to attend the first audition for *The X Factor* at Old Trafford, Manchester. His mum had filled out an application form for him and sent it off. Will joins him for the day and they queue up for more than five hours. Harry subsequently learns he is through to the first televised audition.

June 2010: White Eskimo play their biggest gig so far, at a wedding in the nearby town of Sandbach. They are paid £400.

July 2010: Sings Stevie Wonder's 'Isn't She Lovely' in front of Simon Cowell, Nicole Scherzinger and Louis Walsh, who gives him a thumbs-down. He is rescued by the other two. Simon tells him, 'You could actually be very good.' At Bootcamp, Simon warns there are no second chances. He gives five boys, including Harry, a second chance. Harry sinks to his knees in delight.

Sept 2010: The five teenage boys – Liam, Louis, Niall, Zayn and Harry – settle on One Direction as their name; Harry's idea. They perform 'Torn' at Judges' Houses for Simon and Sinitta and win through to the live finals at the Fountain Studios, Wembley.

Oct 2010: Harry suffers an acute attack of nerves before the band are due to perform 'My Life Would Suck Without You' by Kelly Clarkson. He is anxious he would sing the wrong note, but all is well on the night. Simon finds Harry charming and the easiest member of the group to talk to.

Dec 2010: The band tops the UK charts for the first time when they join the other contestants for the Comic Relief charity record, David Bowie's iconic 'Heroes'. For the grand final weekend, One Direction perform 'She's the One', with Robbie Williams joining them on stage. They finish third behind Matt Cardle and Rebecca Ferguson. Simon signs 1D to a recording contract.

Jan 2011: Harry and the boys visit Los Angeles for the first time, where they meet record producers and he buys lots of Abercrombie & Fitch t-shirts from their flagship store. They are greeted by hundreds of excited fans when they land back at Heathrow.

Feb 2011: One Direction perform five songs as part of *The X Factor* annual tour. When it finishes in April, Harry moves into a flat in North London, which he shares with Louis Tomlinson.

Aug 2011: Their first video is released to promote debut single 'What Makes You Beautiful'. They are filmed frolicking on a beach in Malibu. Harry splashes around and serenades model Madison McMillin. The video has been watched 1.2 billion times. Harry tells the official *X Factor* website that Caroline Flack is 'gorgeous'.

Sept 2011: 'What Makes You Beautiful' is number one in the UK. It would sell more than seven million copies worldwide.

Dec 2011: Harry is photographed leaving Caroline Flack's North London home on a wintry morning. Caroline would face a barrage of newspaper criticism about the age gap as well as online abuse and death threats. One Direction's *Up All Night* tour begins at the Watford Colosseum. He posts a tweet just before Christmas: 'Work hard, play hard, be kind.'

Jan 2012: Harry posts on Twitter following his break-up with Caroline: 'Please know I didn't "dump" Caroline. This was a mutual decision. She is one of the kindest, sweetest people I know. Please respect that.'

Feb 2012: On his eighteenth birthday, in Los Angeles, Harry gets his first tattoo – the outline of a five-pointed star on the inside of his left bicep. 'What Makes You Beautiful' wins Best British Single at the BRITs. He quietly moves in with Ben Winston and his wife Meredith in Hampstead Garden Suburb while his new house nearby is being renovated. He would stay more than eighteen months.

March 2012: Meets Taylor Swift for the first time backstage at the Nickelodeon Kids' Choice Awards in LA. She apparently told Justin Bieber that she thought Harry was hot.

Dec 2012: Taylor and Harry are photographed together walking hand in hand in Central Park, New York. She is also pictured with him on a break in Cheshire, the Lake District and in a pub near Sheffield, where Harry's sister attends Hallam University. One Direction's second album *Take Me Home* tops a million sales in the US. His mum gives him a belly button brush for Christmas.

Jan 2013: Splits with Taylor after reportedly having a big bust-up on holiday in the British Virgin Islands.

Feb 2013: One Direction wins the Global Success Award at the BRITs. They perform their Comic Relief single 'One Way or Another (Teenage Kicks)'. Harry is moved to tears when they visit Ghana and makes a series of video diaries highlighting the country's poverty and the need for improved medical facilities.

June 2013: Harry is best man at the wedding of his mother in Congleton, Cheshire, to local businessman Robin Twist, with whom he has a great relationship.

Sept 2013: Beams with pride at his sister's university graduation with First Class Honours. He tweets: 'She's all clever and that.' Harry is the centre of attention at London Fashion Week, especially when he is seen supporting the supermodel Cara Delevingne at the Burberry Prorsum Show.

Nov 2013: The marathon *Take Me Home* tour ends in Japan after 123 shows and a box office gross of $114 million. Third album, *Midnight Memories*, is released and again tops charts in the UK and US. Most of the album had been written and recorded in makeshift studios in their bedrooms on tour. He is photographed leaving a Hollywood restaurant with Kendall Jenner.

Dec 2013: Harry is crowned the winner of the British Style Award at the British Fashion Awards. He wins a High Court order preventing certain paparazzi from harassing him.

April 2014: Poses happily with fans after arriving in a Porsche for rehearsals at a disused aircraft hangar near Bedford. The all-stadium *Where We Are* tour begins in Bogotá, Colombia.

Sept 2014: Posts a picture online of himself holding a sign that declares HeForShe. Underneath he writes: 'I'm supporting @UN Women and @EmWatson in HeForShe: As should you.' The post is liked nearly half a million times.

Nov 2014: Seems subdued at the recording of Band Aid 30 in Notting Hill. Rumours start that One Direction are on the verge of splitting up. Proceeds of this number-one version go towards fighting ebola in Africa. *Four* is released and they become the first band to have their first four albums debut at number one in the US.

Feb 2015: Turns twenty-one with a glamorous party at Lola's in Hollywood with guests including Harry's gang: James Corden, Kendall Jenner, Cara Delevingne, Rita Ora, Kelly Osbourne, David Beckham and the man who would soon be his manager, Jeffrey Azoff. None of One Direction attends but he is thrilled when Adele gives him a signed copy of *21* with the message: 'I did some pretty cool stuff when I was twenty-one. Good luck!'

March 2015: Zayn Malik leaves the band. An official statement says he wants some 'private time out of the spotlight'. He would later say that he thought One Direction's music was as 'generic as fuck' and that he and Harry had never really spoken to each other.

Aug 2015: After a concert at Soldier Field, Chicago, news leaks that they would be taking a break when the current tour ends.

Sept 2015: Harry is seen for the first time in an eye-catching, geometric-patterned Gucci suit, designed by Alessandro Michele, when he attends a fashion event at a private members' club in Mayfair.

Oct 2015: The last One Direction concert before the group's hiatus is at the Motorpoint Arena, Sheffield.

Nov 2015: Wears an even bolder floral Gucci suit to the American Music Awards in Los Angeles. With longer rock-star hair, he stands out and apart from the rest of the group. The band wins Artist of the Year for the second time and performs 'Perfect', a track from their fifth and last album to date, *Made in the AM*.

Dec 2015: Fittingly, their last appearance on UK television is at the grand final of *The X Factor*. In the US they sing five songs on Carpool Karaoke with James Corden. The video has been watched nearly 184 million times on YouTube.

March 2016: Harry is the first big signing of Jeffrey Azoff's new company Full Stop Management. In a busy start to the year, he has already joined the Creative Artists Agency (CAA) and auditioned for a role in the World War II drama *Dunkirk*, directed by Christopher Nolan, who says Harry has an 'old-fashioned face'.

May 2016: Harry starts his own label, Erskine Records, an imprint that will release his records under the Columbia umbrella. His personal assistant, Emma Spring, is registered as company director.

July 2016: Begins filming his role as young soldier Alex, after two weeks of training in Northern France, swimming while wearing an overcoat with a pack on his back. His first line in a movie is, 'What's wrong with your friend?'

Dec 2016: Finishes most of his debut solo album at a villa and studio at Port Antonio in Jamaica with his new musical entourage, which includes guitarist Mitch Rowland – who was working in a pizza restaurant in Hollywood when he was asked to play at a recording session for Harry. They become great friends and collaborators.

Feb 2017: Columbia Records, which had been the US label of One Direction, confirm they will be releasing Harry's first solo album, *Harry Styles*. He is the only member of the band they sign.

April 2017: His debut solo single 'Sign of the Times' is heard for the first time on Nick Grimshaw's breakfast programme on Radio 1. The six-minute epic had been written in three hours after lunch in Jamaica when Harry started tinkering around on the piano. The song, a thoughtful commentary on the things that matter in the world, goes straight to number one in the UK. In the US, he appears on *Saturday Night Live* and does a hilarious impression of Mick Jagger.

May 2017: The album *Harry Styles* debuts at number one on both sides of the Atlantic and sells more than one million copies by the end of the year. His favourite track is 'From the Dining Table' because 'it's the most personal'. Performs with the legendary Stevie Nicks at the Troubadour, Los Angeles.

June 2017: Harry's stepfather Robin Twist dies aged 57 after a long battle with cancer. Niall Horan describes him as 'the nicest, kindest, most generous, hilariously funny guy you'll have met'.

July 2017: Attends the premiere of *Dunkirk* at the Odeon, Leicester Square, and chats backstage to Prince Harry, who is guest of honour. The movie makes $527 million at the box office.

Sept 2017: Waves a rainbow flag that a member of the audience threw onto the stage at the first *Live on Tour* concert in San Francisco. The LGBTQ+ Pride symbol would become a fixture at his shows. After the concert in LA, he goes out for sushi with his girlfriend, the model Camille Rowe. Writes 'Watermelon Sugar' during a break before his show in Nashville.

March 2018: Tweets in support of the March for Our Lives, the youth-led protest in Washington urging gun control. Camille is seen dancing next to his mum Anne at his Paris concert.

June 2018: He begins Pride month by announcing that the proceeds from a special-edition Treat People with Kindness t-shirt would go to GLSEN (Gay, Lesbian and Straight Education Network), which champions inclusive and safe school environments. Dances with a rainbow flag and a Black Lives Matter flag at his concerts in New York and Chicago.

March 2019: Harry gives the presentation speech in New York in honour of Stevie Nicks when she becomes the only woman to be inducted twice into the Rock and Roll Hall of Fame. They sing a duet of her classic song 'Don't Go Draggin' My Heart Around'.

May 2019: It's a big night for Harry when he is co-host for the famous Met Gala (Met Ball) in New York. The theme of the evening is 'Camp: Notes on Fashion'. Pictures of Harry in a Gucci sheer-black ruffled top with a lace bib go round the world.

Oct 2019: 'Lights Up', the lead single from his second album, is released. While it doesn't reach number one in the US or the UK, the steamy video filmed in Mexico is watched 95 million times. Harry gives evidence behind a screen at Hendon Magistrates Court in North London in a harassment case involving a stalker who had been camped outside his home for months, leaving him 'scared and very uncomfortable'.

Nov 2019: Hosts *Saturday Night Live* in New York and reveals comic talent in a series of sketches including playing a Chihuahua. Show regular Cecily Strong calls his performance 'magical'. Announces *Love on Tour* promoting his album *Fine Line* will begin in Birmingham in April 2020.

Dec 2019: Harry steps in to host *The Late Late Show* in Los Angeles when his friend James Corden dashes off to be with his wife Julia, who is about to give birth. Plays a game of Spill Your Guts or Fill Your Guts with Kendall Jenner. Harry becomes the first UK male artist to have his two albums debut at number one in the US when *Fine Line* reaches the top. Plays a secret gig at the Electric Ballroom in Camden with Stormzy as the special guest.

Jan 2020: Enjoys a Caribbean holiday with friends including Adele and James Corden. Harry and Adele leave their waiter a timely tip of $2,020 (£1,500) at a seafood restaurant in the Virgin Islands and scribble 'Happy New Year' on the receipt.

Feb 2020: Harry is mugged at knifepoint near his London home. Caroline Flack is found dead and Harry wears a simple black ribbon on his Gucci suit at the BRIT Awards in her memory. He performs 'Falling', a moving ballad from the album about his relationship with ex-girlfriend Camille Rowe.

March 2020: Announces postponement of *Love on Tour* owing to Covid-19.

May 2020: Five days after the murder of George Floyd, Harry posts on Twitter, 'Being not racist is not enough. We must be anti-racist.'

June 2020: Takes part in a peaceful Black Lives Matter protest through the streets of Hollywood.

July 2020: Harry tweets on the tenth anniversary of the formation of One Direction. He thanks everyone who helped the band along the way and says, 'To all the fans, I love you and I thank you with all my heart.' His comments are liked more than 10.5 million times.

Aug 2020: 'Watermelon Sugar' finally becomes his first US number one single.

Sept 2020: Harry is cast opposite Florence Pugh as a 1950s husband in the new psychological thriller *Don't Worry Darling*, directed by Olivia Wilde, one of Hollywood's most prominent activists and feminists. He replaces Shia LaBeouf, who, it's alleged, had been fired by Olivia for his poor behaviour on set. She does a 'little victory dance' when Harry agrees to step up.

Dec 2020: Harry becomes the first solo man to appear on the cover of *Vogue*. He is wearing a sky-blue, lace, Gucci ballgown that reaches to the floor and a black Gucci tuxedo jacket. He breaks the internet. He is recognised as the most popular UK celebrity on Twitter with 35.7 million (and rising) followers. He has even more on Instagram – 39 million.

Jan 2021: Releases video for 'Treat People with Kindness' that features him dancing with Phoebe Waller-Bridge in the manner of an old-fashioned Hollywood musical. The world realises Harry and Olivia are a couple when they arrive holding hands at the wedding of Jeffrey Azoff in Montecito, California. Olivia had split from her long-term partner and father of her two children, Jason Sudeikis, in November.

March 2021: Wins first Grammy, claiming Best Pop Solo Performance for 'Watermelon Sugar'. Spends the early summer in London filming *My Policeman*, again set in the 1950s, in which he co-stars with Emma Corrin.

May 2021: Takes a break from filming scenes in Brighton to collect BRIT Award for Best British Single for 'Watermelon Sugar.' Fans are bemused by his semi-American accent when he gives his thanks on stage. The *Sunday Times* Rich List puts his wealth at £75 million, an annual rise of £12 million.

June 2021: *My Policeman* wraps in Venice. Harry and Olivia begin a romantic break in Tuscany before flying back to the US, where he starts rehearsals for his live concerts.

Aug 2021: Harry's beloved grandfather, Brian Selley, dies after suffering from Parkinson's disease for many years. His heartbroken mum praises her 'brave and courageous' father.

Sept 2021: *Love on Tour* finally gets under way in Las Vegas. Olivia is there supporting him and the Pride flag is back. In a rare tweet, Harry says, 'Vegas, you blew me away. I'd been waiting for that. Thank you so much for all the love. I had the time of my life with you. H.'

Nov 2021: Stops the show at his concert in Milwaukee in front of 17,000 people to allow one university student to come out to her mother. Launches own beauty and life brand called Pleasing with the slogan 'Find Your Pleasing.' Closes US leg of *Love on Tour* after performing thirty-nine shows that grossed nearly $95 million.

Jan 2022: Announces world stadium tour. The UK leg beginning in June at the Ibrox Stadium in Glasgow sells out in minutes.

March 2022: Posts on Twitter news of his third album. It says simply Harry's House. May 20th.

April 2022: Releases first single from album on 1 April. Called 'As It Was', it goes straight to number one in the UK and on its first day of release worldwide breaks Spotify records for a male artist. The track is streamed 16,103,849 times. It is exactly twelve years since he skived off school to attend an *X Factor* audition. As he says in the elegiac song, 'It's not the same as it was.'

ACKNOWLEDGEMENTS

As this is a book about Harry Styles, I thought I would start with fashion and specifically thank Alison Jane Reed, who has helped me countless times over the years. She is a very talented writer on many subjects, as well as fashion. She has just started *The Luminaries Magazine* online and I am so jealous! She describes it as 'The Organic Arts, Entertainment, Food and Fashion Magazine: Inspiring You to Live Well and Make a Difference Through the Power of Journalism and Storytelling.' It's well worth checking out at theluminariesmagazine.com.

AJ, as her friends know her, loved looking at Harry and his fashion development over the years. She is hoping he doesn't take any period film roles for a while so he can grow his 'wonderful hair' again because it looks so good with a flower-power Gucci suit.

Many thanks as always to Gordon Wise, my agent at Curtis Brown, who continues to look after my interests so well. Next year we will be having a celebratory lunch to mark fifteen years since I was lucky enough to be taken on as a client; his assistant Niall Harman has once more been a terrific help, especially during such a difficult working year for everyone.

That's also true of everyone at HarperCollins. I don't know how they have managed to get the books out these past two years, so nice one you guys. Thanks in particular to Kelly Ellis for commissioning *Harry Styles: The Making of a Modern Man* and her Desk Editor, Holly Blood, for making sure everything ran smoothly day to day. Thanks also to Georgina Atsiaris, Senior Project Editor; Sarah Burke, Senior Production Controller; Fiona Greenway, Picture Research; Mark Rowland, Designer; Claire Ward, Creative Director; Hattie Evans, Marketing Executive; Anni Shaw, Press Officer; Tom Dunston, Sales Director; Alice Gomer, Head of International Sales; Zoe Shine, Head of UK Rights; Fionnuala Barrett, Audio Editorial Director; and Ajda Vucicevic, who has been in charge of this new paperback edition.

I've been so lucky to have Helena Caldon looking after the words. As well as being a superb copy editor, she went to see Harry Styles' secret Christmas gig at the Electric Ballroom, Camden, in 2019. I wish I'd been there!

I am grateful to Jo Westaway, who once more has helped me with all things online and technical. She is now in her second year of a master's degree in singing at the Royal Welsh College of Music & Drama. The pandemic has made it a tricky time for the acting profession but it's been my good fortune to secure Eleanor Williams as my chief researcher for this book. I hope things are picking up for talented actors now, although I hope she will still have the time to help with my next book. Thanks also to Jen Westaway for transcribing my interviews again and to Madeleine Moore for another fascinating star chart. She is a fixture in all of my books and I urge you to take a look even if you are not particularly interested in the world of astrology. You will be after reading 'Harry's Stars'. I have been fortunate to have the help of PJ Norman at AuthorProfile (www.authorprofile.co.uk) in guiding me through the digital possibilities for my books.

I really enjoyed my trip up to Harry's home patch, Holmes Chapel in Cheshire. I had never been there before. Everyone was charming. I kept on meeting people who had been to the local comprehensive school too, which was a bonus. And of course I had to sample an ice cream from the Great Budworth Ice Cream Farm and a bun from the W. Manderley Bakery. I met a lady there who had once been sold double-glazing by Robbie Williams. What a small world! I wrote about Rob a few years ago and remembered that was his job when he left school. And I had a pint (or two) in the Antrobus Arms where Harry lived at one time as a boy, as well as sweet and sour from the Chinese take-away a few doors down from his home. I love travelling to the places where dreams begin.

Finally, a word for the Harry Styles fans: I hope you enjoy this look at your hero. He is a fascinating, interesting man and I hope I have done him justice. I would like to give a special thank you to Millie Caldon, a devoted Harry fan who has read every word of this book and made sure I stayed on the right track.

You can read more about my books at seansmithceleb.com or follow me on Twitter or Facebook @seansmithceleb.

SELECT BIBLIOGRAPHY

Cowen, Elle, *Harry Styles Photo-Biography*, Plexus, 2013

Flack, Caroline, *Storm in a C Cup*, Simon & Schuster UK, 2015

Jepson, Louisa, *Every Piece of Me*, Simon & Schuster UK, 2013

One Direction, *Dare to Dream*, HarperCollins, 2011

One Direction, *Where We Are*, HarperCollins, 2013

Smith, Sean, *Ed Sheeran*, HarperCollins, 2018

PICTURE CREDITS

Page 1 (Top left) The Sun/News Licensing; (Top right and bottom) Ken McKay/Talkback Thames/Shutterstock; (Middle) Neil Mockford/FilmMagic/Getty Images

Page 2 (Top left) Dave Hogan/Getty Images; (Middle) S.A.M/Alamy; (Bottom left) Ian Horrocks/Newcastle United via Getty Images; (Bottom right) Kevin Mazur/AMA2015/WireImage/Getty Images

Page 3 (Top left) Danny Martindale/WireImage/Getty Images; (Top right) BCR/Bauer-Griffin/GC Images/Getty Images; (Bottom) David M. Benett/Getty Images for Burberry

Page 4 (Top) Richard Young/Shutterstock; (Bottom) David M. Benett/Dave Benett/Getty Images for *Dazed*

Page 5 (Top) Angela Weiss/AFP via Getty Images (Middle) Robert Gauthier/*Los Angeles Times* via Getty Images; (Bottom) Terence Patrick/CBS via Getty Images

Page 6 (Top left) Mario Anzuoni/Reuters/Alamy Stock Photo; (Top right) Dave J Hogan/Getty Images; (Bottom left) Anthony Pham via Getty Images; (Bottom right) JMEnternational/ JMEnternational for BRIT Awards/Getty Images

Page 7 (Top) WENN Rights Ltd/Alamy Stock Photo; (Middle) Backgrid; (Bottom left) Simon Dack/Alamy Live News; (Bottom right) James Boardman/Alamy Stock Photo

Page 8 (Top and bottom) Backgrid

INDEX

Thomas Dixon and Adam R. Shapiro

SCIENCE AND RELIGION

A Very Short Introduction

SECOND EDITION

OXFORD
UNIVERSITY PRESS

OXFORD
UNIVERSITY PRESS

Great Clarendon Street, Oxford, OX2 6DP,
United Kingdom

Oxford University Press is a department of the University of Oxford.
It furthers the University's objective of excellence in research, scholarship,
and education by publishing worldwide. Oxford is a registered trade mark of
Oxford University Press in the UK and in certain other countries

First edition published 2008
This edition published 2022

Impression: 1

Published in the United States of America by Oxford University Press
198 Madison Avenue, New York, NY 10016, United States of America

British Library Cataloguing in Publication Data
Data available

Library of Congress Control Number: 2021949066

ISBN 978-0-19-883102-0

Printed and bound by
CPI Group (UK) Ltd, Croydon, CR0 4YY

Science and Religion: A Very Short Introduction

VERY SHORT INTRODUCTIONS are for anyone wanting a stimulating and accessible way into a new subject. They are written by experts, and have been translated into more than 45 different languages.

The series began in 1995, and now covers a wide variety of topics in every discipline. The VSI library currently contains over 700 volumes—a Very Short Introduction to everything from Psychology and Philosophy of Science to American History and Relativity—and continues to grow in every subject area.

Very Short Introductions available now:

ABOLITIONISM Richard S. Newman
THE ABRAHAMIC RELIGIONS
    Charles L. Cohen
ACCOUNTING Christopher Nobes
ADOLESCENCE Peter K. Smith
ADVERTISING Winston Fletcher
AERIAL WARFARE Frank Ledwidge
AESTHETICS Bence Nanay
AFRICAN AMERICAN RELIGION
    Eddie S. Glaude Jr
AFRICAN HISTORY John Parker and
    Richard Rathbone
AFRICAN POLITICS Ian Taylor
AFRICAN RELIGIONS
    Jacob K. Olupona
AGEING Nancy A. Pachana
AGNOSTICISM Robin Le Poidevin
AGRICULTURE Paul Brassley and
    Richard Soffe
ALEXANDER THE GREAT
    Hugh Bowden
ALGEBRA Peter M. Higgins
AMERICAN BUSINESS HISTORY
    Walter A. Friedman
AMERICAN CULTURAL HISTORY
    Eric Avila
AMERICAN FOREIGN RELATIONS
    Andrew Preston
AMERICAN HISTORY Paul S. Boyer
AMERICAN IMMIGRATION
    David A. Gerber
AMERICAN INTELLECTUAL
    HISTORY
    Jennifer Ratner-Rosenhagen

AMERICAN LEGAL HISTORY
    G. Edward White
AMERICAN MILITARY HISTORY
    Joseph T. Glatthaar
AMERICAN NAVAL HISTORY
    Craig L. Symonds
AMERICAN POETRY David Caplan
AMERICAN POLITICAL HISTORY
    Donald Critchlow
AMERICAN POLITICAL PARTIES
    AND ELECTIONS L. Sandy Maisel
AMERICAN POLITICS
    Richard M. Valelly
THE AMERICAN PRESIDENCY
    Charles O. Jones
THE AMERICAN REVOLUTION
    Robert J. Allison
AMERICAN SLAVERY
    Heather Andrea Williams
THE AMERICAN SOUTH
    Charles Reagan Wilson
THE AMERICAN WEST Stephen Aron
AMERICAN WOMEN'S HISTORY
    Susan Ware
AMPHIBIANS T. S. Kemp
ANAESTHESIA Aidan O'Donnell
ANALYTIC PHILOSOPHY
    Michael Beaney
ANARCHISM Colin Ward
ANCIENT ASSYRIA Karen Radner
ANCIENT EGYPT Ian Shaw
ANCIENT EGYPTIAN ART AND
    ARCHITECTURE Christina Riggs
ANCIENT GREECE Paul Cartledge

For more information visit our website

www.oup.com/vsi/

For Emma Dixon and Stacey Bhaerman

Contents

Preface

Books about science and religion generally fall into one of two categories: those that want to persuade you of the plausibility of religion and those that want to do the opposite. This *Very Short Introduction* falls into neither category. It aims instead to offer an informative and even-handed account of what is really at stake. The polemical passion the subject often generates is an indication of the intensity with which people identify themselves with their beliefs about nature and God, whether they are religious or not. The origins and functions of those beliefs form the subject of this book.

Historical notions about famous individuals, especially Galileo Galilei and Charles Darwin, philosophical assumptions about miracles, laws of nature, and scientific knowledge, and discussions of the religious and moral implications of modern science, from quantum mechanics to neuroscience, are regular features of science–religion debates today. All of these are scrutinized here. Increasingly, people also recognize that 'science' and 'religion' describe two types of thought that first became separated and compared in European cultures—and that the global story of 'science and religion' is one shaped by legacies of colonialism and cultural contact.

It is not our aim in this book to persuade people to stop disagreeing with each other about science and religion—far from it. Our hope is only that it might help people to disagree with each other in a well-informed way.

Acknowledgements

Thomas Dixon

I remain grateful to all the wonderful scholars, colleagues, and friends I thanked in the first edition of this book, including Fraser Watts, John Hedley Brooke, Janet Browne, Hasok Chang, Rob Iliffe, Jim Moore, Jim Secord, Stephen Pumfrey, Geoffrey Cantor, Colin Jones, Miri Rubin, Virginia Davis, Yossi Rapoport, and the late Peter Lipton. Friends who kindly read the first edition in draft included Emily Butterworth, Noam Friedlander, James Humphreys, Finola Lang, Dan Neidle, Trevor Sather, Léon Turner, and Giles Shilson. The first edition was dedicated to my sister Emma, who—many years ago—advised me to become an academic and not a lawyer, and I remain grateful to her and to my whole family for their support, especially Emily, Caleb, and Laurie. My greatest thanks in this second edition, however, are reserved for my co-author Adam R. Shapiro who has done virtually all the work in improving, updating, and expanding this text and extending its life and usefulness for a new generation of readers. Thank you, Adam!

Adam R. Shapiro

Thomas and I first met in 2007 at the conference on 'Science and Religion: Historical and Contemporary Perspectives' at Lancaster University, which marked John Hedley Brooke's retirement. As a new Ph.D., that conference was one of my first opportunities to connect with science and religion scholars from around the globe. Thomas invited me to contribute to the volume that came from that conference and I am very grateful that over a decade later, he asked me to build upon the excellent work he did in creating the first edition of this text. I am indebted to my mentors, Ron Numbers, Adrian Johns, and Bob Richards. I especially wish to thank Sarah Qidwai and Scott Prinster for discussions with me about recent directions in the study of science and religion and what new questions and topics merited discussion (more than could fit!) Lastly, all thanks to Stacey, Yitzy, and Moti—from whose stolen minutes this book was written.

List of illustrations

The publisher and the authors apologize for any errors or omissions in the above list. If contacted they will be pleased to rectify these at the earliest opportunity.

Science and Religion

Chapter 1
What are science–religion debates really about?

In Rome on 22 June 1633 Galileo Galilei went down on his knees. The Inquisition of the Roman Catholic Church had found him 'vehemently suspected of heresy, namely, of having held and believed a doctrine which is false and contrary to the divine and Holy Scripture'. This was the doctrine that 'the sun is the centre of the world and does not move from east to west, that the earth moves and is not the centre of the world, and that one may hold and defend as probable an opinion after it has been declared and defined as contrary to Holy Scripture'. The 70-year-old Florentine philosopher and astronomer was sentenced to imprisonment (later commuted to house arrest) and instructed to recite the seven penitential Psalms once a week for the next three years. His penance included a particularly apt line in Psalm 102: 'In the beginning you laid the foundations of the earth, and the heavens are the work of your hands.' Kneeling before the 'Reverend Lord Cardinals, Inquisitors-General', Galileo accepted his sentence, swore complete obedience to the 'Holy Catholic and Apostolic Church', and declared that he cursed and detested the 'errors and heresies' of which he had been suspected—namely belief in a Sun-centred cosmos and in the movement of the Earth.

According to the mythology that grew around Galileo's trial, after publicly repudiating his beliefs, he supposedly muttered 'E pur si muove' (And yet it moves). There is no proof that Galileo actually said this, but for centuries the Galileo legend has been used to advance a story about science being oppressed by religion. The portrayal of Galileo as the abused martyr who championed empirical truth against the biblical bigotry of organized religion is probably the most famous example of the idea that science and religion are inevitably in conflict. Later episodes of science–religion encounters—debates over the meaning of evolution and the nature of human morality, the origins of the cosmos, even the relationship between human beings and their planetary environment—all take place within the orbit of that Galilean folk tale. Ultimately, Galileo was correct that the Earth does move—it orbits the Sun once a year. But, as we will see, the Inquisition's punishment of Galileo was not the clear-cut case of 'science' versus 'religion' that is often told.

The Victorian agnostic Thomas Huxley expressed this idea of religion battling science vividly in his review of Charles Darwin's *The Origin of Species* (1859). 'Extinguished theologians', Huxley wrote, 'lie about the cradle of every science as the strangled snakes beside that of Hercules; and history records that whenever science and orthodoxy have been fairly opposed, the latter has been forced to retire from the lists, bleeding and crushed if not annihilated; scotched, if not slain.' The image of conflict has also been attractive to some religious believers, who use it to portray themselves as members of an embattled but righteous minority struggling heroically to protect their faith against the oppressive and intolerant forces of science and materialism.

Although the idea of warfare between science and religion remains widespread and popular, most recent academic writing on the subject has undermined this hypothesis of an inevitable conflict. As we shall see, there are good reasons for rejecting simple conflict stories. From Galileo's trial in 17th-century Rome to modern American struggles over acceptance of evolution and human-caused climate change, there has been more to the relationship between science and religion than meets the eye.

Pioneers of early modern science such as Isaac Newton and Robert Boyle saw their study of nature as part of a religious enterprise devoted to understanding God's creation. Galileo too thought that science and religion could exist in mutual harmony. The goal of a constructive and collaborative dialogue between science and religion has been endorsed by members of religious traditions all around the world, as well as many scientists, who continue to see their research as a complement rather than a challenge to their faith.

Does that mean that the story of science and religion is actually one of harmony, rather than conflict? Certainly not. The primary thing to avoid is too narrow an idea of the kinds of conflicts or harmonies one might expect to find between science and religion. Individuals, ideas, and institutions can and have come into conflict, or been resolved into harmony, in an endless array of different combinations.

Historian John Hedley Brooke writes that serious historical study has 'revealed so extraordinarily rich and complex a relationship between science and religion in the past that general theses are difficult to sustain. The real lesson turns out to be the complexity.' That complexity will be explored in subsequent chapters. There has certainly not been a single and unchanging relationship between two entities called 'science' and 'religion'. There are, nonetheless, some central philosophical and political questions that have frequently recurred in this context: What are the most authoritative sources of knowledge? What is the most fundamental reality? What kind of creatures are human beings? What is the proper relationship between church and state? Who should control education? Can either scripture or nature serve as a reliable ethical guide?

Debates about science and religion are, on the face of it, about the intellectual compatibility or incompatibility of some particular religious belief with some particular aspect of scientific knowledge.

Does belief in life after death or free will conflict with the findings of modern brain science? Is belief in the Bible incompatible with believing that humans and chimpanzees evolved from a common ancestor? Does belief in miracles conflict with the strictly law-governed world revealed by the physical sciences? One answer to the question that titles this chapter—What are science–religion debates really about?—is that they are about these issues of intellectual compatibility.

What we especially want to emphasize in this *Very Short Introduction*, however, is that these contemporary contests of ideas are the visible tips of much larger and deeper-lying structures. Our aim will be to look historically at how we came to think as we do about science and religion, to explore philosophically what preconceptions about knowledge are involved, and to reflect on the political and ethical questions that often set the unspoken agenda for these intellectual debates. More often than not, questions about science and religion take place in a wider social and cultural context. Often, what science–religion debates are really about is not just finding some abstract truth about human nature or the cosmos, but using those concepts to negotiate issues that affect our daily lives.

Encountering nature

Scientific knowledge is based on observations of the natural world. But observing the natural world is neither as simple nor as solitary an activity as it might sound. Take the Moon, for instance. When you look up at the sky on a clear night, what do you see? You see the Moon and the stars. But what do you actually observe? There are a lot of small bright lights and then a larger whitish circular object. If you had never learned any science, what would you think this white object was? Is it a flat disc, or is it a sphere? If the latter, then why do we always see the same side of it? And why does its shape appear to change from a thin crescent to a full disc and back again? Is it an object like the Earth? If so, how big is it? And how close? And do people live there? Or is it a smaller night-time equivalent of the Sun? Finally, perhaps it is like one of the little bright lights but larger or closer? In any case, how and why does it move across the sky like that? Is something else pushing it or does it move on its own? Is it attached to an invisible mechanism of some kind? Is it a supernatural being?

You might already know that the Moon is a large spherical rocky satellite which orbits the Earth completely about once a month and which rotates once on its own axis in the same time (which explains why we always see the same side of it). You may know that the Moon does not generate its own light, but reflects light from the Sun. The changing relative positions of the Sun, Earth, and Moon explain why the Moon displays 'phases'—with either the entirety or only a small crescent of the illuminated half of the Moon visible at a particular time. You may also know that all physical bodies are attracted to each other by a gravitational force in proportion to the product of their masses and in inverse proportion to the square of the distance between them, and that this helps to explain the regular motions of the Moon around the Earth and of the Earth around the Sun. You will probably also know that the bright little lights in the night sky are stars, similar to our Sun; that the ones visible to the naked eye are thousands of light years away and those observable through telescopes are millions or even billions of light years away; so that to look up at the night sky is to look into the distant past of our universe. But however much of all this you know, you did not find it out by observation alone. You were told it. You possibly learned it from your parents or a science teacher or a television programme or an online encyclopedia. Even professional astronomers will not generally have checked the truth of any of the statements made in this paragraph by their own empirical observations. Astronomers are not lazy or incompetent, but they know that they can rely on the amassed authoritative observations and theoretical reasonings of the scientific community which, over a period of many centuries, have established these facts as fundamental physical truths.

The point is that while it is certainly true that scientific knowledge is based on and tested against observations of the natural world, there is an awful lot more to it than just pointing your sense organs in the right direction. As an individual, even an individual scientist, only the tiniest fraction of what you know is based directly on your own observations. And even then, those observations only make sense within a complex framework of existing facts and theories which have been accumulated and developed through many centuries. You know what you do about the Moon and the stars because of a long and complex cultural history (a small part of which is told in Chapter 2), which mediates between the light from the night sky and your thoughts about astronomy and cosmology. That history includes challenges to the old Earth-centred world-view by Galileo Galilei, made with the help of Copernicus' astronomy and the newly invented telescope in the early 17th century (Figure 1)—as well as the establishment of Newton's laws of motion and gravitation later in that century and more recent developments in physics and cosmology too. It also includes, crucially, the histories of those social and political mechanisms that allow for, and control, the dissemination of scientific knowledge among the people through books and letters and in classrooms and laboratories.

We should also notice, by the way, that what science often aims to show is that things in themselves are not as they initially seem to us—that appearances can be deceptive. The Earth beneath our feet certainly seems to be solid and stable, and the Sun and the other stars appear to move around us. But science eventually showed that, despite all the sensory evidence to the contrary, the Earth is not only spinning on its own axis but is also hurtling around the Sun at great speed. Indeed, one of the characters in Galileo's *Dialogue Concerning the Two Chief World Systems* (1632) expresses admiration for those who, like Aristarchus and Copernicus, had been able to believe in the Sun-centred system before the advent of the telescope: 'I cannot sufficiently admire the intellectual eminence of those who received it and held it to be

1. The Moon as engraved by the artist Claude Mellan from early 17th-century telescopic observations.

true. They have by sheer force of intellect done such violence to their own senses as to prefer what reason told them over that which sense experience plainly showed them to be the case.'
In more recent times, both evolutionary biology and quantum mechanics have similarly required people to believe implausible

things—that we share an ancestor not only with rabbits but also with carrots, for example, or that the smallest components of matter can behave both as waves and as particles. People sometimes say that science is just a systematization of empirical observations, or nothing more than the careful application of common sense. However, it also has the ambition and the potential to show that our senses deceive us and that our basic intuitions may lead us astray.

But when you look up at the night sky, you may not be thinking about data or theories taken from astronomy and cosmology at all. You may instead be gripped by a wider sense of the power of nature, the beauty and grandeur of the heavens, the vastness of space and time, and your own smallness and insignificance. This could even be a spiritual experience for you, reinforcing your feeling of awe at the power of God and the immensity and complexity of creation, bringing to mind the words of Psalm 19: 'The heavens declare the glory of God; the skies proclaim the work of his hands.'

Such an emotional and religious response to the night sky would, of course, be every bit as historically and culturally mediated as the experience of perceiving the Moon and the stars in terms of modern cosmology. Without some kind of religious education you certainly would not be able to quote from the Bible, and you would perhaps not even be able to formulate a developed concept of God. Individual religious experiences, like modern scientific observations, are made possible by long processes of human collaboration in a shared quest for understanding. In the religious case, what intervenes between the light hitting your retina and your thoughts about the glory of God is a lengthy history of a particular set of sacred stories, passed down orally or as texts, and their interpretation within a succession of human communities. And, as in the scientific case, one of the lessons learned through that communal endeavour is that things are not always as they seem. Religious teachers, as much as scientific ones, try to show

8

their pupils that there is an unseen world behind the observed one—and one which might overturn their most settled intuitions and beliefs.

The political dimension

Among historians of science and religion there have been two primary forms of refutation of the 'conflict narrative' favoured by Enlightenment rationalists, Victorian freethinkers, and modern-day scientific atheists. The first strategy is to replace the overarching image of conflict with that of complexity: to put emphasis on the very different ways that science–religion interactions have developed at different times, in different places, and in different local circumstances. Some scientists have been religious, others atheist. Some religious denominations welcome certain aspects of modern science, others are suspicious. Recognizing that neither 'science' nor 'religion' refers to a simple singular entity is an important part of this approach too, as is acknowledging the existence of considerable national and linguistic differences. To take one well-known example, debates about evolution and religion have developed quite differently in the United States from how they have in Europe and elsewhere. As discussed in Chapter 4, the debates about the teaching of evolution in schools are shaped by the legal and political circumstances that affect how education is regulated.

If this first approach to debunking the conflict narrative is to complicate the plot, the second involves recasting the leading characters. This approach says: yes, there have been real conflicts, but they are not clashes between science and religion. The question then is: who or what are the real antagonists in this story? Sometimes, what appears to be a case of science versus religion is actually a case of one religious world-view against another religious world-view, with scientific theories and observations shaping how the two sides debate. In other cases, a local political issue is redescribed by its partisans as a conflict between science and religion to make the fight seem grander, more epic, and morally justified. By associating with the seemingly timeless debate of 'science versus religion', disputants can describe themselves as martyrs, as patriots, or on the right 'side of history'.

There is certainly not a simple recasting that works for all cases, but the general idea is that the real conflict is a political one about the production and dissemination of knowledge. The opposition of science versus religion is then seen to be standing proxy for some classic modern political conflicts: the individual versus the state, or secular liberalism versus conservative traditionalism.

Questions about the politics of knowledge will arise repeatedly in subsequent chapters. For the moment, let us consider just one other example—the philosopher and firebrand Thomas Paine. An unsuccessful corset-maker, sacked tax-collector, and occasional political writer, Paine left his native England to start a new life in America in 1774. A couple of years later, his polemical pamphlet *Common Sense* (1776) was a key factor in persuading the American colonists to go to war against the British government, and established Paine as the best-selling author of the age. An associate of Benjamin Rush, Thomas Jefferson, and other founders of the United States of America, Paine's democratic and anti-monarchical political philosophy shaped the Declaration of Independence. Paine also attended popular lectures on Newton and astronomy back in England, and he spent many years of his life working on a design for a single-span iron bridge, inspired by the delicacy and strength of one of the great works of nature—the spider's web. He saw revolutions in governments paralleling the revolutions of celestial bodies in the heavens. Each was an inevitable, natural, and law-governed process. Later in life, having had a hand in both the American and French revolutions, Paine turned his sights from monarchy to Christianity. The institutions of Christianity were as offensive to his enlightened and Newtonian sensibilities as were those of monarchical government. In his *Age of Reason* (1794), Paine complained of 'the continual persecution carried on by the Church, for several hundred years, against the sciences and against the professors of science'.

Paine's version of the conflict narrative makes most sense when seen in its political context. Paine was a scientific thinker who was opposed to Christianity. He denounced the Bible, especially the Old Testament, with its stories of 'voluptuous debaucheries' among the Israelites and the 'unrelenting vindictiveness' of their God. To the shock of his friends, Paine wrote of the Bible: 'I sincerely detest it, as I detest everything that is cruel.' Paine also lambasted the 'priestcraft' at work in the 'adulterous' relationship between the Church of England and the British state. What he hoped for, though, was not an end to religion but the replacement of Christianity by a rational religion based on the study of nature—one which recognized the existence of God, the importance of morality, and the hope for a future life, but did away with scriptures, priests, and the authority of the state. His reasons for this were democratic ones. National churches lorded illegitimate power over the people by claiming special access to divine truths and revelations. But everyone can read the book of nature and understand the goodness, power, and generosity of its author. In the religion of Deism recommended by Paine, there was no need for the people to be in thrall either to priests or to the state. Science could replace Christianity by showing that every individual could find God by looking at the night sky rather than by reading the Bible or going to church. 'That which is now called natural philosophy', Paine wrote, 'embracing the whole circle of science of which astronomy occupies the chief place, is the study of the works of God, and of the power and wisdom of God and his works, and is the true theology.'

Looking to the laws of nature to explain moral and political philosophy was not only the recourse of radicals; as we will see in Chapter 3, the idea that the book of nature offers moral and political guidance was also embraced by the more conservative William Paley in his *Natural Theology* (1802). Both Paley's vision

11

of religious toleration and Paine's ideals of the separation of church and state are enshrined in the founding documents of the United States. And in modern America, too, it is competing political visions that come into conflict in debates about science and religion. American politicians who cast doubt upon the scientific theories of evolution, human-caused climate change, or public health efforts often do so to send a signal—to indicate their general support for Christianity, their opposition to excessively secularist interpretations of the Constitution, and their hostility to naturalistic and materialistic world-views.

The interplay of science and religion has also been used as a literary device, memorably in two mid-20th-century stage plays inspired by real moments of historical conflict. Bertolt Brecht's *Life of Galileo* was composed during the 1930s and early 1940s. Brecht was a German communist, opposed to fascism, and living in exile in Denmark and subsequently the United States. The play uses the story of Galileo to investigate the dilemmas faced by a dissident intellectual living under a repressive regime, and also to discuss the importance of pursuing scientific knowledge for moral and social ends rather than purely for its own sake. Brecht saw in the well-known Galileo affair political lessons which could be applied to a world struggling against authoritarian fascism and, in the later version of the play, questioning the ethical actions of scientists after the atomic bombing of Hiroshima and Nagasaki.

Jerome Lawrence and Robert E. Lee's play *Inherit the Wind*, first performed in 1955, and made into a famous film in 1960, was a dramatization of the Scopes 'monkey trial' of 1925. The historical events on which the play was based are discussed in Chapter 4. *Inherit the Wind* used Scopes's prosecution for the crime of teaching about evolution to draw connections between the religious bigotry associated with creationism in the United States in the 1920s and racial bigotry at the dawn of the civil rights era. Both Brecht's *Galileo* and Lawrence and Lee's *Inherit the Wind* used the tension between science and religion to explore themes of intellectual freedom, fascism and censorship, political power, and human morality.

'Science and religion' as an academic field

So far we have looked at science and religion as two distinct cultural enterprises which interact in both the personal and political spheres. There is an important further dimension to add to this preliminary picture, which is the development of 'science and religion' as an academic field in its own right.

Of course theologians, philosophers, and scientists have been writing treatises about the relationship between natural knowledge and revelation for centuries. Many of these works were very popular, especially in the 18th and 19th centuries. The *Bridgewater Treatises on the power, wisdom and goodness of God as manifested in the creation* was a series of eight books endowed by the bequest of the Earl of Bridgewater in the 1830s; they became widely read as both works of theology and texts of popular science. Toward the end of the 19th century, Lord Adam Gifford established a lecture series to promote natural theology at four Scottish universities. The Gifford Lectures remain one of the most prominent lecture series about science and religion. However, from the 1950s onwards 'science and religion' took on a more distinct existence as an academic discipline. The Institute on Religion in an Age of Science (IRAS) began its annual meetings at Star Island, New Hampshire, in 1954, and in 1966 the first specialist journal in the field was founded in Chicago—*Zygon: Journal of Religion and Science*. The same year saw the publication of a very widely used textbook, *Issues in Science and Religion* by the British physicist and theologian Ian Barbour. Since that time, various organizations have fostered this kind of work, including a European Society for the Study of Science and Theology, and an International Society for Science and Religion. There are established academic chairs and research centres devoted specifically to the study of science and religion at many major universities around the world.

Academic work by scientists and theologians seeking to develop a harmonious interdisciplinary dialogue has been supported by a range of institutions, including the Roman Catholic Church, through the work of the Vatican Observatory, and also the John Templeton Foundation in America—a philanthropic organization particularly committed to supporting research that harmonizes science with religion. The Templeton Foundation spends millions of dollars on research grants each year, including an annual Templeton Prize, currently valued at about $1.5 million, given to 'a living person who has made an exceptional contribution to affirming life's spiritual dimension'. Former winners have included scientists, and leaders of several world religions, as well as individuals who have contributed to the academic dialogue between science and religion. They include St Teresa of Kolkata (Mother Teresa), *Zygon* journal founder Ralph Wendell Burhoe, Nobel-winning physicist Charles Townes, the Tibetan Buddhist leader the Dalai Lama, and the anthropologist Jane Goodall. As with many other elite awards, including the Nobel prizes in the sciences, Templeton Prize recipients have disproportionately been men. Many Templeton prizewinners—along with others who have contributed to the creation of 'science and religion' as an academic subject—fall into the category of religiously committed professional scientists (and in some cases ordained ministers). There are also many historians, philosophers, and theologians who have contributed significantly to the field.

Whether arguing for conflict or for harmony, it could be objected that any academic field addressing 'the relationship between science and religion' obscures the true plurality and complexity of the terms. 'Science' and 'religion' are both hazy categories with blurry boundaries and long histories. And different sciences and different religions have clearly related to each other in a variety of ways. Mathematics and astronomy were both particularly nurtured in Islamic societies, for example. In the Middle Ages they were used to calculate the correct times of prayer and the direction of Mecca, as well as for other, more secular, purposes. Muslim scholars working in academies such as the House of Wisdom in Baghdad preserved, tested, and improved upon ancient Greek medicine and optics, as well as astronomy and astrology, between the 9th and the 15th centuries. The motto of these scholars was: 'Whoever does not know astronomy and anatomy is deficient in the knowledge of God.' Their works were also crucial sources for the revival of European learning from the later Middle Ages onwards.

Historically excluded from more mainstream European academic institutions, Jewish communities formed a particularly strong connection with sciences and medicine in early modern Europe. The Roman Catholic Church, despite the high-profile difficulties caused by Galileo's ideas, was one of the largest sponsors of scientific research during the 16th and 17th centuries, especially through the investment of the Jesuit order in astronomical observatories and experimental equipment.

'Science' and 'religion' are terms whose definitions and distinctions emerged primarily in Christian European contexts, and yet questions of modern science–religion 'relationships' have been exported to other cultures, languages, and world regions, with nuances often lost in translation. Here we might consider Buddhist neuroscientific studies of the state of the brain during meditation, the 2009 Hindu Declaration on Climate Change, or even Fritjof Capra's 1975 best-seller, *The Tao of Physics: An Exploration of the Parallels between Modern Physics and Eastern Mysticism*. In much of the world, concepts of religion and science—and a relationship between them—are strongly influenced by centuries of colonial and post-colonial history, and the role that sciences, technology, and religions played in creating and governing imperial territories.

In this book, therefore, we examine the phenomenon of 'science and religion' while acknowledging that the phrase, and the ways of thinking it describes, are not as universal as some of its users imagine. In this book, as in many contributions to the field, the 'religions' under discussion are primarily the Abrahamic monotheistic religions of Christianity, Islam, and Judaism. There are good historical reasons for this emphasis, as it is in the European Christian context that 'science' first emerged. These three monotheisms have shared intellectual histories, including the common view that God is the author of two 'books'—the book of nature and the book of scripture—and that the individual believer will find their understanding and their faith strengthened through the careful reading of both books. The intellectual, political, and ethical implications of that shared commitment to reading God's words and works have developed in comparable, although far from identical, ways in these monotheistic traditions. Many other religions and parts of the world beyond Europe first encountered 'science and religion' as part of the cultural exchanges wrought by Western colonialism. To resist using the word 'science' to describe empirical knowledge about nature in the precolonial non-European world is not intended to belittle that knowledge. On the contrary, it is a recognition that science is something specific, contextual, and limited in scope.

No single example of these relationships can serve as a universal template for understanding engagements between science and religion. Some think that the extent of oversimplification, generalization, and reification involved in even using the phrase 'science and religion' makes it a non-starter as a sensible topic. But there is no denying that 'science and religion' has been a topic of academic and popular discussion for well over a century. The fact that the phrase names an academic field, as well as conjuring up vivid if historically debatable cultural stereotypes, justifies its continued use as a category of thought (and as the title of this and many other books). Academics and journalists alike continue to write as if there were some ongoing general relationship between science and religion, in terms of which particular contemporary episodes might be understood. Even if that relationship really exists only in our imaginations, it is still important to try to understand how it got there. Since Galileo Galilei and his encounter with the Roman Inquisition takes centre stage in many popular accounts of that relationship, his story is an appropriate place to start our enquiry.

Chapter 2
Galileo and the philosophy of science

When Galileo recanted his belief that the Earth moved around the Sun, what did that signify? Was it a victory for biblical Christianity and a defeat for scientific rationality? Was it evidence that science and religion are irreconcilable? Nothing so simple. On all sides of the Galileo case, people agreed that it was proper and rational to seek accurate knowledge of the world through both the observation of nature and the revelations recounted in the Bible. The conflict was not between science and religion but rather between differing views within the Catholic Church about how to interpret nature and scripture.

Nicolaus Copernicus had argued for a Sun-centred astronomy in his book *On the Revolutions of the Heavenly Spheres* long before, in 1543. Galileo's observations of the heavens, his writings about the Copernican system, and his trial, all took place in a different political context. An appreciation of the circumstances of Galileo's trial, the shadow cast over it by the Protestant Reformation, and a century of religious warfare, along with the politics of the papal court at the time, all help to explain how these issues took on the dramatic character that they did in 1633, almost a century after Copernicus.

Before considering the Galileo story as a disagreement among 17th-century Catholics about how to read the Bible, it will be useful to look at some general questions about sources of knowledge. These will help to make sense both of what was at stake in Rome in June 1633 and also of general questions about the philosophy of science that still come up in debates about science and religion.

How do we know anything?

We generally derive knowledge of the world from four sources: our senses, our powers of rational thought, the testimony of others, and our memory. All of these sources are fallible. Our senses can deceive us, our reasoning can be faulty, people can knowingly or accidentally mislead us, and most of us know only too well how partial and distorted our memories can be. The whole project of modern science could be summarized as the attempt to weave these individually relatively feeble threads into a more resilient web of knowledge. So the sense experiences of one person must be witnessed, corroborated, and repeated by many others before being accepted as empirical facts. Observations must be supplemented by carefully designed experiments which test more precisely how things behave under different circumstances. Human powers of perception may be limited, but the inventions of the telescope and the microscope in the early 17th century, and of many other sophisticated devices since then, has enormously increased the scope and accuracy of the observations and measurements that are possible. But experiments could not be designed, nor could observations be interpreted, without the use of reason. Theoretical hypotheses about the nature of reality, and reasoning about what experimental evidence is needed to support or refute them, are prerequisites of scientific knowledge.

Finally, scientific experts must cite the sources of their knowledge and explain their chain of reasoning if their testimony is to be accepted. And the publication of scientific results in treatises, books, specialist journals, and electronic databases provides us with a collective and well-documented memory greater than anything that would be possible by relying on one person's memory alone. The knowledge thus produced is a highly prized possession in human societies. It bestows on us the ability to understand and manipulate not only the natural world but also each other. One of the most important advocates of science in 17th-century England, Francis Bacon, wrote that 'human knowledge and human power meet in one; for where the cause is not known the effect cannot be produced'. In other words, an understanding of the secret workings of nature would allow people to produce machines and medicines to improve the human condition. Bacon also wrote, to justify the new knowledge of the period, that 'all knowledge appeareth to be a plant of God's own planting', whose spread and flourishing at that time had been divinely ordained.

Natural philosophers in 17th-century England such as Robert Boyle and Robert Hooke—the new 'virtuosi' of the experimental method, the founders of the Royal Society of London—were perceived by some as a threat to orthodoxy. Their claims to be able both to discover and to manipulate the laws that govern nature seemed to verge on usurping the role of God. That was why it was important to reassure their readers that in reaping this knowledge they were collecting a harvest which was, in Bacon's words, 'of God's own planting'. In this image, God planted the seed of knowledge and natural philosophers harvested its fruit. This agricultural language draws attention to the fact that human knowledge (at least of the natural kind) is cultivated rather than simply found. Seeds do not become plants and bear fruit unless they are sown in proper conditions, are watered and fed, and are harvested in the right way.

In another popular metaphor, God is imagined not as a cosmic planter, but as the author of two books—the book of nature and the book of scripture. This metaphor describes the same idea—that the ultimate source of truth was God and that humans had to adopt certain techniques to acquire knowledge of that truth. Texts do not generally have obvious meanings, but rather these must be teased out through the collective efforts of many readers using different historical and literary techniques. Even if one decides to approach a text in search of its 'literal' meaning, that is by no means a simple matter. It is well known among literary scholars that the project of discerning an author's intentions in a text is a difficult and controversial one. The histories of science and religion reveal that these difficulties have been experienced in full measure in relation to both of God's books. Neither nature nor scripture offers a transparent account of its author's intentions.

This brings us to the question of whether—in addition to sense, reason, testimony, and memory—a fifth source of knowledge needs to be added, namely revelation. It is a belief shared by many Jews, Christians, and Muslims that the natural world reveals the power, intelligence, and goodness of the Creator and that holy scriptures reveal God's plans and the legal and moral basis according to which people should live. Even believing that a scripture is a revealed text does not make the intentions of the divine author immediately transparent, however. Many within religious traditions suggest that it takes years of study, devotion, and perhaps even divine guidance to come to know the meanings of the scriptures.

Natural knowledge is produced by the human powers of sense and rational thought (these faculties can be applied to scripture as well as about the natural world). Moreover, natural knowledge is reproducible and public—you'd expect other reasonable people to reach the same conclusions you do based on their own senses and rational thought. Revealed knowledge is produced by a supernatural uncovering of the truth—either through a divinely inspired scripture or by a direct revelation—a vision or other miraculous experience. Revealed knowledge is more likely to be individual and private. You would not necessarily expect others to reach the same knowledge that you have just because they had gone through the same actions that you did (such as praying while reading a particular passage of scripture).

The private and subjective nature of some supernatural experiences has led philosophers and theologians to seek a more rational and public way of discussing them. *Natural theology*, as opposed to revealed theology, is such a form of discourse—producing ideas about God based on sense and human reason rather than on revelation. This includes theological works making inferences about God from the design apparent in the natural world—as in William Paley's famous *Natural Theology* (1802)—but it also includes other philosophical works about God's existence and attributes. As we shall see, theologians like Paley thought that complete understanding of God was only possible through bringing together both natural and revealed religion.

Debates over science and religion often involve disagreements about the relative authority of different sources of knowledge, and those debates reflect the larger politics of authority and knowledge in society. Thomas Paine's objection to Christian philosophers was not that they found God in nature—he did too—but that they thought they could also find God in the supernatural revelation of the Bible. For Paine, the only possible kind of revelation was from God directly to an individual. If God ever did act in this way, it was revelation 'to the first person only, and hearsay to every other'. The scriptures were therefore nothing more than mere human testimony—second-hand memories—of an alleged revelation and the rational reader was not obliged to believe them. Some advocates of creationism in the 20th and 21st centuries argue that both 'God's word' and 'human reason' are legitimate sources of knowledge, but that the second must always be subordinate to the first, since revealed knowledge is certain while natural knowledge is fallible. While rationalists have rejected revelation altogether, and fundamentalists have insisted that all forms of knowledge be tested against the Bible, many more have looked for ways to reconcile their readings of God's two books without doing violence to either.

The rise and fall of Galileo

Galileo belonged to this last category of believers—seeking harmony between the Bible and knowledge of nature. He endorsed the view that the Bible is about how one goes to heaven and not about how the heavens go. In other words, if you wanted to know about matters pertaining to salvation you should consult scripture, but if you were interested in the detailed workings of the natural world, then there were better starting points—namely empirical observations and reasoned demonstrations. This was not a particularly unorthodox view in itself, but Galileo failed to persuade the authorities that it was a principle that could be applied to his case. The church was certainly not opposed to the study of mathematics, astronomy, and the other sciences. But Galileo didn't limit himself to the book of nature; his writings openly challenged biblical interpretations that were authorized by the church. To the extent that we can distinguish between them, it was his religious claims, not his scientific ones, that drew the attention of the Inquisition.

At the beginning of the 17th century, Galileo was among a tiny handful of natural philosophers who thought it likely that the Copernican astronomy accurately described the universe. The majority of those who took an interest in such questions, including the mathematicians and astronomers working within the Catholic Church, held to the system of physics and cosmology associated with the ancient Greek philosopher Aristotle. There were two elements in this Aristotelian science which were challenged by Galileo. First, there was the Earth-centred model of the cosmos produced by the 2nd-century Greek astronomer Ptolemy. This was the standard model and, despite certain complexities and technical problems, it worked as well as the Copernican model as a device for calculating the positions of the stars and planets, and had the considerable advantage of according with the common-sense intuition that the Earth was not in motion. The

23

second Aristotelian principle that would come under attack was the division of the cosmos into two regions—the sublunary and the superlunary. The sublunary region consisted of everything within the orbit of the Moon. This was the region of corruption and imperfection and of the four elements of earth, water, air, and fire. In the superlunary region, the domain of all the celestial bodies, everything was composed of a fifth element, ether, and was characterized by perfect circular motion (Figure 2).

2. A 16th-century illustration of Ptolemy's Earth-centred astronomical system. At the centre is the world, composed of the four elements of earth, water, air, and fire, surrounded by the spheres of the Moon, Mercury, Venus, the Sun, Mars, Jupiter, Saturn, and finally the sphere of the fixed stars.

Galileo's first contribution to astronomy came when he made use of a recent invention—the 'telescope'. After learning of Dutch telescopes used primarily for distant viewing on land and sea, Galileo built one with improved magnifying power and turned it upwards to observe the sky. The spectacular results were published in two books, *The Starry Messenger* in 1610 and *Letters on Sunspots* in 1613, which established Galileo's reputation as a brilliant observational astronomer and one of the leading natural philosophers in Europe. These works also made it clear that Galileo favoured the Copernican hypothesis.

Just a couple of examples will give a sense of how Galileo wielded his telescope against Aristotelian science. Perhaps the most telling discovery made by Galileo was that Venus, when viewed through the telescope, could be seen to display phases, like the Moon. Its apparent shape varied between a small crescent and a full disc. This strongly suggested that Venus orbited the Sun. In the Ptolemaic system Venus, which was known always to be close to the Sun in the sky, should have appeared always as a thin crescent. Secondly, Galileo was able to deploy a number of key observations against Aristotelian division of the cosmos into distinct sublunary and superlunary regions. His telescope revealed that the Moon was a rocky satellite with craters and mountains—more like the Earth than like an ethereal and perfect heavenly body. He also discovered four satellites or moons orbiting Jupiter. This helped defeat a common objection to the Copernican theory. In the Ptolemaic theory, the Earth's Moon was treated as the closest of several planets, all of whose orbits centred on the Earth. If Copernicus were right, then the Moon would have to orbit the Earth, while the Earth in turn went around the Sun. Was it possible that a celestial body could move in an orbit with a centre other than the centre of the cosmos? The discovery that Jupiter was accompanied in its orbit (whether that was around the Earth or around the Sun) by four satellites established that such motion was indeed possible. Finally, Galileo's discovery of sunspots further undermined the Aristotelian distinction between perfect heavenly bodies and a changeable and imperfect Earth.

Galileo's publications made Copernicanism a live issue in the 1610s. Galileo knew that his advocacy of the new astronomy was arousing both theological and naturalistic objections. One of the reasons for the former was the apparent inconsistency between Copernican astronomy and the Bible. Several passages refer to the Sun moving through the heavens. An often-quoted passage from the Book of Joshua described God stopping the Sun and Moon in the sky. Seeking to pre-empt biblical objections to the view that the Earth moves, in 1615 Galileo wrote his *Letter to the Grand Duchess Christina*, in which he articulated his views about how to deal with apparent conflicts between natural and revealed knowledge. Galileo relied heavily on the views of the Fathers of the Catholic Church, especially St Augustine's idea of the principle of accommodation. This stated that the Bible was written in language accommodated to the limited knowledge of the relatively uneducated people to whom it was initially revealed. Since the first readers of the Book of Joshua believed that the Earth was stationary and the Sun moved around it, God's word was couched in terms that they would understand. Other biblical references to God's 'right hand' or to God's experience of human passions such as anger were generally understood not as literal, but as accommodations to common understanding. Galileo argued that the same attitude should be taken to biblical passages referring to the movement of the Sun. The other principle Galileo adopted was that the Bible should only be given priority in matters relating to salvation. In matters of natural knowledge, if interpretations of scripture seemed to contradict the best available science, then the text would need to be reinterpreted.

All of this was in tune with St Augustine's 4th-century approach to scripture. However, church doctrine about the interpretation of the Bible had now evolved and been more sharply enforced in response to the Protestant Reformation, which continued to divide Europe both politically and religiously throughout the 17th century. One of the central tenets of Protestant forms of Christianity was the right of individuals to read and interpret the Bible for themselves, and in their own language, in contrast to Catholic views that biblical reading required special mental and spiritual training and the sanction of the church. The Catholic Church's principal response to the Reformation came in the form of a series of meetings which comprised the Council of Trent (1545–63). One of the declarations of that Council was that, in matters of faith and morals,

> no one, relying on his own judgement and distorting the Sacred Scriptures according to his own conceptions, shall dare to interpret them contrary to that sense which Holy Mother Church, to whom it belongs to judge their true sense and meaning, has held and does hold, or even contrary to the unanimous agreement of the Fathers.

In the context of these Counter-Reformation teachings, Galileo's suggestion in his *Letter to the Grand Duchess Christina* that he, an individual layman, had the authority to tell the 'Holy Mother Church' that his astronomical results required scripture to be reinterpreted smacked both of arrogance and of dangerous Protestant leanings. The fact that in 1632 he would publish his *Dialogue* in vernacular Italian rather than scholarly Latin would add further to that impression.

When a committee was asked to report on the question of Copernicanism to the Inquisition in 1616, it declared it to be both false and absurd as scientific doctrine, and additionally to be contrary to the teachings of scripture and thus formally heretical. Galileo was personally summoned into the presence of Cardinal Robert Bellarmine, who instructed him that he must not hold or defend the Copernican astronomy. At the same time, Copernicus' *On the Revolutions of the Heavenly Spheres*, which had been largely ignored since its appearance in print, was now suspended from publication, pending 'correction'.

The election in 1623 of Cardinal Maffeo Barberini as Pope Urban VIII must have seemed like the answer to Galileo's prayers. Barberini was an educated and cultured Florentine. Since 1611 he had been an admirer and supporter of Galileo's work, even composing a poem, *Adulatio Perniciosa* ('In Dangerous Adulation'), in 1620, expressing admiration for Galileo's telescopic discoveries. In 1624, Galileo had several meetings with Urban VIII, who assured him he could discuss the Copernican theory in his work but only as one hypothesis among others. Urban argued that God, in his omnipotence, could make the heavens move in any way he wished, and so it would be presumptuous to claim to have discovered the precise manner in which this end was achieved. Galileo left Rome reassured and was soon at work on the book that would be published in 1632 as his *Dialogue Concerning the Two Chief World Systems*.

This was when the real trouble started. Although the *Dialogue* was presented as an even-handed discussion among three characters—an Aristotelian, a Copernican, and a common-sensical everyman—it was perfectly clear to most readers that the arguments given in favour of the Copernican system were much stronger than those defending Earth-centred astronomy, and that Galileo had in effect produced Copernican propaganda, thus breaching the conditions of the 1616 injunction and the instructions given by Urban in 1624. That was not all. The Aristotelian character was named 'Simplicio'. This was the name of a 6th-century Aristotelian philosopher but also suggested simple-mindedness. Even more provocatively, one of the arguments put forward by simple Simplicio was the one that had been put to Galileo by Urban himself in 1624—that God could have produced natural effects in any way he chose, and so it was wrong to claim necessary truth for any given physical hypothesis about their causation. This apparent mockery of the Pope added personal insult to the already grave injury delivered by Galileo's disobedience. And the timing could not have been worse. The *Dialogue* reached Rome in 1632 at a moment of great political crisis.

Urban was in the midst of switching his allegiance from the French to the Spanish during the Thirty Years War and was in no mood for leniency. He needed to show his new conservative allies that he was a decisive and authoritative defender of the faith. So Galileo was summoned to Rome to be tried before the Inquisition.

As with the Scopes trial in America three centuries later, the trial of Galileo in 1633 was one in which the outcome was never in doubt. Galileo was found guilty of promoting the heretical Copernican view in contravention of the express injunction not to do so that he had received in 1616. It was for disobeying the church, rather than for seeking to understand the natural world through observation and reasoning, that Galileo was condemned. Galileo's political misjudgement of his relationship with Pope Urban VIII played as much of a role in his downfall as did his overreaching of himself in the field of biblical interpretation. Galileo's work was to be one key contribution to the eventual success of the Copernican theory, which, when modified by further scientific insights such as Kepler's replacement of circular by elliptical orbits, and Newton's discovery of the law of gravitation, was virtually universally accepted. However, in 1632 there was sufficient doubt about the relative merits of the Copernican system and the alternatives (including Tycho Brahe's compromise according to which the Sun orbited the Earth but all the other planets orbited the Sun) that an objective observer would have pronounced the scientific question an open one, making it even harder to decide how to judge between the teachings that the church declared to be contained in the book of scripture and those which Galileo had read through his telescope in the book of nature.

Appearance and reality

The Galileo affair, remembered by some as a clash between science and religion, was primarily a dispute about the enduring political question of who was authorized to produce and disseminate knowledge. In the world of Counter-Reformation

Rome, in the midst of the Thirty Years War, which continued to pit the Protestant and Catholic powers of Europe against each other, Galileo's claim to be able to settle questions about competing sources of knowledge through his own individual reading and reasoning seemed the height of presumption, theologically naive, and a direct threat to the authority of the Church.

The case can also be used to illustrate one further philosophical question that has been central to modern debates about science and religion, namely the issue of *realism*. Arguments about realism particularly arise in connection with what scientific theories have to say about unobservable entities such as magnetic fields, black holes, electrons, quarks, superstrings, and the like. To be a realist is to suppose that science is in the business of providing accurate descriptions of such entities. The anti-realist position is to remain agnostic about the ultimate truth of such descriptions and to hold that science is in the business only of providing accurate predictions of observable phenomena. Urban VIII was not alone among theologians and philosophers in the 16th and 17th centuries in taking an anti-realist or 'instrumentalist' approach to astronomy. On that view, the Ptolemaic and Copernican systems could be used to calculate and predict the apparent motions of the stars and planets, but there was no way to know which system, if either, represented the actual way that God had chosen to structure the heavens. Indeed, when Copernicus' *On the Revolutions of the Heavenly Spheres* was first published, it included a preface written by the Lutheran Andreas Osiander stating that the theory was intended purely as a calculating device rather than as a physical description. Galileo, on the other hand, took a realist attitude, extending it to include the religious claim that his observations explained the way God had made the world. It was his insistence on arguing this which resulted in his trial before the Inquisition.

Galileo was a member of one of the earliest scientific societies, the Academy of Lynxes, founded in 1603 by Prince Cesi. The lynx was thought to see in the dark and so to perceive things invisible to others. Using new scientific instruments such as the telescope and the microscope in conjunction with the power of reason and the language of mathematics, Galileo and his fellow 'lynxes' aimed not just to find useful models for predicting observable phenomena but explanations of those phenomena in terms of the invisible structures and forces of the universe. They seemed to be succeeding. In addition to Galileo's telescopic and astronomical discoveries, the microscope was opening up a different kind of previously unseen world. Using an instrument sent to him by Galileo, Prince Cesi made the first known microscopic observations in the 1620s. Cesi's observations of bees were recorded in engravings by Francesco Stelluti and used as a device to seek approval for the Academy of Lynxes from Urban VIII, whose family coat of arms featured three large bees (Figure 3).

Debates between realists and anti-realists continue to form a lively and fascinating part of the philosophy of science. Each side rests on a very plausible intuition. The realist intuition is that our sense impressions are caused by an external world that exists and has properties independently of human observers, so that it is reasonable to try to discover what those properties are, whether the entities in question are directly observable by us or not. The anti-realist intuition is that all we ever discover, either individually or collectively, is how the world appears to us. We live in an endless series of mental impressions, which we can never compare with the nature of things in themselves. We cannot, even for an instant, draw back the veil of phenomena to check whether our descriptions of reality are right. We can have no knowledge of the world beyond the impression it makes on us, and so, the anti-realist concludes, we should remain agnostic about the hidden forces and structures which scientists hypothesize about in their attempts to explain those impressions. There have also been theological arguments made on both sides of this debate. Some have argued that a good God would not seek to deceive us, and so the theories produced by our God-given powers of perception and reason

3. Francesco Stelluti's *Melissographia* (1625), produced using a microscope provided by Galileo, and dedicated to Pope Urban VIII.

should be trusted. Others suggest (like Urban VIII) that an all-powerful God need not have made creation fully comprehensible to finite beings. For them, anti-realism is a form of epistemological humility.

Modern debates about scientific realism have centred on the question of science's success. Realists argue that accurate predictions made by scientific theories that rely on entities that are unobservable—quantum physics, for instance—would be inexplicable unless those entities, such as electrons, actually existed and had the properties scientists ascribed to them. Anti-realists have a couple of good responses to this. First, they can point out that the history of science is a graveyard of now-abandoned theories which were once the most successful available but which posited entities we now do not believe existed. This would apply to the 16th-century theory that the planets were carried in their orbits by crystalline spheres; the 18th-century theory that explained combustion, according to which a substance known as 'phlogiston' was given off when things burned; or the 'ether' of 19th-century physics—a physical medium that was supposed to be necessary for the propagation of electromagnetic waves. Since theories we now take to be untrue have made successful predictions in the past (including also Ptolemaic astronomy, which was hugely successful for many centuries), there is no reason to suppose that today's successful theories are based on accurate descriptions of unobservable entities. Both true and untrue theories can produce accurate empirical predictions.

A second anti-realist argument was put forward by two influential philosophers of science in the 20th century—Thomas Kuhn and Bas van Fraassen. Kuhn's book, *The Structure of Scientific Revolutions* (1962), has become a classic in the field and remains one of the most widely read books about scientific knowledge. The book focused on what Kuhn called 'paradigm shifts' in the history of science, when one dominant world-view was replaced by another, as in the case of Copernican astronomy replacing the

Ptolemaic theory, or Einsteinian physics replacing pure Newtonianism. Kuhn did not think that newer paradigms replaced old ones because they were more accurate descriptions of reality, but rather that they had been chosen by the scientific community from among the various proposed theories because of their improved predictive power and puzzle-solving ability. Van Fraassen's 1980 book *The Scientific Image* made use of a 'Darwinian' explanation of the success of science. Since scientists will discard theories that make false predictions (as nature discards non-adaptive variations) and keep hold of those that make successful predictions, the fact that as time goes on their predictions get better is no surprise at all. They were selected for precisely their instrumental success, and there is no need for a further appeal to unobservable realities to explain that success.

Science and religion have a shared concern with the relationship between the observable and the unobservable. The Nicene Creed includes the statement that God made 'all that is, seen and unseen'. St Paul wrote in his letter to the Romans that 'since the creation of the world God's invisible qualities—his eternal power and divine nature—have been clearly seen, being understood from what has been made'. However, there are theological anti-realists too. The intuition here is similar to that of the scientific anti-realist. We have no way (at least not yet) to check our ideas about God against ultimate reality, and so propositions about God derived from scripture, tradition, or reason should not be treated as literally true but only as attempts by finite, fallible humans to make sense of those ideas. Theological anti-realism is sometimes misinterpreted as agnosticism or atheism, but the claim that God cannot fully be known is distinct from the claim that there is no God (or that we cannot know if there is). There is also a more orthodox tradition of mystical and 'negative' theology which emphasizes the gulf between the transcendence of God and the limited cognitive powers of mere humans, and draws the conclusion that it would be presumptuous to suppose any human formulation could grasp divine reality. Theologians in several religious traditions have responded to anti-realist calls for epistemic humility by claiming that the prospect of certainty, knowledge of real truth, is not a feat of human intellect, but requires divine intercession itself. For that reason, many have continued to try to look beyond the seen to the unseen, hoping to succeed in the apparently impossible task of drawing back the veil of phenomena to discover how things really are.

Galileo believed that what he saw through his telescope was real and that the Copernican model was not just instrumentally useful, but a true description of a universe governed by real unseen forces and laws. He explained the apparent contradiction of some biblical passages with this view of the solar system by treating scripture, in those cases, as instrumentally useful, rather than literally true. Among the many who, like Galileo, believe they have succeeded in seeing behind the veil of phenomena, there are conflicting accounts of what is to be found there—an impersonal cosmic machine, a chaos of matter in motion, a system governed by strict natural laws, or an omnipotent God acting in and through his creation. Which should we believe?

Chapter 3
God and nature

Even before there was science, people had intuitions about how the world around them typically behaved. Liquids flow downhill. Wounds take time to heal (and some are beyond complete healing). The realist might explain these ordinary phenomena as consequences of laws built in to the very structure of the universe itself, while an anti-realist might emphasize the way that repeated observations and shared experiences shape people's intuitions of what's ordinary. A religious philosopher might interpret the recurrence of everyday events as proof that God ordered the world in a purposeful, understandable way. But when something extraordinary happens, when something seemingly impossible or unexpected is observed, other explanations have to be considered.

Extraordinary events have historically performed an important social function. They have sometimes been interpreted as signs and wonders that mark out individuals, movements, or institutions as endowed with special God-given authority. The ability to perform miracles has been ascribed to revolutionaries, teachers, prophets, saints, and even to places and objects. The apparent power to resist the most irresistible of all forces—the laws of nature—has provided inspiration and hope to many communities facing persecution, poverty, or disaster.

4. St Agatha carrying her breasts on a plate, as depicted by the
17th-century painter Francisco de Zurbarán.

Take, for example, the story of Agatha, a 15-year-old girl in 3rd-century Sicily, then part of the Roman empire (Figure 4). She rejected the amorous advances of a local official, who banished her to a local brothel as revenge. When Agatha still refused to give up either her chastity or her Christian faith, she was tortured, including having her breasts cut off with pincers. A vision of St Peter appeared to her and healed her wounds. Agatha was then condemned to further abuses, including being dragged across burning coals and broken glass. During this ordeal, an earthquake was sent by God, killing several Roman officials. Agatha herself died in prison soon after.

The story of St Agatha did not end with her death. She was adopted by the people of Catania (in Sicily) as their protector and patron saint. According to local folklore, in the year after her martyrdom Mount Etna erupted. When her veil was held up towards the lava, it changed direction, leaving the city unharmed. Agatha's veil is reported to have protected the inhabitants of Catania from volcanic eruptions in the same miraculous way on several subsequent occasions. St Agatha's intercession is also credited by some believers with preventing the plague from spreading to Catania in 1743.

Natural and supernatural

Seeking miraculous intervention as protection against natural disasters shows one facet of the complex interaction between the natural and supernatural in religious thinking. For many who assert that God created the world, this includes the creation of natural principles that dictate, for instance, how volcanoes form or how lava flows. A volcano may be a part of nature, but for the believers of Agatha's day it was also created by God. God cared for the people of Catania and, because of St Agatha, would protect them, even if it meant momentarily suspending or contravening natural processes.

God's ability, either directly or through the intercession of saints and prophets, to contravene the laws of nature has long been central to many beliefs asserted by the Abrahamic religious traditions. God's various revelations to Moses, to St Paul and the apostles, and through the angel Gabriel to Muhammad are presented as miraculous. The Bible records that God sent plagues upon the Egyptians to punish them, divided the Red Sea, and provided manna from heaven to feed his chosen people. The Gospels assert that Jesus walked on water, healed the sick, brought the dead back to life, and was himself miraculously resurrected after dying on the cross. The Qur'ān includes reports of miracles performed by Moses and Jesus, including an episode, not included in the Christian Bible, when Jesus is said to have fashioned clay into the shape of a bird and miraculously breathed life into it to create a real bird. Although Muslims debate whether Muhammad himself performed miracles, there is a reference in the Qur'ān to the splitting of the Moon, which was interpreted as miraculous confirmation of Muhammad's prophetic status.

Reports of miracles persist to this day. They frequently come in the form of miraculous cures, such as those sought by pilgrims to the shrine of the Blessed Virgin Mary at Lourdes in France, or by those who attend revivalist religious meetings presided over by charismatic preachers offering divine healing. In 1995, milk sales across the world increased after reports that statues of the Hindu deities Ganesh and Shiva had seemed to drink spoonfuls of milk. In 2018, a Catholic church in New Mexico reported that its bronze statue of the Virgin Mary appeared to 'weep' olive oil.

In most cases, a rational and scientific explanation is soon forthcoming. In the case of the Hindu deities apparently drinking milk, it seemed the liquid was being drawn out of the spoon by capillary action (the same process that allows sponges and paper towels to absorb liquid), and was then simply running down the front of the statue. There was also a political explanation readily to hand. The ruling Congress Party in India claimed that news of the alleged miracle was being spread by their Hindu nationalist opponents for electoral gain. The leader of one right-wing Hindu party, speaking in defence of the miracle, said: 'Scientists who dismiss it are talking nonsense. Most of them are atheists and communists.'

Signs, wonders, and miracles have a central place in many religious traditions, whether as evidence of the special status of particular individuals, as proofs of particular doctrines, or as support for the broader social and political aspirations of a movement. Although some believers welcome miracles as apparent proofs of the reality and power of God, others are embarrassed by them. Reports of supernatural phenomena are all too often debunked, shown to be the results of wishful thinking, gullibility, or even fraud. Easily refuted claims of miracles can make religion seem superstitious and primitive.

But scepticism about miracles isn't the same as doubting religion entirely. Not every doctrine is rooted in either direct revelation from God or supernatural explanations of events. As mentioned previously, some religious groups envision God as author of a 'book of nature' as well as a (miraculously revealed) book of scripture. Justifications for arguments pertaining to God's existence, goodness, or power—or the moral rules people ought to live by—are often found in the natural world instead of (or in addition to) a sacred text. For many people, the distinction between science and religion is not the same as the difference between the natural and the supernatural; it is drawn instead between different explanations of both apparently natural and apparently non-natural phenomena.

The theologians' dilemma

Pity the poor theologians! They are faced with a seemingly impossible dilemma when it comes to making sense of divine action in the world. If they affirm that God does act through miraculous interventions in nature, then they must explain why God acts on some occasions but not on numerous others; why miracles are so poorly attested; and how they are supposed to be compatible with our scientific understanding of the universe. On the other hand, if they deny that God acts through special miraculous interventions, then they are left with questions about how much power God has to affect our lives and why one should bother with prayer or with following rules of ethical behaviour. The theologian seems to have to choose between a capricious, wonder-working, tinkering God and an absent, uninterested, undetectable one. Neither sounds like a suitable object for love and worship.

The theologian's task is to articulate how God can act in and through nature while avoiding the two unattractive caricatures indicated above. Various distinctions have been employed to try to achieve this. One of these differentiates between the basic primary cause of all reality, which is God, and the secondary, natural causes employed to achieve divine purposes. Another distinguishes between God's 'general providence'—the way that nature and history have been set up to unfold according to the divine will—and rare acts of 'special providence', or miracles, in which God's power is more directly manifest. If those acts of special providence are restricted to a very small number—perhaps only those attested in scripture, or those associated with the lives of a very small number of important prophetic individuals—then God's interventions in the world might seem less capricious. Among Christians, Muslims, and Jews there are those who believe that the age of God's revelations and miracles has now passed.

'As if God lived in the gaps?'

Protestant theologians have traditionally been somewhat more suspicious than Catholics about miracles (other than those explicitly recorded in the Bible). At the time of the Reformation, Protestants used the Catholic veneration of saints—especially the

Blessed Virgin Mary—and belief in the miraculous powers of holy relics, to portray the Church of Rome as superstitious and idolatrous. In more recent times, evangelical and Pentecostal forms of Protestant worship have involved wonders and miracles such as healings and speaking in tongues. However, there has been a continuous tradition of Protestant thought asserting that the age of miracles has passed and that divine activity is to be perceived in nature and history as a whole rather than in special interventions.

Two Protestant theologians illustrate this reinterpretation of the miraculous. The German thinker Friedrich Schleiermacher went so far as to redefine 'miracle' as 'merely the religious name for event', rather than as a happening which violated the laws of nature. In other words, a miracle was in the eye of the believer. In a series of lectures delivered in Boston in 1893, the Scottish evangelical theologian Henry Drummond, engaging the question of the proper Christian attitude to the theory of evolution, declared that a miracle was 'not something quick'. Rather, the whole, slow process of evolution was miraculous. Through that process God had produced not only the mountains and valleys, the sky and sea, the flowers and stars, but also 'that which of all other things in the universe commends itself, with increasing sureness as time goes on, to the reason and to the heart of Humanity—Love. Love is the final result of Evolution.' Drummond's conclusion was that it was this result—love—rather than the particular process, natural or supernatural, which was the real miracle.

In these same lectures Drummond introduced the idea of the 'God of the gaps'. He spoke of those 'reverent minds who ceaselessly scan the fields of Nature and the books of Science in search of gaps—gaps which they will fill up with God. As if God lived in the gaps?' God, he said, should be sought in human knowledge, not in human ignorance. He pointed out that if God is only to be found in special and occasional acts, then God must be supposed to be absent from the world the majority of the time. He asked whether the nobler conception was of a God present in everything or one present in occasional miracles. Drummond concluded that 'the idea of an immanent God, which is the God of Evolution, is infinitely grander than the occasional wonder-worker, who is the God of an old theology'.

The whole history of modern science could be read as a parable reinforcing Drummond's warning against placing God in the gaps of our current knowledge of nature. When Isaac Newton faced questions about why the planets remained in their orbits rather than gradually slowing down and falling towards the Sun and why distant stars were not drawn towards each other by gravity, he was prepared to hypothesize that God must intervene occasionally to keep the stars and planets in their proper positions. Newton's rival and critic G. W. Leibniz attacked this hypothesis on theological grounds. Newton's God, Leibniz wrote in 1715, lacking sufficient foresight to make a properly functioning universe at the first attempt, apparently needed 'to *wind up* his watch from time to time' and 'to *clean* it now and then' and 'even to *mend* it, as a clockmaker mends his work; who must consequently be so much the more unskilful a workman, as he is oftener obliged to mend his work and to set it right'. Leibniz preferred to see God's involvement in the universe as one of perfect and complete foresight. As theoretical and mathematical models of the solar system became even more accurate during the 18th and 19th centuries, there were those who went even further. When asked by Napoleon about the place of God in his cosmological system, the French physicist Pierre Simon de Laplace allegedly replied that he 'had no need for that hypothesis'.

The histories of geology, natural history, and biology reveal a similar pattern of supernatural explanations for things in the world (floods, volcanoes, and earthquakes; separate creations of different species; intelligent design of individual adaptations of creatures to their environments) gradually being pushed out in favour of more gradual, uniform, and lawlike natural processes. Even Charles Darwin's *The Origin of Species* made references to God, but only as the author of the laws of nature—those 'secondary causes' which seemed to be able to achieve the most wondrous results when impressed on matter, without apparent need for further interventions by the Creator.

The laws of nature

It was never the intention of the pioneers of modern science—people such as Isaac Newton, Robert Boyle, or René Descartes—to undermine religious belief. Far from it. They envisaged nature as an orderly system of mechanical interactions governed by mathematical laws and they hoped that people would see in this new vision the strongest possible evidence of divine power and intelligence. In 1630 Descartes wrote to the Catholic theologian Marin Mersenne: 'God sets up mathematical laws in nature as a king sets up laws in his kingdom.' Most early modern European scientists believed that God, who was responsible for determining the regular way in which nature would normally operate, was also capable of suspending or altering that normal course of nature at any time. Natural and supernatural explanations sometimes went hand in hand. Accepting supernatural events did not mean simply rejecting natural law. In fact, without a belief about the way nature 'normally' behaves, it would be impossible to recognize specific events as supernatural. Nonetheless, the method they adopted was one that favoured a view of God as lawgiver rather than as interventionist wonder-worker.

The collaborative enterprise inaugurated by these scientific pioneers has proceeded on the assumption that natural phenomena are indeed governed by strict laws. Does the success of science in explaining nature in terms of such laws amount to proof that God cannot act in nature, or is the coherent lawlike behaviour of the universe itself proof of God's creative power? One common explanation for the tendency of nature to follow laws (articulated in different degrees by various European early modern philosophers and theologians) is that God chooses to act within the bounds of natural laws, not because God is prevented from doing otherwise, but because God wants to be understood. As Descartes put it, God, being good, is not a 'deceiver' and would not trick people into believing in natural laws that were not real. Taking this further, English thinkers like Boyle and later William Paley both argued that God wanted people to observe divine presence through public evidence, whose experience we can share and discuss with others, not just through private miracles and revelations.

There are different ways of thinking about laws of nature. Realists and anti-realists have different opinions about whether such 'laws' have a real existence as entities or forces that constrain the world we observe. Natural laws can be interpreted in a more modest way as the best empirical generalizations we have so far arrived at to describe the behaviour of particular systems in particular contexts (often highly restricted experimental conditions that can be created only in laboratories). In addition, historians and other scholars of science and society debate whether laws of nature are solely rooted in the physical properties of the external world, or reflect the cultural norms of science in the times and places they were discovered and expressed.

Those who hold that the laws of nature are really built into the universe itself (regardless of whether or not they believe that this was done by a God creating the universe) sometimes insist that the patterns described as laws in various scientific fields ought to integrate with one another. This is sometimes called *reductionism*. For example, Descartes sought to discover and express laws of the physics of motion that were consistent with his theories of the human body and human psychology (and possibly also with his Catholic belief in free will). In the 20th century, some philosophers sought to 'unify' science by using logic to analyse statements used to describe observations and theories in different fields. These logical positivists hypothesized that statements in one science, say meteorology, could be 'reduced' or translated into statements that made sense within the language of another science, like physics. Critics of this reductionism argue that more complex systems, such as the biological processes of life, or psychological or sociological phenomena, cannot be explained in terms of the more 'fundamental' laws of physics that govern atoms and energy.

Reconciling natural laws at different levels has proven to be a complicated task for scientists and philosophers for the past century. Two of the most successful physical theories—general relativity and quantum mechanics—are both supposed to apply universally and yet are not compatible with each other. As the philosopher of science Nancy Cartwright has put it, what modern science seems to show is not that we live in a world governed by a single systematic set of natural laws that apply at all times and in all places, but rather that we live in a 'dappled world' in which pockets of order emerge, or can be made to emerge, using a patchwork of different scientific theories (from physics, to biology, to economics), none of which is applicable across all domains.

In contrast to reductionism, some philosophers of science speak of 'emergence', a phenomenon whereby properties that are not present at a more 'basic' physical level become apparent only in more complex systems. Ecosystems, which rely upon complex interactions among various species and their environment, follow certain laws which may not be observed when constituent species are considered separately under laboratory conditions. Even non-living systems, such as complex meteorological phenomena, cannot be explained or predicted purely through the laws governing the physics of gases and liquids. This idea of 'emergence' has also long been favoured by theologians seeking to reconcile religion and science as an argument against a deterministic universe in which everything in the universe unfolds according to natural laws without any ongoing creative input.

Emergence is also put forward as a potential explanation for spiritual realities that can be seen or felt socially or psychologically, but are not explained at the atomic level.

Quantum mechanics

In addition to the considerable philosophical perplexities involved in articulating, let alone defending, any kind of determinism, an important scientific challenge to the doctrine arose in the early 20th century in the form of quantum mechanics. Quantum theory resulted from physicists' attempts to understand the world of the very small—the behaviour of atomic and subatomic particles. Max Planck and Albert Einstein showed that light, then understood as an electromagnetic wave, also behaved as if it were made up of discrete particles, which came to be known as 'photons'. The implications of the theories later developed in the 1920s by quantum pioneers such as Erwin Schrödinger and Werner Heisenberg were wide-ranging, and their interpretation is still the subject of controversy. Einstein himself was unhappy with the probabilistic and indeterministic interpretations of quantum theory that came to predominate, saying that 'God does not play dice with the universe.' Some philosophers and physicists still share Einstein's unease. Having an instinctive preference for deterministic explanations, they hope to find a different interpretation of the laws of quantum physics.

Quantum theory is controversial because it seems to suggest that physics can no longer be reduced to a series of deterministic interactions between particles of matter. According to quantum theory, entities such as photons and electrons behave like either particles or waves depending on how the experimental apparatus interacts with them. Heisenberg's uncertainty principle further dictates that there is a limit to the precision with which the momentum and the position of a quantum entity can be known; exact knowledge of both at the same time is impossible. Finally, quantum phenomena can only be understood as functions of statistical probability. We might be able to predict that a certain percentage of radioactive atoms will decay over a specified period of time (this is where the concept of 'half-life' comes from and this process is crucial to studies concerning the age of the Earth and fossils found within it). However, quantum mechanics states that we cannot predict exactly when any given atom will decay.

Even this brief and inexpert summary of some of the findings of quantum physics is hopefully enough to give a sense of how far we have come from the world of classical materialistic determinism. Quantum mechanics suggests that at the most basic level material reality is not deterministic (nor does it always seem to be 'material'). We are in a world of clouds, of wave functions, of probabilities—not the reassuringly picturable clockwork universe of the Enlightenment. Quantum theory may even undermine the idea that the physical world exists objectively and independently of human observers, since the act of observation or measurement causes changes in physical objects.

Quantum physics is an absolutely central part of present-day science, and the fact that the picture of physical reality that it offers is so counter-intuitive and indeterministic has proved of great interest to philosophical and religious thinkers. The prospect of a new and more holistic philosophy of nature in which the observer is integrally involved and in which determinism is denied is one that appeals to proponents of many different world-views, from traditional religions to more modern 'New Age' ideologies. Attempts by theologians to make use of quantum physics as a more permanent source of 'gaps' in which God might be able to act have had a mixed reception. Such attempts do not help to answer the question of why God would act on some occasions rather than others; nor do they satisfy those religious believers who hold that, as the author rather than the slave of the laws of nature, God can override or suspend them at will without needing to tinker with the states of quantum systems. The fact that 'gaps' in natural explanation are frequently closed by new scientific knowledge or the concern that a God-of-the-gaps seems limited in power or scope are important criticisms of such arguments. But for centuries, theologians and many religious scientists professed a more general objection to such reasoning. For them God was not found by the failure to explain things according to nature, but by the very fact that nature worked and showed evidence of a divine plan. This was a central idea within the domain of natural theology.

Natural theology

Natural theology is the practice of trying to draw inferences about God using our natural powers of sense and reason, rather than relying on revelation or scripture. This has often included arguments based on the natural world and its apparent design. In the traditions of the major monotheistic religions, natural theology was not developed to replace revealed scripture, but to work in tandem with sacred texts to further knowledge about divine intention, moral behaviour, and even the appropriate legal and political systems used to govern nations. In a sense, natural theology is the exact opposite of what Henry Drummond called the 'God of the gaps'. Rather than finding evidence for God in phenomena that cannot be explained by natural laws, natural theology often draws argumentative force from the very fact that the world does obey some sort of governing principles. The result is not just an argument that science and religion might be compatible, but a different view of what God might be and how knowledge of a deity is found.

In the 13th century, Thomas Aquinas penned the *Summa Theologiae*, perhaps the most influential work of Christian theology of the entire millennium. In part of this magisterial work, Aquinas put forward the 'quinque viæ'—the 'five ways' to infer God's existence. Looking at phenomena such as the ability of one natural cause to lead to a natural effect, which in turn causes other natural effects, Aquinas reasons that there must have been some initial first effect that had no natural cause. Another argument infers a designing mind from the observation that natural objects seem to act together in ways that accomplish unified purposes. Everything we observe exists temporarily and eventually decays or ends. Nothing on Earth has inevitable existence, but rather comes about as a contingent or accidental effect. Aquinas argues that such temporary things could not have come into being from nothing, thus there must be something in the world whose existence is necessary and permanent.

Though the five ways have sometimes been spoken of as 'proofs' of the existence of God, we should not imagine that these arguments were the only thing standing between Aquinas and atheism. The point of his 'five ways' was to examine both the justifications for faith that Christians already professed and to consider what else might be known about God besides sheer existence. The God Aquinas argued for has the ability to create and change things, is eternal, and has a purpose in mind for creation. From these attributes, Aquinas builds his system of theology.

Aquinas's theology has had a lasting impact on Christian thought, especially in shaping the way that the Catholic Church has responded to new scientific discoveries in the 20th and 21st centuries. In 1951, Pope Pius XII addressed the Pontifical Academy of Sciences discussing 'The Proof of God in the Light of Modern Natural Science'. The speech was widely misreported as a papal endorsement of the Big Bang theory (a cosmological account of the universe's beginning that at the time was not yet widely accepted). But Pius's real intention was to show that 20th-century discoveries about the changing nature of atoms, the impermanence of stars and galaxies, and even new understanding about heredity and evolution only demonstrated that Aquinas's arguments held up in the newly understood realms of the macrocosm and the infinitesimal.

The assertion that people could do theology—could determine truths about God and divine intentions—through examining nature, and more broadly by using their unaided powers of natural reason, had an especially complicated impact on Christian thought in the centuries after Aquinas, especially as European philosophy began to envision 'religion' and 'science' as distinct and independent forms of knowledge. Francis Bacon argued that 'the contemplations of man' could be divided into three categories, those which 'penetrate unto God', those 'circumferred to nature', and those 'reflected or reverted upon himself'. He placed natural theology in the first of these categories (distinct from inspired or revealed theology), describing it as 'that knowledge or rudiment of knowledge concerning God which may be obtained by the contemplation of His creatures'. Natural theology made use of natural knowledge, but not for the sole sake of understanding or explaining the natural world.

Natural theology and the idea that the natural world was a source of knowledge about God played an important role in 17th- and 18th-century England, when conflicts between members of the established Church of England, English Catholics, and dissenting English Protestants continually reshaped the relationship between the monarchy, parliament, and the people. The Royal Society of London, today the oldest continuous scientific society in existence, was established in 1660 upon the Restoration of the English monarchy. Explicitly established to be a religiously tolerant body, the Society prohibited discussion of religion or politics at its meetings. As the historians Steven Shapin and Simon Schaffer argue, its founder Robert Boyle believed that shared public experience and consensus could establish 'matters of fact', empirical knowledge distinct from its theological or metaphysical implications. Not that Boyle was unconcerned with natural theology. He posthumously endowed a series of lectures devoted to illustrating the harmonious relationship between Christianity and natural philosophy. The series was revived in 2004. The annual Boyle lecture has since been delivered at St Mary-le-Bow church in London.

In 1691, a year before the first Boyle Lecture, English naturalist John Ray published *The Wisdom of God Manifested in the Works of the Creation*. Ray was a member of the Royal Society and one of the first people to propose a formal classification system for plants and animals. His book drew on his unequalled knowledge of living creatures, showing how various species had bodies and behaviours that demonstrated their part in a divine plan. Ray argued that natural theology was not just about refuting atheism or logically inferring the powers and attributes of God. Deep understanding of the natural world and how creatures relate to one another and to their environment inspires a deep emotional response, producing feelings of awe and wonder wherein God is truly found. In one of the most striking passages, Ray argues that human beings were created with the ability to bend their necks to look straight up—which many other animals cannot do—precisely because the Creator wanted people to be able to gaze upon the heavens and be inspired by them.

This increased focus on natural theology as more than just a logical proof of God's existence illustrates how the genre of natural theology evolved over the 18th and 19th centuries. Building upon works like Ray's, a number of lectures and publications in English began to view the goal of natural theology as something more than drawing inferences about God from the evidence of nature. They invoked the idea that God was all knowing or good, or had human well-being in mind as a way to explain how nature itself worked. By the middle of the 19th century, natural theology and the kind of thinking it entailed had a strong influence on a new genre of publishing that came to be known as 'popular science'. The *Bridgewater Treatises*, a series of eight books on natural theology, were published in the 1830s. Though the theological arguments presented in the treatises were often unoriginal, the great appeal of these best-selling books lay in the rigour of their descriptions of the natural world. In practice, historian Jonathan Topham argues, their success was rooted in giving a religiously respectable cover to studying the natural world. 'They presented the pious middle classes with a largely nontechnical and religiously conservative compendium of contemporary science.'

Hume, Paley, and the politics of natural religion

Natural theology, both as a form of popular science communication and as a way of thinking about religion, flourished greatly in England and Scotland in the 17th and 18th centuries—more so than in most other Christian countries of Europe. Some historians have attributed this to a tradition of British empiricism that developed in contrast to 'continental' rationalism. But also important is the place of religion in Britain. Although many religious Protestants who dissented from the established Church of England gained the right to profess their faith with the Toleration Act of 1689, Catholics and Unitarians (as well as non-Christians) were excluded from this toleration. Throughout the 1700s anyone wishing to attend Oxford or Cambridge universities, or to hold public office, was required to swear their subscription to the Church of England's Articles of Faith.

In this political context, the critiques of natural and revealed religion developed by the Scottish philosopher David Hume (1711–76) were in no small part a rejection of the use of state power to compel belief.

Hume was the author of some of the most famous expressions of rationalist scepticism about religion—taking aim at both supernatural and natural theological ideas. In a 1748 essay 'Of Miracles', for instance, Hume argued against miracles on the basis of the relative weakness of the evidence in favour of them. Since the laws of nature are, by definition, generalizations that conform as closely as possible to the universal experience of humanity, Hume said, then they are as empirically well grounded as any statement can be. However generous we wish to be about the strength of the evidence in favour of miracles—that is, the reports of supposed eye-witnesses to the events, such as those recorded in the scriptures and in lives of saints—that testimony will never be as strong as the evidence that supports the laws of nature. Which, Hume asked, would be the greater miracle—that the laws of nature had actually been overturned or that those attesting to the miracle (possibly even including yourself) were mistaken? A rational person, Hume concluded, would have to answer that the falsity of the testimony was the more likely option. In short, a rational person could not believe in miracles. To put this in terms of the different sources of knowledge discussed in Chapter 2, Hume's argument was that collective sense experience trumps testimony.

In earlier writings, Hume had introduced what philosophers of science often call the 'problem of induction'. The practice of drawing general conclusions from patterns of separate observable facts—the process of induction—cannot be philosophically validated except through circular reasoning. That is, the justification for why induction seems to work is through an inductive process of observing its utility in previous cases. Although it might at first seem that natural theology, in the form modelled by Royal Society members like Boyle and Ray, might be the kind of collective sense experience that Hume would prefer to testimony or revealed religion, Hume extended his philosophical scepticism to religious arguments inferred from nature in his posthumous *Dialogue Concerning Natural Religion* (1779).

Much like Galileo's *Dialogue Concerning the Two Chief World Systems* (which Hume refers to), the *Dialogue* is written in the form of a three-way discussion among people representing different philosophical positions. The scientific sceptic Philo demolishes the arguments of both Demea (who argues dogmatically for a God based upon a priori rational argument and revelation) and Cleanthes, who serves as the mouthpiece for natural theology. Philo tells Cleanthes that reasoning that nature looks as though it is designed because it resembles human inventions is flawed. To claim to know what God's purposes are is to imagine a God who is limited and anthropomorphic, not infinite and all powerful. Moreover, Philo claims, knowing only this one particular world created by God (or perhaps even by a number of deities working at cross purposes) we cannot even infer that this world is good. 'In a word, Cleanthes, a man, who follows your hypothesis, is able, perhaps, to assert, or conjecture, that the universe, sometime, arose from something like design: But beyond that position he cannot ascertain one single circumstance, and is left afterwards to fix every point of his theology, by the utmost licence of fancy and hypothesis.'

Hume's arguments against natural theology have long been viewed as formidable by philosophers of science. It is not uncommon to see philosophers claim that Hume refuted the arguments of William Paley (1743–1805) despite the fact that Paley's *Natural Theology* was published a quarter-century after Hume died. Paley's work is in part a response to Hume, as well as a commentary on the religious politics of his time. An Anglican clergyman, philosopher, and theologian, Paley was one of the most popular English religious writers of the 18th and 19th centuries. His *Principles of Moral and Political Philosophy* (1785) became a standard text at Cambridge and many American universities. Although part of the Church of England, Paley was also outspoken against the requirement of demanding oaths of adherence to the established church as a prerequisite for positions of authority and power. This was not because he thought that other religious interpretations might also be correct, but because he thought that providing incentives for dissenters to swear oaths they did not believe in put their souls in greater peril than simply holding to unorthodox ideas. In part, he wrote his major works as a means to persuade his audience of Anglican interpretations of God's place in nature without using the brute force of economic and social pressure.

Paley argued for a kind of utilitarianism, arguing that the world that God created was so constructed as to bring about the greatest possible amount of well-being and happiness. This did not mean a world without suffering—Paley observed that creatures must sometimes die for others to live—but he argued that in human affairs, a principle of optimizing well-being was both possible and desirable. Paley's politics were conservative and wary of social change; he argued that people were endowed with God-given instincts that suited them towards different occupations. When people went against divine inclinations—when the manual labourer wanted to act as the ruler—a well-ordered society breaks down. Paley attributed much of the suffering in France that followed its Revolution to this kind of failure. Paley's social theories were in dialogue with those of another Anglican clergyman, Thomas Malthus.

Science and Religion

Malthus's concern was with human populations. He believed that these had a natural tendency to increase at a geometric rate from one generation to the next (1, 2, 4, 8 . . .), while the amount of food that a society could produce increased only arithmetically (1, 2, 3, 4 . . .). This led, in each generation, to a struggle for resources. The strong would survive but the weak would perish. Malthus's *Essay on the Principle of Population* (1798) argued that human suffering, such as war and famine, was unavoidable because human populations naturally grow faster than the resources needed to support them. This opposed Paley's idea that God had ensured that such widespread suffering could be avoided by rulers and societies that adhered to a divinely ordained moral order. Malthus interpreted this inevitable suffering theologically, arguing that God designed nature this way to spur humanity's intellectual and spiritual progress. 'Had population and food increased in the same ratio, it is probable that man might never have emerged from the savage state.'

Paley's *Natural Theology* attempted to show that his moral utilitarianism was illustrated in the natural world, demonstrating the goodness and personal interest of God in creation. At the same time, indebted to Hume, Paley's arguments were constructed more narrowly than precursors like John Ray. For Paley, the primary argument for God lay in evidence that the created world demonstrated purpose. For Paley, it did not logically matter how some object came to be created or even if it had existed perpetually in a universe of infinite duration. He deliberately set aside arguments about origins. Also sensitive to Hume's criticism that ascribing human-centred purposes to the natural world produced an anthropomorphic image of God, Paley even conceded that in some cases, the purpose of some feature of the natural world may not be known. However, Paley argued that the existence of purpose, what were often called 'final causes', could still be inferred by the fact that material objects in nature showed some kind of adaptation to the laws of nature. Thus, even if we did not know that vision was a form of sensation that creatures use to observe the world around them, the fact that the parts of the eye seem to demonstrate great attunement to the laws of optics is evidence that whatever caused eyes to exist had some purpose in mind that made use of the way light would pass through them.

Later defenders of natural theology, including many of the authors of the wide-selling *Bridgewater Treatises*, explicitly acknowledge Paley's work as definitive, even though the examples he cited from the natural world were sometimes seen as outdated by discoveries made in the 19th century. But some of these writers defended Paley's conclusions, that there was a single, beneficent, omnipresent God, by reverting to older natural theological arguments less carefully responsive to Hume. By the 1820s and 1830s, when Charles Darwin was a student, British natural theology had restored its focus on questions about how things in the world came to be created.

The political and ideological debates of this era were not seen as a conflict of science against religion, but instead were disagreements between different religious interpretations of how much nature and natural laws should shape understanding about God, in conjunction with questions about divine action, miracles, and revelation. Such questions are among the most difficult with which religious believers have to grapple. As Henry Drummond put it, 'If God appears periodically, He disappears periodically. If He comes upon the scene at special crises, He is absent from the scene in the intervals.' Science and philosophy certainly do not require us to believe in determinism or to deny the possibility of miracles. However, the theologians' dilemma will not go away: divine action and divine inaction are both hard to explain. And believers continue to disagree about whether God acts through the creation of natural laws, the violation of natural laws, or both.

Chapter 4
Darwin and evolution

When he died at his Kent home in April 1882, the English naturalist Charles Darwin was a worldwide celebrity, famed as the author of the theory of evolution that had transformed science and become the defining philosophy of the age. Despite lingering doubts about Darwin's religious beliefs, it was soon agreed that no other tribute would be adequate than a grand funeral at Westminster Abbey. The great and the good gathered to mark the astonishing theoretical achievements, the decades of patient research, and the dignity and modesty of this unassuming English gentleman. At the funeral, the Reverend Frederic Farrar's sermon compared Darwin's genius with that of his countryman Isaac Newton, next to whose memorial in the abbey Darwin's final resting place would be. Farrar explained that Darwin's theory was quite consistent with an elevated sense of the actions of the Creator in the natural world. The funeral symbolized the Anglican establishment's acceptance of Darwin and biological evolution, just over 20 years after the publication of *The Origin of Species* in 1859.

It was a somewhat suspicious and hesitant kind of acceptance, though. Not everyone in the Church of England, nor society at large, was happy to 'go the whole orang'—as geologist Charles Lyell described the belief that evolution applied to humans too. Indeed, it has always been *human* evolution in particular, rather than the evolution of bacteria, beetles, barnacles, or bats, that has really captured the imagination and unsettled the beliefs of the wider public. Religious ideas about the elevated place of humanity in creation, and especially about the soul and morality, were the ones most directly challenged by the evolutionary science that Darwin's career helped to establish as a new orthodoxy. The idea of evolution's conflict with a 'literal interpretation' of scripture was initially a fringe movement, gaining more traction only in the second half of the 20th century. For many others who have resisted Darwinism for religious reasons, their concern has been rooted in the theory of evolution's apparent incompatibility with free will, moral responsibility, and a rational and immortal human soul.

In this chapter, we explore these and other reasons why the theory of evolution has been considered so dangerous, starting with Darwin's religious views and the reception of his theory around the globe, before looking specifically at controversies about teaching evolution in schools. The personage of Charles Darwin himself continues to haunt these discussions. The theory of evolution by natural selection has become identified with this single iconic historical individual. The most frequently used pictures of Darwin are those from his old age in which his white beard and portentous expression conjure up images of biblical prophets, perhaps even of God. Darwin's personal scientific and religious beliefs are often discussed and sometimes cited as evidence of the real relationship between evolution and religion. It is important therefore to have a grasp of what this revolutionary scientific thinker really thought and why.

Darwin's odyssey

In his early 20s, Darwin was planning a career in the Church of England. He had embarked on medical training in Edinburgh a few years earlier but had found lectures boring and demonstrations of surgery disgusting. His father sent him off to

Christ's College, Cambridge, where young Charles signed up to the Thirty-Nine Articles of the Church of England and set about studying mathematics and theology with a view to entering holy orders. But Darwin found that theology appealed about as much as surgery. His real passion was for beetle-hunting rather than Bible-reading, and he had an early triumph when one of the specimens he had identified appeared in print in an instalment of *Illustrations of British Entomology*. In 1831 this enthusiastic young amateur naturalist was invited to join the HMS *Beagle* as a companion to the ship's captain, Robert Fitzroy, and to undertake collections and observations on matters of natural-historical interest. Perhaps he was not, after all, destined to become the Reverend Charles Darwin.

The primary purpose of the *Beagle*'s expedition was to complete the British Admiralty's survey of the coast of South America, but its five-year itinerary also took in Australia, New Zealand, and South Africa. Such expeditions were acts of hegemony and dominion over a vast proportion of the world's land, sea, and people. As Britain expanded its empire throughout the 19th century, collecting and interpreting the world's natural diversity, including geology, biology, and anthropology, became both a symbolic and very real tool of colonial power.

Darwin's observations of rock formations, plants, animals, and indigenous peoples were also central to his own intellectual development. Aboard the *Beagle*, Darwin's religious views started to evolve too. He had no doubt that the natural world was the work of God. In his notebook he recorded his impressions of the South American jungle: 'Twiners entwining twiners—tresses like hair—beautiful lepidoptera—Silence—hosannah.' To Darwin, these jungles were 'temples filled with the varied productions of the God of Nature', in which no one could stand without 'feeling that there is more in man than the mere breath of his body'. He even admired the role of Christian missionaries as colonizers, observing that 'so excellent is the Christian faith, that the outward conduct of the [indigenous] believers is said most decidedly to have been improved by its doctrines'.

After the voyage, however, Darwin would start to have doubts. His grandfather, father, and elder brother had all rejected Christianity, adopting either Deism or outright unbelief. He seemed to be heading in a similar direction. His reasons were many. His travels had revealed to him at first hand the great variety of religious beliefs and practices around the world. All these different religions claimed to have a special revelation from God, but they could not all be right. Then there was his moral revulsion at the Christian doctrine that while the faithful would be saved, unbelievers and heathens, along with unrepentant sinners, would be consigned to an eternity of damnation. Darwin thought this was a 'damnable doctrine' and could not see how anyone could wish it to be true. This objection hit him with particular force after the death of his unbelieving father in 1848. The death of his beloved young daughter Annie in 1851 prompted further painful thoughts about the question of an afterlife, along with grave reflections upon the cruelty of the natural world.

At the time he wrote *The Origin of Species* Darwin was still a theist, although not a Christian. By the end of his life he preferred to adopt the label 'agnostic', which had been coined by his friend Thomas Huxley in 1869. Darwin, for the most part, kept his religious doubts to himself. He had many reasons to do so, not least his desire for a quiet life and social respectability. The most important reason, though, was his wife Emma. In the early years of their marriage, Emma, a pious evangelical Christian, wrote a letter to Charles of her fears about his loss of faith in Christianity and the consequences for his salvation. She could not bear the thought that his doubts would mean they were not reunited after death in heaven.

Darwin's religious views changed during the same decades that he was developing his theory of evolution by natural selection, but it would be too simplistic to suggest that evolution made him a non-believer. His personal tragedies, experiments, journeys, and observations, his social position, and his education all informed the scientific and religious world-view he came to. What is true is that Darwin's understanding of the political, theological, and scientific thought of his time shaped his understanding of a new theory of biological change.

The theory of evolution by natural selection

When Darwin got back to England he began to focus on the 'species question'. This was the 'mystery of mysteries' for those seeking a naturalistic explanation of the origins of the different forms of life. In the 1830s, Darwin was confronted with two alternative explanations which were both equally unpalatable to him. Either each species had been created at a particular time and place by God, or else all life had started, perhaps spontaneously, in a simple form and had gradually climbed the ladder of life in the direction of greater complexity and perfection. The first option was unattractive because it posited a whole series of miraculous interventions in the history of life. What Darwin wanted to find was an explanation in terms of natural laws. The second option, the French naturalist Jean-Baptiste Lamarck's theory of 'transmutation', developed in his *Philosophic zoologique* (1809), involved too many unacceptable theoretical assumptions for Darwin, such as the idea that life was continuously being spontaneously generated and starting its ascent up the ladder of life, that all life was climbing in the same direction up this single ladder, and that a creature's own voluntary efforts could alter its physical structure. Lamarck's theory was also widely believed to be connected to religiously unacceptable ideas of materialism and determinism—in other words, to the view that all phenomena, both mental and physical, could ultimately be explained in terms of causal interactions between particles of matter. Radicals in England, some inspired by revolutionary events in France, also took Lamarckism as evidence against a hereditary upper class, arguing that differences in aptitude and intelligence were shaped by the environment and could improve or degenerate from one generation to the next.

A key component of Darwin's world-view was provided by a book he read during the *Beagle* voyage, Sir Charles Lyell's *Principles of Geology*, published in three volumes between 1830 and 1833. Lyell's book argued that the history of the Earth was one of gradual changes operating over long periods of time rather than one of regular violent catastrophes. This argument also implied that geological events like earthquakes and volcanic eruptions had natural causes, as sudden culminations after aeons of slow change. If geology could be explained by such gradual modifications over time, perhaps biology could too. Darwin later confessed, 'I always feel as if my books came half out of Lyell's brains.'

The animal life of the Galapagos islands—its finches and giant tortoises, its iguanas and mocking birds—was later to provide one of the keys to unlocking the 'mystery of mysteries'. Each island had its own species of finch, with differences in the sizes and shapes of their beaks (Figure 5). Did this require Darwin to believe that there had been a separate act of creation by God on each island, and another one on the mainland too? This seemed scientifically and theologically inelegant, to say the least. A unidirectional transmutationist model would not work either, since there was no obvious way to arrange these different species in a single line with one developing into the other. From the late 1830s, Darwin filled notebooks with arguments and counter-arguments trying to solve these sorts of problems. He thought about the way that breeders of pigeons selected particular individuals among each generation when trying to produce unusual new varieties. The analogy with artificial selection would be central to his argument. Even more central, though, was the idea of scarcity and competition for resources, which he borrowed from Malthus's *Essay on the Principle of Population*.

1. Geospiza magnirostris.   2. Geospiza fortis.
3. Geospiza parvula.   4. Certhidea olivasea.

5. An illustration from Darwin's *Journal of Researches into the Natural History and Geology of the Countries Visited During the Voyage of H.M.S. Beagle* (1845), showing a selection of the different species of finch collected during the voyage.

Darwin read Malthus's *Essay* in 1838 and saw how it could be applied to the species question. Looking at the entangled creepers of the South American jungle, the parasitic and murderous instincts of insects, and even at the plants and weeds in his own back garden, Darwin could see something similar going on—a competition for resources which those creatures with even a slight advantage over their competitors would win. This struggle for existence and the resulting 'survival of the fittest', as the evolutionary philosopher Herbert Spencer would call it, became the central idea of Darwin's theory. Alfred Russel Wallace, who came up with the idea of natural selection in the 1850s (20 years later than Darwin but before Darwin had published his theory), also credited Malthus as a source of inspiration.

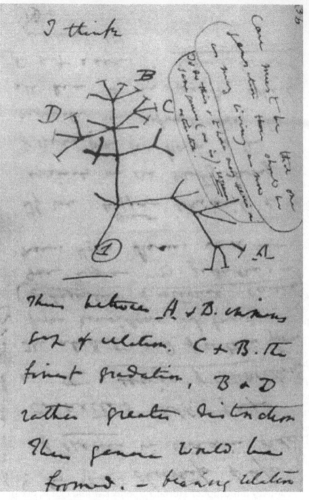

6. One of Darwin's first sketches, in his notebooks of the late 1830s, of his idea of a branching tree of life connecting all organisms through a shared ancestry.

Darwin now had his solution. The adaptation of organisms to their environment, and the origins of separate species, should be explained not in terms of direct divine acts of creation, but by geographical distribution, random heritable variation, competition for resources, and the survival of the fittest over vast spans of time. Natural selection could come in many different guises—as a disease, a predator, a drought, a shortage of your favourite food, a sudden change in the weather—but those individuals in each generation who happened by good luck to be the best equipped to cope with these natural assaults would flourish and leave offspring, while the less well adapted would perish without issue. Repeat that process for hundreds of millions of years and the whole panoply of species now observed could evolve from the simplest forms of life (Figure 6).

In 1858, Darwin received a letter from Wallace written from Ternate, part of the Dutch East Indies colony. The letter outlined a theory virtually identical to Darwin's and spurred him into a more rapid publication of his ideas than he had planned. At a hurriedly arranged meeting of the Linnaean Society, an announcement was made of Darwin's and Wallace's theories. The following year saw the publication by John Murray of Albemarle Street, London, of *The Origin of Species by Means of Natural Selection, or The Preservation of Favoured Races in the Struggle for Life*.

'Our unsuspected cousinship with the mushrooms'

On opening the *Origin* in 1859, the first words a reader would have come across were two theological epigraphs—one a quotation from William Whewell's Bridgewater Treatise, the other from Francis Bacon, one of the leading lights of the scientific revolution of the 17th century. Whewell stated that in the material world 'events are brought about not by insulated interpositions of Divine power, exerted in each particular case, but by the establishment of general laws'. According to Bacon, one could never have too much knowledge of either the book of God's word or the book of God's works, divinity or philosophy, 'rather let men endeavour an endless progress or proficience in both'.

Those first readers of *The Origin of Species* were presented with a view of nature in which God had been pushed to the margins but not banished completely. God was no longer needed to create each individual species but Darwin, whether for the sake of convention or out of his own remaining religious convictions, presented his argument as favouring a kind of theistic evolution. When it came to the concluding section of the book, Darwin reiterated Whewell's view that God acted in a lawlike rather than a miraculous fashion. 'To my mind,' Darwin wrote,

> it accords better with what we know of the laws impressed on matter by the Creator, that the production and extinction of the past and present inhabitants of the world should have been due to secondary causes . . . When I view all beings not as special creations, but as the lineal descendants of some few beings which lived long before the first bed of the Silurian system was deposited, they seem to me to become ennobled.

In the famous closing sentences of the book, Darwin marvelled that from 'the war of nature, from famine and death', the highest forms of life had been produced. He concluded:

> There is grandeur in this view of life, with its several powers, having been originally breathed into a few forms or into one; and that, whilst this planet has gone cycling on according to the fixed law of gravity, from so simple a beginning endless forms most beautiful and most wonderful have been, and are being, evolved.

From the second edition onwards, in case there was any doubt about his meaning, he changed the phrase 'breathed into a few forms or into one' to 'breathed by the Creator into a few forms or into one'.

Darwin's rereading of the book of nature also gave him reasons to rethink his religion. Some theologians argued that the 'perfection' of organs was proof of their direct and divine creation. Hard though it was for him to believe it himself—the human eye could still give him a shudder of incredulity—he came to think that all these adaptations came about by natural processes. Variation and natural selection could, over time, produce 'organs of extreme perfection'. Even after abandoning the idea of distinct and supernatural acts of creation, Darwin still respected more subtle arguments like Paley's about nature's benevolent purpose, even citing Paley in the *Origin* to counter 'difficulties of the theory'. But eventually the suffering he'd seen both in his own life and in the natural world led him to conclude that Paley's argument 'which formerly seemed to me so conclusive, fails, now that the law of natural selection has been discovered'.

Darwin had observed all sorts of cruelty and violence in nature, which he could not believe a benevolent and omnipotent God could have willed. Why, for example, would God have created the ichneumon wasp? The ichneumon lays its eggs inside a caterpillar, with the effect that when the larvae hatch they eat their host alive. Why would God create cuckoos which eject their foster siblings from the nest? Why make ants that enslave other species of ant? Why give queen bees the instinct of murderous hatred towards their daughters? 'What a book a Devil's chaplain might write', Darwin exclaimed, 'on the clumsy, wasteful, blundering low & horridly cruel works of nature!'

There were some within the Christian churches who embraced Darwin's variety of natural theology. There was indeed greater grandeur and nobility, they agreed, as well as more simplicity and order, in a world where God had created through a lawlike process of evolution, rather than one in which God periodically intervened to top up the planet's flora and fauna after particularly destructive catastrophes.

Henry Drummond was one such individual. The historian, Christian socialist, and novelist Charles Kingsley was another. His famous children's story *The Water Babies*, published in 1863, included an allusion to his approval for Darwin's new theory. The little boy Tom approaches 'Mother Carey', a personification of nature, and says, 'I heard, ma'am, that you were always making new beasts out of old.' Mother Carey replies, 'So people fancy. But I am not going to trouble myself to make things, my little dear. I sit here and make them make themselves.' A future Archbishop of Canterbury, Frederick Temple, was another Anglican who supported the idea that God might have created through variation and natural selection rather than by a succession of miracles. On the other side of the Atlantic also there were individuals, such as the Harvard botanist and Presbyterian Asa Gray, who adopted theistic interpretations of Darwinian evolution.

But there were instances of conflict too, most famously in a dramatic confrontation at the British Association for the Advancement of Science in Oxford in 1860. Darwin himself was not present, but his theory was discussed in a paper applying Darwinian ideas to the question of intellectual and social progress. The general issue of Darwinism was then opened up to the floor for further debate. First, the Bishop of Oxford, Samuel Wilberforce, spoke at length about Darwin's theory. We do not have a record of exactly what he said, but we can infer from his review of the *Origin* published in the conservative *Quarterly Review*. Wilberforce conceded that the book's conclusion that 'mosses, grasses, turnips, oaks, worms, and flies, mites and elephants, infusoria and whales, tadpoles of today and venerable saurians, truffles and men, are all equally the lineal descendants of the same aboriginal common ancestor' was certainly surprising, but one which he would have to admit if the scientific reasoning were sound. He could not object to Darwin's inference of 'our unsuspected cousinship with the mushrooms' on biblical grounds, since it was most unwise to try to judge the truth of scientific theories with reference to revelation. However, drawing heavily on the work of the country's leading anatomist, Richard Owen, Wilberforce raised plenty of scientific objections to the theory, focusing especially on the lack of fossil evidence of transitional forms, and on the fact that, however many varieties of pigeons and dogs may have been produced under domestication, pigeons had always remained pigeons and dogs always dogs. There had been no hint of a new species.

Although he did not base his objections on a literal reading of the Bible, Wilberforce's resistance to evolution, like that of many religious believers since his day, did derive from a commitment to a biblically inspired world-view in which human beings were separate from and superior to the rest of the animal world. The Christian teaching that God took on human form in the person of Jesus Christ also gave that human form a unique significance. To claim that man was nothing more than an 'improved ape' rather than 'Creation's crown and perfection' was, Wilberforce pointed out, demeaning to God as well as to humanity. At the end of his remarks at Oxford, Wilberforce is reported to have turned to one of Darwin's staunchest advocates, Thomas Huxley, and asked whether he was descended from an ape on the side of his grandmother or his grandfather. It was intended as a joke, but Huxley was apparently white with anger as he rose and replied severely that he would rather be descended from an ape than from a man who used his intellect and influence to introduce ridicule into a grave scientific discussion. As the temperature in the packed auditorium rose, Darwin's old companion from HMS *Beagle*, Captain Fitzroy, stood up holding a Bible aloft with both hands and denounced Darwin's theory. Another of Darwin's inner circle, the botanist Joseph Hooker, then weighed in with what was, on Hooker's own account, a decisive intervention on the side of Darwinism.

It is a colourful story, and one that has become part of Darwinian folklore. In 1860, Wilberforce, Huxley, and Hooker all thought that they had won the day. But by the time the tale came into wider circulation a couple of decades later, Huxley and Hooker, who had long been pressing for the autonomy of science from the church, had risen to positions of greater influence. The ascendancy of the professionalizing agnostics within the British scientific establishment was witnessed by the fact that both Hooker and Huxley were chosen to serve as presidents of the Royal Society. The Huxley–Wilberforce story was then used retrospectively, as a piece of victors' history, to suggest a clearer triumph for scientific naturalism over Anglican conservatism than had really been achieved in Oxford in 1860. It suited the new elite to be able to tell the story in a way that seemed to foreshadow and legitimize their own rise to power, while simultaneously depoliticizing the issue. The 1860 confrontation between Samuel Wilberforce and Richard Owen, on the one hand, and the young Darwinians, on the other, had resulted from a struggle for dominance within the institutions of British science and education—a conflict between competing social interests as well as between competing interpretations of the scientific evidence for evolution. The later recasting of the Huxley–Wilberforce debate as one more instance of a simple and timeless conflict between 'science' and 'religion' helped to suggest that the agnostics' rise to power was the result of an inexorable historical process rather than a deliberate political campaign.

Evolution and theology

Wilberforce's review of *The Origin of Species* identified the theological issues which would play out repeatedly among Christians, Jews, Muslims, and others as they considered the implications of evolution for their religious beliefs in the 19th century and afterwards. Some of these were not new. Discoveries in astronomy and geology had already given theologians plenty of opportunity to discuss the relative authority of science and scripture in determining natural knowledge. Darwin's view of nature drew particular attention to suffering, violence, and death. But people hardly needed Darwin to tell them that these were features of the natural world in general and of human life in particular. Again, theologians were already aware of the problem of evil, and had various responses to it. One common response to human evil was to explain that God must allow his creatures free will, which could be turned to either good or evil ends. Bishop Wilberforce's response to Darwin's remarks on imperfections in nature, and on the apparent cruelty of such creatures as the ichneumon wasp, was to refer to the Christian idea of the Fall. On this view, when Adam and Eve, the crowns and rulers of creation, were expelled from the Garden of Eden for their disobedience, it was not just they and their human descendants who fell from grace into a disordered state; it was the whole of nature. As Wilberforce put it, the 'strange forms of imperfection and suffering amongst the works of God' were the ongoing expression of 'the strong shudder which ran through all this world when its head and ruler fell'.

What was theologically new and troubling was the destruction of the boundary securely separating humanity from the 'brute creation' (and, to a lesser but significant extent, the destruction of the boundaries separating kinds of plants and animals from each other). The publication of Darwin's theories about human evolution in *The Descent of Man* (1871) and *The Expression of the Emotions in Man and Animals* (1872) provided further material for discussions about the relationship between humanity and the other animals. In these works Darwin speculated, as he had not dared to in 1859, on how even the most elevated of human faculties—the emotions, the moral sense, and religious feelings—might have evolved by natural means.

By the end of the 19th century, there was no serious scientific opposition to the basic evolutionary tenets of descent with modification and the common ancestry of all forms of life. There was considerable dispute about the explanatory sufficiency of the mechanism identified by Darwin and Wallace as the main driving force of evolution, namely natural selection acting on random variations. Lamarckian mechanisms of the inheritance of acquired characteristics were still discussed, and the process of heredity was a matter of dispute. From 1900 onwards, there were debates about whether Gregor Mendel's work on all-or-nothing units of inheritance that came to be known as 'genes' was compatible with a Darwinian model of gradual change over generations. That debate was not resolved until the 1930s and 1940s with the modern evolutionary synthesis of neo-Darwinism. That framework combined Mendelian genetics and the theory of natural selection, and led to the rejection of evolutionary theories that appealed either to the inheritance of acquired characteristics or to some innate life-force driving evolution from within.

Throughout these decades, theologians continued to make various uses of evolutionary ideas. The early 20th century saw a flourishing of ideas about creative evolution and guided evolution that appealed to religious thinkers. Since then, the triumph of neo-Darwinism has posed different theological questions. Within each faith tradition, there have been those who embrace evolution but also those who question or reject it.

Evolution, religion, and empire

Darwin's journey on the *Beagle* was both enabled by and representative of the global power of the British empire. Throughout the 19th century, and well into the 20th, Britain and other national powers exercised various forms of colonial control over much of the world, including many parts of Africa and Asia—and used economic and military clout to influence cultural and political affairs elsewhere. While science and religion were sometimes thought to be in conflict by warring elite factions within these nations, they often worked together in promoting this kind of colonial domination. We have spoken already of Darwin's admiration for Christian missionaries, who, in his view improved the lot of more 'primitive' peoples by bringing them European religion. Darwin saw this first hand, when the *Beagle*'s

Captain Fitzroy abducted several children in Tierra del Fuego and brought them to England to be 'civilized'. As missionaries, explorers, military leaders, and imperial officials sought to assert knowledge of and control over local populations, they also used their scientific systems of analysis and classification to justify their claims. The separation of knowledge into distinct categories of 'science' and 'religion', although still relatively new to Europe, was used by Europeans as a mark of civilization and sophistication that could justify their moral authority to govern people from other parts of the world and to lay claims to their lands, bodies, and resources. That other peoples had not segregated their knowledge in this way was seen (by Western colonizers) as proof of their inferiority.

Malthus's view that scarcity, competition, and limited survival had spurred the progress of civilization towards deeper theological and philosophical truths, and the natural theological idea that the created world had an ultimate purpose shaped by God's goodness, had been incorporated into Darwinian theories of species change to give rise to what is sometimes called 'Social Darwinism'. These ideas travelled with European and North American colonizers and were used to interpret the people they encountered. In framing a narrative of evolutionary progress, colonizers placed their own physical characteristics as most fully evolved away from other animal species and interpreted others as closer to animal relatives. The same was true of non-Western religions and cultures. Reports that indigenous people were animists (believers that physical objects were infused with spirits) or were polytheistic—or that they had not conceived of a distinction between rare miracles and natural law—were used to justify claims that they had not evolved as much as Europeans.

In using themselves as the standards by which the assessment of other peoples was calibrated, colonizers placed their own invention—the knowledge tradition they called 'science'—as the most highly evolved form of thought. Other forms of natural knowledge, if they could not be explained in a scientific way, were often dismissed. In realist terms, it did not matter whether indigenous forms of knowledge—about navigation, medicine, agriculture, or astronomy—'worked'; what mattered was that they didn't describe objects and laws that had been established as the true basis of reality by Western science.

Colonial assertions of moral and intellectual supremacy over other peoples had the effect of raising both the science and religion of European and Western cultures to a place 'above' the knowledge of other peoples. On one hand this seemed to bolster monotheistic religion, particularly interpretations which saw Christianity as superseding more 'primitive' religions that had come before it and saw an arc of progress in the history of Christian reformation. On the other hand, this concept of social evolution also gave weight to arguments that even reformed Christianity would be superseded by an enlightened secularism. Out of such ideas came the late 19th-century language of science at war with religion, which erupted into social conflicts in several ways. Debates over evolution have long been a staple of these, perhaps most famously in political and legal fights over the teaching of biology in the United States.

The anti-evolution movement from Dayton to design

On 21 March 1925, Austin Peay, the Governor of Tennessee in the United States, put his signature to an Act making it unlawful for teachers to 'teach any theory that denies the story of the Divine Creation of man as taught in the Bible, and to teach instead that man has descended from a lower order of animals'. Other states, including Mississippi and Arkansas, adopted similar anti-evolution measures in the 1920s, but it was in the town of Dayton, Tennessee, that the issue came to a head.

The American Civil Liberties Union (ACLU) saw the Tennessee law as an opportunity to take a stand in defence of intellectual freedom. They placed an advertisement seeking a volunteer to bring a test case. Some of the lawyers and businessmen of Dayton, grasping the opportunity to put their town on the map, persuaded a local science teacher, John Scopes, to put himself forward. What followed generated more publicity than the townsfolk of Dayton could possibly have envisaged.

At first glance, it seems strange that a misdemeanour charge levied against a small-town schoolteacher—for which the maximum penalty was only a small fine—would attract such massive attention. But it was not the legal issue itself, but the opportunity to use the courtroom to debate science and religion that turned the Scopes trial into a public spectacle. Scopes had agreed to stand trial in the hope that (after he was convicted, and had appealed the decision) the US Supreme Court would rule that anti-evolution laws were unconstitutional. With his defence attorneys making no effort to have Scopes acquitted, the trial turned into an internationally discussed drama whose attraction was not a legal question, but philosophical and moral ones. Were evolution and religion compatible? Was it wrong or harmful to teach children that they were descended 'from a lower order of animals'?

The trial's promise of a great debate between science and religion—breathlessly covered in newspapers across the USA and internationally, and taking advantage of new media including cinema newsreels and broadcast radio—also attracted the participation of two of the most famous orators in America: William Jennings Bryan acting for the prosecution, and Clarence Darrow for the defence. Bryan had run three times for president, as the candidate of the Democratic Party, never succeeding. Bryan's support for popular sovereignty against the economic elite had gained him unwavering support in much of the rural United States—especially in regions that felt their way of life threatened by America's rapid urbanization, its increasing industrialization, and those trends' reliance on the nation's diversification through influxes of immigrants. (In the late 19th and early 20th century, the United States welcomed a greater number of immigrants from Europe who were not Protestant, including Jews and Catholics, which gave rise to anti-immigrant sentiment and restriction on migrants enacted in 1924.) Darrow had made his reputation defending politically unpopular clients, including labour union leaders and racial minorities. In 1924, he convinced a judge to withhold the death penalty from two University of Chicago students who had pleaded guilty to abducting and murdering a child.

Although some saw the Scopes trial as a simple confrontation between science and religion, the political speeches made by William Jennings Bryan at the time reveal that the more powerful dynamic was a generally conceived conflict between the fundamentals of Christianity and the evils of the modern world. Bryan was a defender of the newly formed movement for Christian 'fundamentalism'. For the fundamentalists, the spread of Darwinism was both a cause and a symptom of the degeneration of human civilization which they witnessed all around them, from the barbaric violence of the First World War in Europe to the cultural and demographic changes in 1920s America (Figure 7). A new science curriculum that was pushed out across the nation in the 1910s and 1920s had reflected these changes. Not only did many schools teach evolution for the first time; they also emphasized urban hygiene concerns and the industrial uses of science and technology.

Protestant Christianity and a literal reading of the Bible were bulwarks against these developments. Bryan and others feared that teaching children they were animals would brutalize and degrade them:

> Does it not seem a little unfair not to distinguish between man and lower forms of life? What shall we say of the intelligence, not to say religion, of those who are so particular to distinguish between fishes

7. A fundamentalist cartoon from the 1920s depicting the theory of evolution as the tune played by a new 'Pied Piper'—'Science falsely so-called'—stealing away the children of America.

and reptiles and birds, but put a man with an immortal soul in the same circle with the wolf, the hyena and the skunk? What must be the impression made upon children by such a degradation of man?

Bryan and the fundamentalists got what they wanted. In the decades after Scopes was convicted, evolution rarely featured in US classrooms, even in states where it was not illegal. In 1927, the Tennessee Supreme Court overturned Scopes's conviction on a technicality: it should have been the jury and not the judge who had set the amount of the fine. With the ruling, Scopes and the

ACLU no longer had grounds to appeal his conviction and challenge the law itself. It would be another 40 years before an anti-evolution law would finally be challenged in front of the United States Supreme Court.

Creationism, science, and the law

The Establishment Clause of the First Amendment to the US Constitution forbids the government from passing any law 'respecting an establishment of religion'. The original intention was not to exclude religion from public life altogether but to ensure that no particular form of Christianity become an official state-supported religion akin to the Church of England. Participation in public life would not require a 'test' like the requirement to affirm acceptance of the Thirty-Nine Articles of Religion. There was also from the outset a broader hope that this amendment would help to build, in the words of Thomas Jefferson, 'a wall of separation between Church and state'. The enactment of statutes forbidding teachers in state-funded schools from contradicting the 'story of the Divine Creation of man as taught in the Bible' would seem on the face of it to put something of a hole in that wall.

From the middle of the 20th century onwards, the US Supreme Court became increasingly active in applying the Establishment Clause to state-level laws, including those governing schools. State laws allowing time for silent prayer in schools, or for the reading of denominationally neutral prayers, or requiring the Ten Commandments to be posted on classroom walls were all declared unconstitutional. When the US Supreme Court ruled in *Epperson v. Arkansas* (1968) that Arkansas's anti-evolution law (modelled after the 1925 Tennessee law) was unconstitutional, it did so on the grounds that the law gave preference to one religious viewpoint (that saw the Bible as irreconcilable with evolution) over another religious viewpoint (one that interpreted scripture as compatible with Darwinism). The Court declared, in November 1968, that 'fundamentalist sectarian conviction was and is the law's reason for existence'. The *Epperson* case marked the beginning of the legal process which would arbitrate new forms of anti-evolutionism into the 21st century.

In theory, a US state could decide to stop teaching a secular subject in its schools, be it science, history, or literature. But by singling out evolution and by emphasizing the interpretation that Darwinism contradicted the Bible, the courts ruled that the point of Arkansas's anti-evolution law (as was said about Tennessee's in 1925) was to endorse creationism, a religious doctrine.

'Creationism' is a term that has loosely been used to describe religious opposition to a belief in the shared ancestry of different species, including humans. Some creationists may accept gradual evolutionary change within species or closely related families over time (that one original dog kind could evolve into wolves, foxes, Pomeranians, and bloodhounds) but insist that separate divine acts created distinct 'kinds'. This doctrine of separate creations distinguishes creationism from a religious view sometimes called 'theistic evolution': the belief that evolution from a common ancestor was a purposeful, divinely intended, or guided process.

Most creationists base their resistance to evolution at least partly on the authority of their sacred text. The Book of Genesis, for instance, relates that God, over a period of six days, created each kind of living creature separately, made man and woman in his own image, and set them above the rest of creation, before resting on the seventh day. As the King James translation put it:

> And God said, Let us make man in our image, after our likeness: and let them have dominion over the fish of the sea, and over the fowl of the air, and over the cattle, and over all the earth, and over every creeping thing that creepeth upon the earth.

The question of how to interpret sacred texts and to what extent observations of the natural world shape those interpretations has been debated in almost every religious tradition. Creationist religious views typically derive from scriptural accounts of creation whose authorship is held to be divinely inspired or dictated. As we have already seen in the case of arguments about Copernican astronomy, however, it is not easy to specify which parts of the scriptures are to be taken absolutely literally. As William Jennings Bryan explained during the Scopes trial, when the Bible said, 'Ye are the salt of the earth', the text did not mean that 'man was actually salt or that he had flesh of salt, but it is used in the sense of salt as saving God's people'. The term 'literalist' is sometimes used to describe people who believe that a sacred text is entirely true, and that all other knowledge claims must be accommodated to what is given in the text. This does not mean that all literalists agree on what the text means when they read it. At the Scopes trial, Bryan defended the literal truth of the Bible, but admitted that the Bible may have stated those truths in language that even its most devout readers could not interpret with certainty.

What Bryan intended as humility, Darrow attacked as hypocrisy. When the Bible said that the Sun had been stopped in the sky, did that mean that in those days the Sun went round the Earth? No, Bryan said, he believed that the Earth went round the Sun and what the passage meant was that the Earth was stopped in its rotation. Then what about the age of the Earth? Many bibles had the date 4004 BC printed in the margin to indicate the date of creation, as calculated from the text itself. Did Bryan believe the Earth was about 6,000 years old? 'Oh, no; I think it is much older than that.' 'How much?' He could not say. What about the six days of creation in Genesis? Were they 24-hour days? Bryan was clear on that one: 'I do not think they were twenty-four-hour days.' Rather, they were 'periods'. God could have taken six days, six years, six million years, or six hundred million years to create the Earth. 'I do not think it is important whether we believe one or the other,' Bryan said. Soon afterwards, this famous exchange descended into acrimony. Bryan claimed that Darrow was trying to use the courtroom to attack the Bible. Darrow told Bryan he was merely examining 'your fool ideas that no intelligent Christian on Earth believes'.

This famous moment during the Scopes trial reveals two important things about creationism generally. First, even among Christian creationists there has been disagreement about how to interpret Genesis. In the early 20th century, many adopted the 'day-age' interpretation favoured by Bryan according to which each biblical 'day' was in fact a geological 'age' during which many different species were created. Others maintained belief in a very ancient Earth by inferring a long 'gap' between the first moment of creation and the six-day creation of modern Earth and its living species. Within that gap there might have been multiple cataclysms and new creations, responsible for producing the fossil record.

Even before the Scopes trial, creationists sought to use the natural world to justify their biblically derived claims about the age of the world or the creation of species and to raise doubts about Darwinism. The Seventh-Day Adventist geologist George McCready Price was an early and influential example. His *Illogical Geology: The Weakest Point in the Evolution Theory* (1906) and *New Geology* (1923) explained the formation of geological strata and the fossils found within them by arguing that they resulted from a recent universal deluge—which he saw as confirming the biblical account of Noah's flood.

Price's books were an inspiration for the 'creation science' revival of the 1960s and 1970s, led by a Texan Baptist teacher of civil engineering, Henry M. Morris. The Creation Research Society was founded by Morris in 1963, and the Institute for Creation Research in 1970. These promoted a more extreme and allegedly more scientific form of fundamentalist creationism than had ever existed before. As with the anti-evolution campaign of the 1920s, the creation science movement was born of a desire to protect white Christian Americans from modern social changes that they derided as corrosive and degenerate. In 1954, the US Supreme Court ruled that racial segregation in public schools was unconstitutional and creation science flourished at the same time that racial segregationists were decrying the interference of federal courts in local school policies. Like the anti-evolutionists of Bryan's time, creationists in the 1960s attempted to frame the debate over evolution as a moral issue, rather than just one about the scientific or historical truth of the Bible account of creation. The range of evils thought to grow out of a belief in evolution in the 1970s were graphically illustrated in R. G. Elmendorf's 'Evolution Tree', which bore fruit ranging widely from secularism, socialism, and relativism to alcohol, 'dirty books', 'homosex', and even terrorism (Figure 8).

The popularizers of creation science made an attempt to distinguish it from the earlier creationism of Bryan and Scopes-era anti-evolutionists. Creation *science*, they argued, was not a religious doctrine per se. It observed nature and sought to confirm theories about the natural world. That those theories were inspired by biblical accounts of creation did not, they argued, make the scientific evidence for those theories religious. This argument had legal ramifications. The US Constitution might prohibit teaching religion, but says nothing about what kinds of science may be taught.

Soon after the State of Arkansas lost the *Epperson* case and had to abandon its anti-evolution law, it enacted a new statute requiring 'balanced treatment' between 'evolution science' and 'creation science' According to the law:

> Creation-science includes the scientific evidences and related
> inferences that indicate: (1) Sudden creation of the universe, energy,

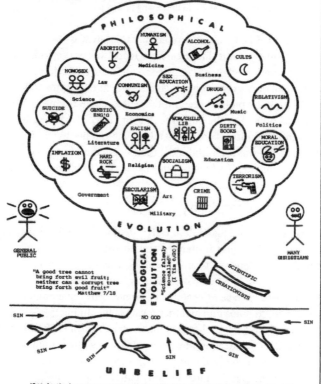

8. A creationist image of the 1970s: the 'Evolution Tree' is nourished by sin and unbelief, and its fruits include a range of secular ideologies, immoral activities, and economic and social evils.

and life from nothing; (2) The insufficiency of mutation and natural selection in bringing about development of all living kinds from a single organism; (3) Changes only within fixed limits of originally created kinds of plants and animals; (4) Separate ancestry for man and apes; (5) Explanation of the earth's geology by catastrophism, including the occurrence of a worldwide flood; and (6) A relatively recent inception of the earth and living kinds.

In 1982, a US Federal Court ruled that this law was unconstitutional and that 'creation science' was not science. Even though creation science attempted to use nature as evidence, the practice of only interpreting such evidence in the context of confirming the biblical account made it a religious enterprise. This was upheld by the Supreme Court in 1987. Not long after that, anti-evolutionists began to talk about another hypothesis that they claimed was scientific and, because it had nothing to do with scripture, not at all religious. They called this 'Intelligent Design'.

Explaining complexity

Proponents of intelligent design (ID) do not invoke the Bible, let alone try to interpret it literally, and do not explain geological and fossil evidence in terms of a biblical flood. They accept the antiquity of the Earth and of humanity, and, in the case of some ID theorists, such as Michael Behe, do not deny the common ancestry of humans and all other forms of life. In his 1996 book *Darwin's Black Box*, Behe accepted more or less all of the standard evolutionary picture but identifies certain key phenomena, such as the biochemistry of the first cells, which he insists cannot be explained without the intervention of an intelligent designer. Structures like the flagellum, a tail-like mechanism that allows some bacteria to move, exhibit 'irreducible complexity'. It could not have evolved gradually because without all of its several pieces working together, it would not provide an evolutionary advantage. Thus, it must have been created all at once.

Arguments about 'irreducible complexity' are a new form of a very old anti-Darwinian argument, namely that complex structures could not have evolved by natural selection because the intermediate forms containing only some of the parts would not have been adaptive. What use is a part of an eye, half a wing, or three-quarters of a flagellum? In general terms, evolutionists have been able to answer this objection by finding, either in fossils or in living species, evidence of intermediate structures that did exist and were in fact adaptive. In the case of the eye, Darwin himself listed various forms of eyes, from a small patch of light-sensitive cells to the complex 'camera' eyes of humans and other animals, showing how each was adaptive and could have evolved into the next in the series. Scientists now estimate that this entire evolutionary process could even have been achieved within a mere half a million years.

Advantages were also conferred by the precursors to fully fledged wings. Feathers, for instance, seem first to have evolved as a form of insulation before being co-opted by natural selection to aid a quite different function—flight. It is harder to produce these scenarios in the case of biochemistry because chemical reactions, unlike feathers, do not fossilize. However, using evidence from currently living species it is possible to reconstruct evolutionary scenarios. This has been done, for instance, in the case of the famous bacterial flagellum, which, it has been suggested, evolved through the co-option of a very similar existing structure used by bacteria for injecting toxic proteins into the cells of their hosts. So the answer to the question, 'What use is a part of an eye, half a wing, or three-quarters of a flagellum?', is 'Light-detection, warmth, and toxin-injection, respectively.'

Some accounts of ID rely upon negative argumentation. They argue that Darwinian natural selection is wrong, or, more often, insufficient to explain nature. Critics sometimes claim that this is simply the 'God of the Gaps' argument refurbished for the age of molecular biology. In other instances, ID arguments look like appeals to the wonderfulness of nature familiar from older natural theology texts, albeit with more modern examples.

When ID advocates first sought to argue for inclusion of their ideas in schools, they tended to mention a 'designer' and 'intelligence', but avoided addressing questions about whether the designer was God, whether there were one or many designers, or how an idea in the mind of some intelligence became manifested in the physical world of matter. This was necessary in order to make the case that ID was 'science' and not 'religion' within the dichotomy that the courts had effectively turned into precedent in the earlier creationism cases.

The first court challenge to ID came after a school board in Dover, Pennsylvania, adopted a rule in October 2004 requiring students to be read a statement asserting that 'Gaps in the [evolution] Theory exist for which there is no evidence' and telling them that 'Intelligent design is an explanation of the origin of life that differs from Darwin's view.' In the lawsuit that followed, Judge John E. Jones III ruled that intelligent design is not a science. Despite its lack of explicit theological conclusions about the Bible or the age of the world, its insistence on supernatural causation disqualified it as science. Based in part on the conclusion that ID is not science, Jones ruled that promoting it represented an endorsement of religion. The historical connection between ID and other forms of anti-evolution also factored into the judge's opinion. Trial testimony revealed that the publishers of the intelligent design textbook *Of Pandas and People* had originally prepared the book about 'creation science' and had simply substituted the phrase 'intelligent design' after the Supreme Court ruling in 1987.

By the 1990s, biblical anti-evolution laws had been declared unconstitutional; laws requiring 'balanced treatment' for evolution and 'creation science' had gone the same way; but opinion polls continued to find that between 45 and 50 per cent of the population of the USA believed that human beings were created by God in their present form at some time in the last 10,000 years. (This figure is about 40 per cent in most recent polls, with most of the rest of the population believing that humanity evolved through an evolutionary process somehow guided by God.)

Since the Dover trial ended in 2005, anti-evolution-minded school boards and politicians have shifted away from promoting specific forms of anti-evolution alternatives and instead emphasize the 'academic freedom' of teachers to teach what they believe to be true or the religious freedom of teachers and students to have their viewpoints included. The Louisiana Science Education Act of 2008 is the most politically successful of these efforts. The law was based upon language drafted by the Discovery Institute, a think tank that has spent millions of dollars to try to create political, scientific, and legal legitimacy for intelligent design.

At the Dover trial, witnesses compared ID to Paley's *Natural Theology*. While the two share superficial similarities, they're actually very different. Paley's insistence that evidence for divine design is found in objects being well adapted to natural laws is almost exactly the opposite of an argument that claims that intelligent design is found in the phenomena where natural laws are not enough. Given the theological vagueness of most ID, it may be surprising that the movement has found strong appeal among evangelical Protestants who endorse a literal reading of the Bible. In light of the larger cultural anxieties that the evolution debate in America evokes, support for ID and other forms of creationism are more comprehensible.

But is it science?

US courts have ruled that creation science and ID are not actually science. This raises complex questions of how one distinguishes between science and non-science, and whether it's the case that everything that is religious is non-scientific or vice versa. There are various candidates for such 'demarcation criteria'. Some say that true science must be empirically testable, others that it must make 'falsifiable' claims, others that it must offer explanations only in terms of natural laws and natural processes.

Philosophers of science are much less optimistic than they were a few decades ago about the possibility of finding any complete and coherent demarcation criteria. It is accepted that many scientific claims—including many of the most interesting ones—are not directly empirically testable but only become so as part of a complex network of auxiliary theoretical assumptions and scientific instruments. For instance, a mathematical model of the Big Bang cannot be tested by direct observation, but only indirectly through predictions about the behaviour of measuring apparatus when a particular reaction is set off in a massive particle accelerator. On the other hand, creation scientists made very clearly testable claims about the age of the Earth and the separate ancestry of all species.

It is also accepted that good scientists will often hold on to their theories in the face of inconsistent empirical evidence and seek to reinterpret that evidence rather than declare their theory 'falsified'. Some philosophers speak instead of the 'robustness' of theories which can generally overcome apparent inconsistencies and can explain a wide range of observed phenomena. The modern framework of evolutionary theory successfully explains and unifies a huge body of evidence accumulated and interpreted over many generations. It makes sense of the fossil record, the geographical distribution of species, the physical similarities between related plants and animals, and the vestigial organs that testify to earlier evolutionary forms. Recent advances in genetic sequencing have provided a huge new mass of evidence which confirms evolutionary theory while identifying a whole new range of puzzles and anomalies. In the face of puzzles and anomalies a good scientist, especially when working with such a well-confirmed theory, does not declare their theory falsified, but designs new experiments and develops new theoretical models to solve those puzzles and resolve those anomalies. This model relies on the good faith of a scientific community; that their decisions to solve puzzles or to alter their hypotheses are taken without regard for political, cultural, or financial considerations. As we shall see in Chapter 6, some forms of science denial abuse that good faith.

Evolution worldwide

In the English-speaking world, debates over evolution and religion have often centred upon Christianity. This is perhaps unsurprising since this was the world that Darwin himself came from and most closely influenced. The experiences of other cultures and religions with evolution have been shaped by their encounter with both the idea of evolution and the people who introduced it.

One month after Darwin's and Wallace's theory of species change was read before the Linnaean Society of London, the British parliament, meeting a mile away, voted to grant Queen Victoria sovereign authority over India. Although the British colonial presence in India had already been felt for centuries, the consolidation of imperial control under the Crown coinciding with the rise of evolution as the intellectual framework to interpret nature and progress influenced the way that colonized Indians experienced Darwinism, and the twinned concepts of science and religion.

As historian Peter Gottschalk relates in his study of science and religion in colonial India, people there had various systems of observing and interpreting the world around them, and applying that knowledge to practice long before European imperialism. What British colonizers brought with them were their own systems of categorizing different kinds of knowledge, and a demand to align beliefs, practices, and explanations that they encountered with the ones they had developed at home. Just as domestic British society had experienced debates and wars over church authority, toleration, and political participation by requiring very explicit distinctions between people by religion, colonial efforts to administrate also involved efforts to classify everyone by religious identity. 'The modern view of India as a primarily religious country, insolvably split between Hindus and Muslims,' Gottschalk observes, 'worked within a system of knowledge largely shaped by models originating in the West and generally controlled by Westerners.'

Some scholars of Indian religion go so far as to say that British imperialism 'invented' India's most populous religion, Hinduism. By this they don't mean that British colonizers came up with the texts, beliefs, and practices of people, most of which pre-date the colonial age by many centuries. Instead they mean that the British imperial view of Indian people created a singular category of 'Hindu' to describe a wide range of such beliefs and practices largely defined by contrast to Muslims and Sikhs. Debate about this supposed invention of Hinduism has divided scholars for decades, and has taken on political importance in India itself, where claims of the unity and antiquity of Hinduism shape some interpretations of national identity. These controversies are rooted in British and other European concepts of religion that in colonial times were often defined by their distinction from science and rationality. These definitions were tools of colonial control, as they served to allow British colonizers in India to treat indigenous forms of knowledge as less evolved than their own.

Indians' engagement with European concepts of science, imposed by colonial power, affected the way that Darwin's ideas of evolution were interpreted. Race and racism figured substantially in this. Interpretations of Darwin were frequently used to justify a hierarchy of races, which British administrators and naturalists used in conjunction with their interpretation of religious 'caste' to create hierarchies among Indians. For example, T. H. Huxley argued that different Hindu castes had resulted from different proportions of racial mixing.

Among Hindus today, there is a range of interpretations of evolution, with a much higher proportion of Hindus in India responding that they accept an evolutionary account of species change than the proportion of Protestants who do in the United States. Many point out that Hindu cosmology has no difficulty accepting an Earth that is billions of years old. (In fact, some interpretations of the *Rig Veda* date the Earth as over 8 billion years old, nearly twice the scientifically accepted age of about 4.5 billion.) Several Hindu texts speak of a series of incarnations of the god Vishnu in different animal, animal–human, and then human forms in a progression of complexity that many consider to parallel the emergence of more complex species in Darwinian evolution. While this is not the same thing as saying that ancient Hindu scriptures anticipated natural selection, this is often cited to support claims that Hinduism is not in conflict with evolutionary science.

This is not to suggest that all Hindus find evolution compatible with their religious belief, but to observe that acceptance or rejection of the theory is conditioned by the colonial and post-colonial authority of science. Arguing that Hinduism is inherently compatible with science has been one way in which the formerly colonized Hindu people of India translate their own intellectual and religious heritage into the modern frameworks that hold science up as a uniquely valid form of knowledge.

For some groups of colonized and marginalized peoples, the use of science as a tool of hegemonic power and the way that colonizers used dualistic concepts of science and religion to categorize and evaluate indigenous knowledge has created wariness of the scientific claims and the validity of the knowledge it creates. Scepticism about evolution, even when articulated in ways that contrast it with traditional beliefs about the origin of humanity or the creation and age of the Earth, should therefore be regarded differently when looking outside the Christian European context in which Darwin and his contemporaries worked.

A telling example of this is among Native American peoples who have frequently been used as objects of scientific study. As Kim TallBear observes, knowledge about human evolution and theories of race ancestry often made use of the first human inhabitants of the Americas, often without their consent. European colonizers used Native American bodies, blood, and other artefacts to create knowledge about race that they then used to justify the dispossession of indigenous peoples. That colonial project was aided by the use of scientific narratives to replace indigenous cultural histories with accounts of people and their past that they had no say in creating. Several years after some members of the Havasupai tribe (native to the Grand Canyon of Arizona) allowed the collection of blood samples to research high incidents of diabetes among their people, it came to light that scientists had continued to use these samples for other purposes without consent, including research into the genetic origins of the Havasupai people (which not only contradicted their creation narratives, but which could be used to question their territorial claims). As TallBear concludes of indigenous critics of evolutionary sciences, 'to characterize them as simply anti-science, or as religious zealots not only misses their sophisticated historical analyses and political insights, but misunderstands indigenous creationism as no different from the type of Christian creationism currently challenging the biological sciences and school curriculums.'

Around the world, in the past and today, the ways that scientific and religious ideas affect people cannot be separated from who they are: their own identity, history, and culture. One reason why evolution has remained a central issue in the science and religion story for so long is that it transforms those very issues, raising questions about how we understand our human selves, the origins of our societies, and how we act and interact with one another.

Chapter 5
Mind, brain, and morality

Perhaps the most important reason that evolution has been more controversial than many other scientific topics has to do with the implication that it provides a biological and historical account of what it means to be human. It speaks to a deeper concern over what we are as human beings, whether our bodies and minds define us, whether our selves change over the course of our lives, and whether anything exists as fundamentally 'us' after our bodies cease to function. If we are defined by our biology, by the genes and evolutionary processes that determine how our brains think and control our actions, what place is there for morality?

Since the 19th century, scientific studies of mind, brain, and morality have been providing challenges to religious ideas about identity and ethics. What if the part of the self we call the 'soul' is merely a by-product of chemical and electrical brain activity? If people's actions are a combination of genetics, brain activity, and social and cultural conditioning, what place does such a view leave for belief in moral responsibility in this life or the prospect of rewards or punishments in the next?

For many people, these questions about mind and morality drive the whole debate about science and religion. As in other areas of theology, so in ethics, some look to revelation or a sacred text for answers, while others look to human instincts or moral sentiments, and yet others look to the natural world around them (or some combination of all of these). Many believers resist the idea that human consciousness, morality, and even religion itself can be explained scientifically. If religious experience and human morality can be explained as natural phenomena, there seems to be no further need for supernatural accounts of such things.

Consider the famous and extraordinary case of Phineas Gage. In 1848, Gage was a railroad construction worker when a dynamite accident propelled a metre-long iron tamping rod through his cheek and out of the top of his head (Figure 9). Astonishingly, Gage survived. But it soon became clear that the damage to the frontal lobes of his brain had altered his personality. He had lost the ability to empathize with others, and his social behaviour became unpredictable and erratic. Accounts of people like Gage spurred interest in the brain and its role in making people act in certain ways, leading to new fields of scientific research into the relationship between our mental and physical selves.

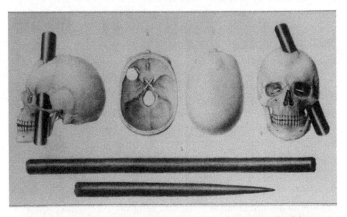

9. Illustration showing the tamping iron that went through Phineas Gage's head in 1848, and the route that it took through his skull.

Brain and mind

Nineteenth-century attempts to specify the exact nature of the connection between brain and mind saw the emergence of the science of 'craniology' or 'phrenology', according to which the extent of the development of different sections of the brain could be discerned from the shape of someone's skull. The different parts of the brain under the 'bumps' on the skull were correlated with different mental traits, such as love of children, secretiveness, self-esteem, and so on. Phrenologists could thus tell people what the shape of their head revealed about their mental capacities. It became a popular craze for a while in Victorian Britain. People were eagerly told what their skulls revealed about their character traits and their future destinies, by those with a special understanding of the secret workings of nature. Queen Victoria even arranged phrenological readings for her children. Some phrenologists of the era claimed that diagnosing mental traits was essential to helping people improve themselves morally. Thus, they presented phrenology as a respectable science that helped create an ethical society aligned with religious values.

At the same time, phrenology and other 19th-century efforts to study the brain and skull were used to make claims of gendered and racial differences in intelligence, and thus to justify the political inequalities of the day. Most famously, in the 1830s and 1840s the American natural historian Samuel George Morton acquired a large collection of skulls from different cultures and regions of the world, and concluded that different races had been separately created by God with varying abilities of mind and body. Morton's comparisons of European-American and African-American skulls in particular were cited to justify the continued practice of slavery in the United States.

Although in many ways phrenology was wrong-headed, the basic idea that different mental functions correlated with particular parts of the brain turned out to be fruitful. Studying patients who had suffered brain damage, scientists started making more informed statements about localization. In the 1860s, the French physician Paul Broca discovered the area—still known as 'Broca's area'—in the frontal lobes of the brain that was responsible for speech production. The more recent invention of brain-scanning technologies has allowed this project to be pursued with greater precision, revealing the dynamic interactions of different parts of the brain, and offering insights into the working of intact brains as well as damaged ones. Neuroscientists can even stimulate parts of the brain experimentally and study the mental effects on their intrepid subjects. These techniques have all been applied specifically to religious experiences as well as to many other mental capacities. A study of Carmelite nuns carried out in 2006 by Mario Beauregard and Vincent Paquette, for example, identified different brain areas that were activated during their spiritual experiences.

Dualism and physicalism

What are the implications of this scientific research for religion? One newspaper report of Beauregard and Paquette's study ran under the headline: 'Nuns Prove God Is Not Figment of the Mind'. The somewhat tortuous idea behind the headline seemed to be that if the whole brain is involved in religious experiences then that contradicts the theory that there is one special 'God spot', perhaps in the temporal lobes, and with it the associated belief that religious experiences are 'nothing but' the activation of that one brain area. Why it would be any less religiously or theologically troubling to find that spiritual feelings were produced by the activation of many parts of the brain, rather than just one, is not clear. This is a good example of the theological and philosophical ambiguity of empirical neuroscientific studies.

Since the 1980s, there have been several studies which use functional Magnetic Resonance Imaging (fMRI) to study the brains of Buddhist monks during periods of meditation (Figure 10). Some results from these studies suggest that 'expert meditators' develop certain cognitive abilities through repeated practice—including sensory processing and mathematical abilities. Public interest in these studies has coincided with increased interest in recreating the effects of these meditative practices—under the general banner of 'mindfulness'—without necessarily understanding the spiritual and supernatural explanations that Buddhists have traditionally used to explain their own experiences of meditation.

However, some Buddhist groups have embraced this scientific reinterpretation of millennia-old practices and have encouraged it. The Dalai Lama, leader of a Tibetan Buddhist movement, has been a strong supporter of neuroscientific research on Buddhist meditation and encouraged his followers to participate in fMRI studies. His engagement with science in this way has not been without controversy. Some scientists have protested his speaking at neuroscience conferences, claiming that inviting him promotes

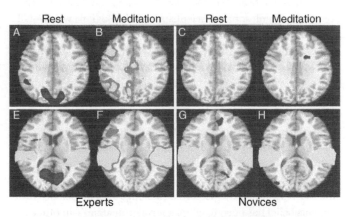

10. **Figure from a 2008 research paper studying the effects of meditation on neurological states. The article concludes that 'expert meditators' with more than 10,000 hours experience in Buddhist meditation show different brain activity than 'novice meditators'.**

religion in what should be a secular setting. Some critics claim that these efforts are an attempt to co-opt science's cultural prestige to bring attention and credibility to political movements for Tibetan sovereignty, implying parallels between repression of Tibet and repression of science itself. In part because of his efforts to promote this harmony between Buddhism and neuroscience, and to see science as legitimizing religious experience rather than superseding it, the Dalai Lama was awarded the Templeton Prize in 2012.

The success of neuroscience in showing that there are correlations between certain states of the brain and certain mental experiences, including religious ones, has been interpreted by some as a direct refutation of traditional beliefs about mystical experiences and the immortality of the soul. According to this sceptical stance, an experience can be caused by the brain or by an immaterial being (God or the soul) but not both: a neurological explanation of an experience rules out a supernatural or religious one. Science has explained away the supernatural. That might seem a reasonable and simple enough assumption. However, there are plenty of philosophers, scientists, and theologians who would deny it. To offer neurological or, for that matter, evolutionary explanations of where our religious and moral beliefs come from is an interesting scientific enterprise. It flourishes today as one part of the ambitious programme of research known as 'cognitive science'. But since absolutely all our beliefs—religious, scientific, or otherwise—are, on this hypothesis, the products of the same evolved neurological apparatus, drawing attention to that fact does not get us any further forward in the philosophical endeavour of distinguishing between the true ones and the false ones.

Another response to the perceived challenge of neuroscience to religious belief has been to adopt a form of 'dualism'—in other words, to assert that there exist two distinct kinds of substance, or properties, the mental and the physical, which interact with each other, especially in human beings. The dualist would interpret the close correlations discovered by neuroscientists not as evidence that the mind is nothing but brain activity, but rather that the mind interacts with the brain, or uses the brain as its instrument. René Descartes's 17th-century version of this philosophy is the one that has received most scholarly attention, but there are plenty of modern successors to his view, both among philosophers and more widely. Key problems in making sense of dualism include the question of how the physical and the non-physical can causally interact with each other, and explaining why dualism is to be preferred to the apparently simpler alternative of physicalism, according to which mental properties are properties of the brain.

Even if all mental experience is, in some sense, physical, it is still not straightforward to articulate what that sense is. Why is it that particular bits of matter (exclusively, as far as we know, complex networks of nerve cells within the brains of living animals) exhibit the properties of consciousness and others (such as rocks, vegetables, or even computers) do not? Philosophers and theologians interested in this question have discussed concepts such as 'emergence', 'supervenience', and 'non-reductive physicalism', all of which try to articulate how mental realities can be both dependent on and yet autonomous from the physical. To say that the mind is 'emergent' or 'supervenient' is to suggest it is autonomous, not in the sense of being able to exist independently of the brain, but in the sense that it exhibits properties and regularities that are not susceptible to systematic reduction to the neurological level.

In a somewhat different way, social scientists also point to culture as an emergent phenomenon that can't be determined at a purely neurological level. Morality exists as a shared set of norms and practices rooted in a common experience among people in a society. Such an account does not easily answer the question of whether the moral values of a society are 'good' in any absolute or objective sense. But these accounts explain why communities are aligned by shared values and why they respond to perceived deviance in the ways that they do. From this perspective, it is the belief in some immaterial part of oneself, and in a system of rewards and punishments, rather than the reality of that world-view, that explains why people seek to act morally.

Selfishness and altruism

When freethinking and anti-Christian works such as Thomas Paine's *Age of Reason* (1794) started to become more widely available, one of the leading concerns of the faithful was that if people ceased to believe in heaven and hell, then they would feel free to indulge their most sensual passions and selfish appetites. Without religion, it was feared, human society would descend into animalistic anarchy. As one judge said when sentencing a London bookseller to imprisonment for selling Paine's works, if these books were widely read and believed then the law would be deprived of 'one of its principal sanctions—the dread of future punishments'.

This same logic, that denying immortality would lead to immorality, was what drove William Jennings Bryan's movement to halt the teaching of evolution in the 1920s. Many today still echo the sentiments of this 18th-century judge and argue that religious beliefs are necessary to provide moral guidance and standards of virtuous conduct in an otherwise corrupt, materialistic, and degenerate world. Religions certainly do provide a framework within which people can learn the difference between right and wrong. An individual might consult the scriptures to discover that God has told his people to be truthful, faithful, and respectful towards their parents; and not to steal, nor commit adultery, nor worship false gods. Believers can also hope to receive moral guidance from the voice of God within, in the form of their conscience. If they follow the divine path faithfully, they will be deemed to be among the righteous rather than the wicked at the day of judgement. The unbeliever, in contrast, is supposed to be a sensuous, self-indulgent, selfish creature whose motto is 'Let us eat and drink; for tomorrow we die.'

The alleged connection between unbelief and selfishness has been strengthened by a particular interpretation of evolution as a process driven by self-assertion and competition. Standard explanations of evolution have emphasized the fact that a trait or behaviour cannot evolve unless it is for the good of the individual organism. This would seem to rule out the possibility of altruism (except as a sort of enlightened self-interest). If evolution cannot produce genuine altruism, then perhaps the only explanation for the self-sacrifice displayed by saintly individuals is that they are inspired or empowered by God. Even the former director of the Human Genome Project (and 2020 Templeton Prize winner) Francis Collins suggests in his book *The Language of God* (2006) that the existence of the 'moral law' of love and altruism within every human heart cannot be explained by science alone.

Others seeking natural explanations for altruism, selflessness, and moral behaviour have turned to evolution. Some interpretations of evolution seem to suggest that selfish behaviour that increases the likelihood of reproducing will be retained by the process of natural selection. For the arch-atheist science writer Richard Dawkins, author of *The Selfish Gene* (1976), it was not individual organisms, but genes themselves that exhibited this tendency to value their own reproduction, and which he described as 'selfish' in an extended and metaphorical sense. A year earlier, in 1975, biologist E. O. Wilson had published *Sociobiology: The New Synthesis*, which looked to group-selection rather than gene-selection to provide an explanation. Wilson argued that groups evolve to have certain behaviours that may not be beneficial to the individual, but which ensure greater survival and success for the overall group. Such explanations don't explain instincts and behaviours in terms of whether they are morally good or bad, but on whether they contribute to the overall fitness of a community who practises them. This kind of group-level thinking about evolution provides one way of thinking about human behaviours that don't seem to immediately benefit the individual.

Dealing with deviance

The moral and legal codes of the monotheistic traditions reveal preoccupations with all sorts of different social problems, including how to get on with neighbouring tribes, how to deal with religious dissent, how to enforce regulations relating to many details of everyday life including diet, dress, and domestic arrangements, and how to punish those who break the rules. One set of concerns that recurs frequently relates to sex, sexuality, and gender expression. Sexual desire has produced as much conflict and anxiety as it has pleasure for as long as human civilizations have existed. And many religions dictate rules and regulations to cope with this very powerful human drive. Generally speaking, sex between men and women, within marriage, to produce children, has been approved of (although St Paul thought it was better to remain completely celibate while awaiting the imminent final judgement), while virtually any other kind of sex, most notably sex with oneself, or with someone of the same sex, or with someone in one's own family, has normally been condemned.

In addition to regarding some forms of sexuality as deviant, many religious groups enforce strictly defined gender norms—including prescriptions on dress, rules regarding access to certain religious rituals or offices, even insisting upon the inequality of partners within marriage. Some religious groups draw upon scriptural language to justify equating gender identity with the sexual characteristics of one's body and insisting upon strict binaries between men and women. Other religious communities, including some forms of Hinduism and some indigenous American societies, have long-standing traditions of a 'third gender' or non-binary conception of gender that pre-date modern scientific interpretations of gender and sexual identity. This complex view of gender is not restricted to humans. The Hindu deity Arthanariswara is depicted as half-man, half-woman.

In modern societies where science and medicine have gradually taken over from traditional religious beliefs as the most acceptable sources of publicly agreed distinctions between the normal and the deviant, two parallel trends can be discerned: a de-moralization of previously moral issues, but also a concomitant medical and scientific imposition, reinforcement, and naturalization of existing social divisions and inequalities. Modern science has proved just as ideologically malleable as the Bible when it comes to arguing either for or against such divisions. As we have seen with historical debates about racism and colonialism, scientific and religious arguments have similarly been invoked to justify a range of interpretations regarding sex, gender, and identity.

The naturalistic fallacy

Science and religion have both been used in pursuit of all sorts of different political goals. Neither is inherently liberal or conservative, racist or egalitarian, repressive or permissive. Each provides a way of understanding the world which might be made consilient with almost any ideological vision. But while we are used to the idea that religious believers will look at ethical and political questions through the lenses of their particular faith commitments, we have not yet learned to be quite so attentive in the case of those who claim to speak for science. On the face of it, a scientific approach to ethics promises to be a balanced and objective one—and one which takes its lead from nature rather than from human prejudices. Does nature not speak with a clear and impartial voice?

Some philosophers, driven by the desire to develop a more scientific approach to morality, have constructed whole systems of 'evolutionary ethics'. For such thinkers, the fact that humanity's conscience and moral feelings are the product of evolution requires that ethics should be understood from an evolutionary rather than a religious or even a philosophical point of view. The problem that all such schemes encounter is that there is more to ethics than following nature. Even if it can be shown that we are endowed with a particular 'natural' instinct by our evolutionary history, that observation does not get us any closer to answering the ethical question of whether it is right to follow that instinct. Presumably the instincts that incline people towards violence, theft, and adultery have evolutionary origins too. Whichever interpretation of evolutionary biology we care to endorse, it is perfectly clear (as it has been to moral philosophers through the ages) that human beings are born with the propensity both to seek their own good and also the good of (at least some) others. The question of whether the altruistic instinct, for instance, is a natural one is completely separate from the question of whether it is one that we should follow, and to what extent. That question will be answered only by thinking about the rules and goals according to which we, individually and communally, wish to live our lives.

The natural theologians of centuries past had justification for this. They reasoned that morality was reflected in the natural word because of the benevolence of the God who created it. But without presupposing divine goodness, inferences from natural facts to moral truths no longer seem so logical. The mistake of supposing that something is ethically desirable just because it can be shown to be natural, or evolved, is sometimes referred to as the 'naturalistic fallacy'. This strange phrase is taken from the English philosopher G. E. Moore's 1903 book *Principia ethica*. Here Moore stated that any system of ethics which tried, misguidedly as he thought, to define the ethical predicate 'good' in terms of a naturalistic predicate such as 'pleasurable' or 'useful' or 'for the good of the species' was guilty of committing the 'naturalistic fallacy'.

Some religious thinkers have invoked the 'naturalistic fallacy' as a reason to resist all secular and scientific approaches to ethics. However, it should be pointed out that Moore's ban on translating the word 'good' into any non-ethical term was applied by him to metaphysical and philosophical systems of ethics too. In fact, Moore's view really amounted to complete moral mysticism. A system of ethics which identifies 'good' with 'in accordance with God's will' or 'for the greatest good of the greatest number', or anything else at all (apart from Moore's own favoured sense of goodness as an intuited quality of beauty) is equally guilty of committing the 'naturalistic fallacy'. From this point of view, religious and scientific approaches to ethics are each in an equally bad position.

Beyond nature

Recent debates about science and ethics have often proceeded as if moral goodness and altruism were synonymous. Some claim that altruism is natural and so we should follow nature. Others insist that we have evolved to be essentially selfish and so we need to struggle against nature. But both views are based on a very limited understanding of what it is to live a good life. Individualism and self-development have traditionally been valued by both secular and religious moralists. As several commentators have pointed out, when Jesus told the rich young man to sell all his possessions and give the proceeds to the poor so that he might have 'treasure in heaven', that advice was given for the good of the young man, not for the good of the poor. There are political connotations too. The ideology of altruism is one that is open to manipulation by ruling elites. The idea of living for others sounds like a noble one. But it can be used both by totalitarian governments seeking to persuade their subjects that the interests of the whole must come before their own individual rights, and also by public leaders who may exploit the good will and generosity of their supporters to serve their own aims. Again, the value of altruism is something to be decided by political and moral discussion, not by an appeal to nature.

As any practical discussion of moral values becomes inseparable from the political realities in which those values will be invoked, another sense of identity must come into the conversation in addition to the mind, soul, and brain. Our human selves are shaped by social factors that do not necessarily exist in our genes or brains, but are emergent properties of the societies that we are born into, complete with histories, cultures, and other contexts. Even though concepts like 'race' or nationality may not exist as purely biological phenomena, they exist as social factors that impact who we are just as our bodies and minds do.

Philosophers of science have also observed that these kinds of social realities impact the nature of scientific enquiry itself, and even call into question whether scientists can obtain a kind of 'objective' truth independent of cultural biases or moral values. Since the 1980s, feminist epistemology of science has raised questions about what Donna Haraway refers to as 'situated knowledge' in science: that access to knowledge about nature and the ability to make claims about knowledge are shaped not just by the natural world scientists observe but also by their relationships to other knowers, their embodiment, and social status. These concepts have not only shaped how philosophers and other scholars view the practice of science but also the relationship of its knowledge claims to other systems, including religious ones.

In the modern world, it seems as though science, technology, and medicine increasingly dominate attempts to make moral meanings. For much of the 19th and early 20th centuries, scientific visions of the future were often laced with optimism, and a belief in progress and improved human flourishing. Visions of people travelling through space, of cheap and clean energy, of cures to all major diseases, were common themes of science fiction and of speculative portrayals of the world of tomorrow. If moral crises were triggered by wars, scarcity of food and natural resources, and economic inequality, science and technology could solve those problems and open up a world where moral behaviour was made easier. But in recent decades, scientific optimism has given way to realities that sound as darkly apocalyptic as some visions from revelation.

Instead of being warned by the great religious prophets of the past that we must mend our wicked ways or face the wrath of God and cosmic cataclysms, we are now warned that our social behaviour, gluttony, and greed will spread disease, result in obesity, and lead to the flooding, burning, and destruction of our planet as a result of catastrophic levels of global warming. And the age of Covid-19 has illustrated moral questions about selfishness and altruism in concrete ways. The details have changed, and of course these projections of future disaster are based on scientific evidence, but the structure of the argument remains the same. Science and medicine now provide us with frightening visions of the future which policy-makers and political leaders use to try to persuade us, as did the prophets of old, to repent and change our ways before it is too late. Whatever our views about morality, it is hopefully clear by now that there is no straight path from either religion or science to simple ethical pronouncements. We should be sceptical of a political figure claiming they are 'following the science' just as we might be of a religious demagogue claiming they are following the will of God. There are no shortcuts in the complex and communal worlds of ethics, identity, and politics.

Chapter 6
The worlds of science and religion

In Hawaii on 17 July 2019, 38 elders went down on their knees. Along with hundreds of other protesters, they blocked a road leading up a mountain. The mountain in question was Maunakea. Its name is a contraction of 'Mauna a Wākea', meaning the birthplace of the god Wākea. The elders were the first to be arrested during protests to prevent construction of a scientific instrument known as the Thirty Meter Telescope (TMT) (Figure 11).

In the four centuries since Galileo turned his telescope skyward, the science of astronomy has expanded beyond measure. Earth- and space-based telescopes have empowered astronomers to see phenomena in increasingly detailed resolution, observe wavelengths outside the limits of human vision, and penetrate into far greater distances beyond the Earth. Because of the finite speed at which light travels, the ability to see across intergalactic distances in space corresponds to looking 'backwards in time'—making it possible for scientists to construct their own account of the beginnings of the universe, trying to describe what could have happened in the earliest moments after an initial Big Bang approximately 14 billion years ago.

At a basic level, modern telescopes function in much the same way as Galileo's: optical tools collect and focus electromagnetic waves

11. A 2014 photograph from protests against the building of the Thirty Meter Telescope in Hawaii. Advocates of the TMT have often dismissed the concerns of protesters as 'religious'.

(visible light, X-rays, microwaves, or radio waves, for example). But the images we 'see' could never be observed with unaided eyes, even if we were somehow transported to the right vantage point. These images are composites of data that have no direct visual counterpart. Telescopes are calibrated to record variations in electromagnetic signals and data is filtered and analysed according to mathematical models that factor in assumptions about how light, gravity, mass, and space all function over large distances and timescales. With each new 'discovery' made by these telescopes, debates about realism—about the existence of apparently 'unobservable' things like black holes, exoplanets, dark matter, and dark energy—are reopened and re-examined. The 2015 discovery of gravitational waves (fluctuations in space and time caused by accelerating masses) has made possible a new form of telescope—one that does not rely upon electromagnetic waves.

Also different from Galileo's time, no one person could design, build, or operate today's advanced telescopes. From casting and polishing mirrors, to writing computer code for rapid adjusting for fluctuations in the air, to manufacturing the housing to hold and aim the device, to rendering a widely published image, a 'telescope' is a complex combination of technologies. Thirty metres refers to the diameter of the telescope's primary mirror, but overall, the TMT design calls for a telescope 55 metres wide and 50 metres tall housed in a building that would be by far the largest structure on Maunakea. Modern telescopes represent a major investment of time and money. Like many large-scale observatories and laboratories, the TMT is also a product of international collaboration (including the USA, China, India, Canada, and Japan), both a product and a tool of modern diplomacy and state power as well as science.

Advocates of the TMT assert that atmospheric and weather conditions make the summit of Maunakea the best possible location for the telescope. But the mountain is also a place that figures centrally in the religious beliefs and ritual life of many native Hawaiians. As the political scientist Iokepa Casumbal-Salazar has explained, a sense of the sacred nature of Maunakea is tied into indigenous accounts of creation. Maunakea was created by the same gods who created the people themselves, making humans and mountain part of a spiritual family. Native Hawaiians have held this peak as sacred land since long before European and American colonization and conquest.

This is land where the god was born, where rituals still take place. Building the TMT, according to the protesters, threatens both that way of life and the spiritual realities that inspire them. Does that make opposition to the telescope 'religious'? As discussed previously, the category of 'religion' is often difficult to separate from other parts of 'culture', especially when looking at areas of the world where those specific and distinct concepts were imposed by colonialism. Native Hawaiian beliefs about the natural world, the gods who created it, and the ongoing relationship between people and the land are in part shaped by descriptions of spiritual realities; but they are also shaped by a long history of political disenfranchisement. In the 19th century, American government and business interests overthrew the independent kingdom of Hawaii, eventually annexing it as a territory and later as a US state. For much of the 20th century, indigenous language and culture was suppressed or denigrated, and assimilation into an English-speaking predominantly Christian lifestyle was rewarded with social advancement. Lands including Maunakea were seized and turned over to government control. By the late 20th century, the state of Hawaii had allowed construction of several telescopes atop Maunakea with little input from indigenous people.

In many ways, the protests at Maunakea resemble indigenous rights movements elsewhere in the USA and across the globe. Since the TMT site was chosen in 2009, protesters have raised concerns about the preservation of their culture and environment, and their inclusion in the political and economic life of the island. They identify the continued construction on Maunakea as assertion of state power over land that was seized from their ancestors. The spiritual or religious meaning of Maunakea to the protesters has always been part of those concerns, but never separated from these other issues. Even as TMT opponents have made use of the law to try to prevent the telescope's construction, they have largely been wary of using a concept of religion that draws a sharp line between religious rights and the cultural, environmental, economic, and political rights that they assert.

Unlike some Christian groups that have fought government seizures of land elsewhere in the United States, TMT protesters have not attempted to argue that their First Amendment constitutional rights to religious freedom are being violated.

Perhaps because the protests in Hawaii are specifically concerned with a telescope, TMT supporters and much of the media coverage beyond Hawaii have been quick to interpret these protests as merely the latest example of a science–religion conflict. Reducing the TMT issue to a story of religion protesting against science made it easier for popular media to describe the protests without acknowledging the nuance of Hawaiian colonial or environmental history or treating it as a local variation on a universal theme. Some commentators equated the concerns of indigenous Hawaiians with religious superstitions, making it possible to dismiss them as unworthy of consideration. A 2014 *New York Times* article argued that TMT protesters were, in effect, 'creationists' indistinguishable from those who held to a literal interpretation of Genesis, but were tolerated 'out of a sense of guilt over past wrongdoings'. This same article even compared the Hawaiian protesters blocking the TMT to the role the Roman Catholic Church played in blocking the dissemination of Galileo's writings. In this conflict narrative, astronomy is always oppressed by religion. A 2015 *Atlantic Magazine* article, however, pointed out that the TMT controversy was more than 'a clash between religion and science'. 'The battle for Mauna Kea', the article argued, 'is ultimately a debate about what is truly sacred, what it means to be human, and who gets to decide.'

In the first chapter, we discussed how it was only through a deliberate and specific process that 'science' and 'religion' became understood as separate categories of knowledge, without which the question of conflict or harmony cannot even make sense. For much of the world outside Europe, that binary way of thinking about science and religion was part of a colonial legacy. In the case of the TMT, it's difficult to distinguish religious elements from other concerns about cultural disregard, political exclusion, environmental degradation, and economic dispossession. A story that imagines marginalized indigenous Hawaiians are the modern equivalents of the 17th-century church, and that a consortium of scientists and universities supported by several of the world's superpowers plays the role of the bullied Galileo, seems preposterous. Nonetheless, the TMT controversy, like the Galileo affair with which we started, shows how debates that seem to be between 'science' and 'religion' tend to conceal struggles for power and control that go beyond those labels.

Like the idea of an inherent science–religion conflict itself, the distorted legacy of Galileo lives on as a convenient mythology in the 21st century. But in the context of Maunakea, these myths are not helping answer questions about the intellectual compatibility of ideas. Instead they are shaping perceptions regarding whose ideas matter at all. Supporters of the TMT can use the framework of science versus religion to argue that opposition to the telescope is 'anti-science' and that concerns about cultural erasure, land seizure, and civil rights are merely 'religious' beliefs that can be dismissed as supernatural. Especially in societies impacted by colonialism and conquest, we see the concepts of science and religion working together like this to establish credibility and authority for certain kinds of knowledge and supplant others.

Medical missions

Perhaps the most visible examples of scientific and religious authority working together in a colonial effort to displace local forms of knowledge is the practice of medicine and knowledge about health. In the 19th century, European nations established hegemony over much of Africa, Asia, and Oceania. In most of these regions, it was not colonial governments but religious societies who assumed the (in their view charitable) task of providing medical care to local populations. For many European Christian organizations, the provision of medical care was often a way to establish credibility and goodwill that could eventually be turned to proselytizing (Figure 12).

As Megan Vaughn has detailed in her history of colonial medicine in Africa, the boundary between secular and religious medicine was often blurry—as Europeans working in medical missions applied knowledge that had itself been developed with particular notions about health, pain, and well-being that were shaped by their own religious world-view. Medical missionaries often combined spiritual messages and prayer with more 'scientific' remedies and frequently interpreted the diseases and conditions they encountered abroad as embodiments of the moral conditions they perceived in the local population. In Africa, European missionaries believed that what they perceived as widespread disease was a consequence of people's non-Christian behaviours. By this they didn't necessarily mean that diseases were a form of divine punishment, but rather that the moral and scientific understanding of the world that (to them) embodied enlightened

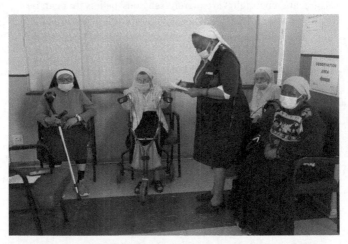

12. A Catholic nun working at a health care facility administering Covid-19 vaccinations in Pretoria, South Africa in 2021.

Christianity naturally resulted in better, healthier outcomes. In some cases, this mindset was an extension of natural theological thinking—particularly the notion that correct understanding of God's book of nature provides moral and political guidance that ensures well-being. Just as William Paley diagnosed the human suffering caused by the French Revolution as the moral and political consequences of its rejection of divine order, European medical missionaries sometimes referred to Africa as a 'sick' continent for which the cure was spiritual as well as medical. A small number of medical missionaries, such as Scottish physician and explorer David Livingstone, at least acknowledged the role that centuries of slavery and exploitation had played in creating the 'sickness' of Africa, but from this they inferred that their missionary work was not only an opportunity to save lives and souls. It also represented an act of expiation for the sins of slavery perpetrated by their ancestors.

The experience of Africa as a 'sick' continent by European Christians also illustrates the dynamics of scientific and religious knowledge in colonialism. Missionaries who documented their experiences treating patients inferred that diseases abroad were more prevalent and more dangerous than those in Europe. But if there's credibility to this claim, those conditions can at least partially be ascribed to the spread of diseases from Europe into Africa. In nearly all places where new forms of human colonial contact took place, diseases spread between populations, often to populations with little natural resistance to unfamiliar germs. Infamously, smallpox and other diseases, sometimes deliberately spread by European colonizers, devastated the native peoples of the Americas. European diseases also decimated the island-insulated Hawaiians, weakening their government and economy just as American business interests plotted their coup.

In the case of Africa, not only did colonialism bring new diseases, outbreaks were exacerbated by colonial governments disrupting established local health practices. A few physicians, like Livingstone, attempted to make sense of medical practices he witnessed in Central Africa and understand why they seemed to work. Most, however dismissed out of hand local knowledge that had developed over centuries, especially when healers proffered cures that seemed to rely on supernatural causes. Colonial laws prevented a host of religious healers from practising, and people often had no alternative to missionary medicine, even when it was less effective. The tendency of colonial leaders to view indigenous health practices through the perspective of (good) science and (bad, non-Christian) religion hindered health efforts. In British colonial Kenya, for example, laws against 'witchcraft' made no clear distinctions between a variety of healers and others who performed supernatural works. Colonial categories did not match the way local people understood their own knowledge.

Missionary medical care was frequently supported by church organizations, not as a direct function of the official government. Consequently, religious health organizations sometimes remained in place after colonized regions of Asia and Africa became independent nation-states. In Ghana, the first sub-Saharan African nation to achieve independence, state authorities work with Christian hospitals to advance 'scientific' medicine and to dislodge people's reliance on 'traditional' forms of health practice. Anthropologist Damien Droney has observed that scientific herbal medicine combines modern technology and chemical and biological laboratory analysis with long-used plant-based remedies. This practice establishes scientific credentials that ensure state approval and convince people to use herbal medicine instead of 'magical' alternatives. Part of establishing that this medicine is 'scientific' involves defining scientific herbal medicine as entirely different from the 'religious' identity of 'traditional' medical practices. Droney observes, however, that because of Ghana's history of missionary medicine and education, the concept of 'science' is deeply associated with Christian identity

and Ghanaian herbal medicine relies upon church-affiliated
hospitals to endorse its claims to be scientific.

Science, religion, and medical knowledge

It is not only the postcolonial world where blurred boundaries
between scientific and religious authority affect health and
medicine. In 1998, *The Lancet*, one of Britain's most prestigious
medical journals, published a study by Andrew Wakefield
claiming that the measles, mumps, and rubella (MMR) vaccine
caused autism in children. Although the study was eventually
determined to be fraudulent and the article was retracted in 2010,
the immediate response to Wakefield's study was a decline in
vaccination rates in the UK, USA, and elsewhere, followed by
outbreaks of once-rare preventable diseases. Although Wakefield's
study does not at first seem to invoke any religious views
regarding the human body or the efficacy of vaccines, the panic it
created found fertile ground in a legal and cultural environment
that had been shaped by religious anti-vaccination movements
that developed in Europe and North America over centuries.

Vaccinations and inoculations are medical procedures in which a
strain of a disease vector (a virus or bacteria, in some cases
weakened or killed) is deliberately introduced into a person's
body. Typically, this allows the body to develop immunity and
reduce the likelihood of becoming sick. Christians in both Europe
and North America learned of this practice in the 1700s. In Boston,
Massachusetts, the theologian and clergyman Cotton Mather was
told about the procedure by Onesimus, an enslaved man brought
from West Africa and sold to Mather in 1706. Mather's advocacy
of smallpox inoculation was strongly condemned by other clergy
in Massachusetts colony, some of whom decried it as going against
the will of God. Some of the opposition to Mather also probably
stemmed from resentment of his role as the instigator of a series
of witch trials in Salem in 1692. Over 200 women and men were

tried, and sometimes convicted of gaining supernatural powers from the Devil and using them to harm others. Twenty people were executed, and others died in prison.

News of inoculation first reached Christian parts of Europe in 1717, in letters from Lady Mary Wortley Montagu, wife of the British Ambassador to Constantinople, who witnessed the practice performed by women in the Muslim Ottoman Empire. On both continents, Christian audiences were deeply sceptical of knowledge that came from non-Christian lands, and in both England and the USA the first inoculation trials were primarily attempted upon people who could not consent: condemned prisoners and enslaved Africans, respectively. Attitudes changed after a smallpox outbreak in 1721 devastated Boston, but nearly all of those who had been inoculated survived. One should not imagine that even those who came to accept inoculation in this era understood it as a purely natural phenomenon, nor that it replaced prayer or other healing remedies rather than added to them. It was several years after these trials, after all, that many believed a miracle of St Agatha had saved Catania from the plague.

As these procedures gained credibility, eventually some people went from tolerating vaccinations to requiring them. The US Supreme Court ruled in 1904 that states had the authority to mandate vaccinations, prompting many US states to pass laws creating exemptions on religious grounds. By the late 20th century, these exemptions were little used; however, following the Wakefield fraud, the number of people invoking a religious exemption to vaccination rose dramatically. This does not seem to be because of any major changes in religious attitudes towards vaccines; most major religions not only tolerate but encourage vaccination as part of a moral obligation to preserve life. The rise of religious exemptions speaks instead to a tendency to use legal protections for religious belief as a tool.

Similar circumstances arose in 2020 as the Covid-19 pandemic spread across the globe. Caused by the coronavirus named SARS-CoV-2, the pandemic prompted a range of major public health measures by nearly every nation on Earth. Misinformation about the disease, its effects, and treatments spread almost as rapidly as the virus itself, which affected both how various nations managed the crisis, and how well their population accepted or resisted measures mandated or advised by scientists (Figure 13). In the United States in particular, requirements to close public

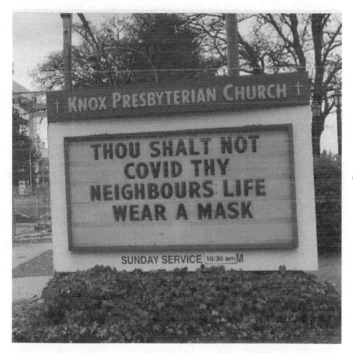

13. A sign outside Knox Presbyterian Church in New Westminster, British Columbia encouraging mask wearing during the Covid-19 pandemic in 2020. The sign is a play on the biblical phrase 'Thou shalt not covet'.

venues, including churches, were met with resistance. In May 2020, as cases of Covid-19 continued to increase, several churches in Illinois wrote an open letter threatening to defy the governor's decree prohibiting in-person church gatherings. Some followed through on this threat and were fined. Several other religious groups which defied orders to restrict in-person prayer saw major outbreaks among their communities.

Although some critics claimed that this was yet another example of religious groups refusing to acknowledge scientific fact, most of the churches were less hostile to medical science and more opposed to the government's role in restricting religious practice. In their letter to the governor, the Illinois churches outlined a series of precautions they would take to prevent viral transmission among their members, including the use of sanitizers and social distancing. These congregations were both aware of and accommodating scientific ideas, but they were also asserting the priority of religious freedom over state-mandated health practices.

This is not to say that there were no moments when scientific and religious ideas came into actual conflict during the Covid-19 pandemic. Congregations of Orthodox Christians around the world debated the practice of using a common spoon to partake in communion, with some theologians insisting that because the bread and wine are transubstantiated into the blood and body of Christ, there could be no transmission of the coronavirus through communion. (A similar debate regarding the practice of taking communion from a shared cup took place among some American churches in the early 20th century, as the germ theory of disease became better known. In that case, some denominations split into separate churches over the issue.) More common than these moments of science–religion disagreement, however, were stories of religious communities making use of science and technology to adapt to the pandemic. At Easter, Pope Francis addressed an empty St Peter's Square, and yet his message probably reached a larger audience than any previous one because it was available online. Despite long-standing practices among some Jews not to use electricity on major holidays, several rabbis lifted this prohibition to discourage in-person gatherings and permit virtual Passover Seders and other events to be shared online. And in many parts of the world, religious institutions funded and provided frontline medical services. Many religious organizations also played a key role in ensuring that accurate scientific information reached their communities, helping to limit the spread and deadliness of this plague.

Science 'denial'

In the 21st century, false claims about vaccine safety or misinformation about the treatment and prevention of Covid-19 are among the more dangerous examples of what is often called science 'denial'. This term refers to an organized effort to undermine confidence in well-established scientific knowledge claims, either through casting doubt on scientific evidence or the impartiality of scientists, or by creating seemingly scientific (or pseudoscientific) alternatives to explain the observed world. Anti-evolutionism—particularly versions that promote creation science or intelligent design as 'scientific' alternatives to Darwinian natural selection—is often cited as one of the most widespread and persistent examples of science denial. The idea of the science–religion conflict thesis emerged at a time in the late 19th century when several new religious movements—Jehovah's Witnesses, Christian Scientists, Adventists—all offered as part of their messages claims about science and health that were contrary to prevailing scientific beliefs; and some of the most prominent forms of science denial—such as anti-evolutionism or spiritualism—seemed to be motivated by supernatural ideas or by the perceived threat that scientific ideas presented to religious power and authority.

But increasingly, the motivations for science denial are secular, not religious. Inquiries into the *Lancet* article fraud showed that

Wakefield had hoped to profit from lawsuits against vaccine makers. As historian Robert Proctor has shown, tobacco companies spent years funding studies attempting to refute scientific evidence of a link between smoking and cancer. And protests against scientific recommendations regarding the prevention and treatment of Covid-19 were often fomented along lines of secular political ideology rather than religious belief. Nonetheless, by emphasizing the religiosity of science denial, science advocates portray their opponents as dogmatic and corrupt and themselves as objective and oppressed. Astronomers using a science–religion narrative to dismiss concerns about the TMT on Maunakea is perhaps the most egregious instance of this, considering the balance of political and economic power. As seen in cases regarding quarantine or vaccine refusal, some science deniers embrace a religious identity because by doing so they are able to argue that their views and actions are protected by rights to religious freedom. We began this book by asking: What are science–religion debates really about? Today, they are still less about a substantive debate between particular scientific and religious ideas and more about how the binary thinking they symbolize expresses power and cultural authority.

How it ends

Most of the substantive science and religion issues addressed so far in this book deal with questions of origins (how and when did the Earth and its human inhabitants begin?), morality (how should we act and how can we know whether our ethical beliefs are correct?), or purpose (why are we here and is there anything beyond the natural world itself?). Yet many major religions also address questions of eschatology—how the world ends and what happens to humanity when it does. Almost every religion has traditions or texts that provide predictions and accounts of how things will end, and how humanity's current state of being will culminate. In some Hindu interpretations, a tenth and final incarnation of the god Vishnu will come to the Earth in about

400,000 years, bringing about an end to the current age and leading to a new cycle of birth and growth of the universe. Most Christian traditions believe in a second coming of Jesus, with some interpreting the Book of Revelation to posit times of conflict followed by a final judgement.

Over the past two centuries, scientists have also developed theories about the end of the Earth and the universe. The Sun is a star like many others, and astronomers have detected and described the fate of many similar to our own. Several billion years from now, the Sun will have depleted much of its hydrogen and will expand into a red giant before collapsing into a white dwarf star. Scientists who have studied mass extinctions such as that which killed off the dinosaurs (thought to be the result of an asteroid striking the Earth) consider the possibility of similar catastrophes happening to humanity. In recent years, cosmologists have determined that the expansion of the universe, observed as the movement of galaxies away from one another since the Big Bang, is accelerating. This suggests that one probable outcome for the universe is an ultimate 'heat death' when all mass and energy (or heat) is so thinly spread across the cosmos that no further interactions are possible. There are other potential models for the fate of the cosmological universe many billions of years from now, including the possibility of a 'Big Crunch', a reversal of the expansion that followed the Big Bang. Observations from new, more powerful tools like the TMT may help determine what outcome is most likely.

On questions regarding the end of the world, science and religion may present intellectually incompatible ideas but rarely have been the crux of social conflict. For a long time, scientific eschatology focused on natural processes far beyond the possibility of human intervention. This started to change in the 19th century. One phenomenon that had challenged natural theologians was extinction. For what possible purpose would God create species that would die out, especially in eras long before humanity was present? The question became more complicated as naturalists realized that some species, like the dodo (which had last been observed almost 200 years earlier), had gone extinct due to human activity. Colonists who came to Mauritius in the 17th century cut down much of the dodos' forest habitat and introduced other animals, such as pigs and monkeys, that attacked dodo nests. The religious implications of human-caused extinction were complicated. If each species was distinctly created by God, was permanently destroying a species undoing divine will? Was it inconsistent with the interpretations of the biblical creation story in which God instructed Adam and Eve to have 'dominion' over every living thing on Earth? By the late 19th century, intentional extinction was used as a tool of colonial conquest. US efforts to exterminate the population of American bison were intended to deprive Native Americans of a major food source, legally expropriate their lands (which had been defined in some treaties with reference to their hunting range), and undermine their culture. Lakota consider bison to be sacred animals. By the late 19th century, fewer than 1,000 bison were left alive.

By the 20th century, the reality of long-term and potentially permanent human impacts on the environment were undeniable. In 1962, environmental scientist Rachel Carson published the book *Silent Spring*, whose title evoked the spectre of a world made quiet due to the extinction of wildlife. Carson identified chemical poisoning in the environment as a threat to many species, particularly the agricultural insecticide dichlorodiphenyltrichloroethane (DDT). It had been a century since Darwin had shown how species evolved to fit well with their environment. What happens when that environment drastically changes?

Carson's work inspired a great rise in environmental activism, in the USA and elsewhere. Though *Silent Spring* focuses on the impact of chemicals, it begins by discussing recently discovered effects of radioactive fallout on human beings, another secular apocalyptic threat looming in the midst of the Cold War. However, even before *Silent Spring* reached bookshelves, a concerted effort to cast the book as false had been orchestrated by the American chemical industry that produced DDT and other environmental pollutants. They funded and publicized studies claiming to refute Carson's claim that chemicals lingering in the environment accumulated in animal bodies and disrupted their ability to survive and reproduce. This response was one of the first concerted corporate efforts at science denial. The controversy was mostly secular, but insinuations that Carson was a Communist sympathizer were used to imply that she was an atheist and therefore her morality and loyalty were suspect. Even as US sales of DDT eventually stopped, the chemical industry found profits in much of the tropical postcolonial world, where insecticides were presented as the scientific solution to the scourge of malaria and other insect-transmitted diseases.

The environmental movement that emerged in the 1960s brought together fears of a secular apocalypse caused by new developments in science and technology and long-standing traditions of religious conservationism that had antecedents in natural theology. Historian Mark Stoll traces this history, observing that at various eras in US history, efforts to set aside land as parks and nature reserves were often led by religious individuals for whom nature was a pathway into understanding and appreciating divine creation.

Exemplifying this is the thought of Holmes Rolston III, an American philosopher and theologian whose work helped create academic interest in 'environmental ethics'. Raised in a family of Presbyterian ministers and deeply inspired by natural theology, Rolston attempted to articulate an ethical mandate for environmental stewardship that was not justified by appealing to its direct benefit to humans. Instead, Rolston argued that people, the environment, and non-human nature all have intrinsic value; therefore humanity has obligations to act responsibly and in a caring way for the natural world. In his 1997 Gifford Lectures, Rolston took issue with the evolutionary account of altruism epitomized by Wilson's sociobiology and argued that ethical values—how one goes from describing what behaviour is to what it ought to be—cannot be determined by biology alone. By combining a theological basis for ethics with Wilson's evolutionary insights into the viability of altruism as a moral strategy, Rolston promotes an environmental ethics that not only includes altruism between humans, but also between people and the rest of creation.

According to Rolston, 'Environmental ethics, in this sense, is the most altruistic, global, generous, comprehensive ethic of all, demanding the most expansive capacity to see others, and this now especially distinguishes humans. This is not naturalized ethics in the reductionist sense; it is naturalized ethics in the comprehensive sense, humans acting out of moral conviction for the benefit of nonhuman others.' Rolston and similar thinkers paved the way for some Christian groups that had previously ignored environmental issues, contributing to the rise of lines of thinking sometimes called ecotheology. His work in this field was recognized with the Templeton Prize in 2003.

That Rolston's work was seen as transformative is a result of his efforts to frame such ideas within a new religious and political context, but it also speaks to an intellectual colonialism that took ideas found in other cultural practices and repackaged them as new, whether it's the technique of inoculations or the proposition that people have an ethical duty to the natural world. In this way, the academic field of science and religion uses its proprietary terminology to make new discoveries.

In recent decades, scientists have become increasingly unified in expressing concern about climate change and amassed substantial evidence that human activity—particularly energy consumption associated with increased use of technology—has played a key role in this process. Gases released through fossil fuel burning accumulate in the atmosphere, resulting in more of the Sun's heat trapped on the planet's surface. This can cause prevailing winds and ocean currents to shift, sea ice and frozen land to thaw, and results in both an overall trend of warming and a greater tendency towards more extreme weather events. The planetary climate is a complex, chaotic system, not a reductionistic one, and its patterns are only seen as an emergence from more localized causes and effects. The natural laws that describe it may allow for probabilistic descriptions, but not deterministic accounts of cause and effect.

The complexity of climate science helps explain why climate change denial has been so effective in its message. For decades efforts to take coordinated action to mitigate climate change have been affected by deliberate science denial. There are clear economic and political incentives for this; energy, fuels, and energy technologies play an unparalleled role in global politics. Historians Naomi Oreskes and Eric Conway have found evidence that petrochemical companies deliberately concealed or attempted to cast doubt upon much of the scientific evidence of human-caused climate change, in many cases looking to the history of anti-evolution for strategic inspiration. While most forms of climate change denial do not explicitly invoke religion or theology, some of the rhetoric invoked echoes of themes introduced in earlier debates over extinction. If this is the world that God has made, can any human force be so great as to undo it?

With the harmful effects of climate change becoming more visible to a larger population, it will increasingly loom as the great challenge that science and religion will need to speak to in the decades to come. Although much of the well-funded sophisticated efforts to spread climate change denial are secular in both origin and rhetoric, it's not unusual to hear claims that human impacts cannot possibly undo the whole of creation, or that the effects of climate change are part of a period of tribulation that precedes divine redemption. But growing louder are religious voices who speak to an ethical responsibility to care for creation. The effects of climate change and other forms of environmental damage often weigh most heavily on the postcolonial world and on impoverished and marginalized people in every country. Yet it is the countries that historically have been colonial powers that have been responsible for consuming the majority of the fossil fuels and producing industrial pollutants that have led to environmental degradation. Finding a just reconciliation of this history requires more than simply a technological solution. As the climate crisis contributes to lands lost to sea rise, droughts, and extreme storms, this is likely to result in people migrating from ancestral lands, and, as Malthus hypothesized, conflict over scarce resources.

It is important to recognize the influence of thinkers like Rolston while also acknowledging that an ethical mandate for environmental care and belief in common kinship between humanity and non-human elements of nature is a long-standing feature of other religions and cultures. It is present in Hindu and Buddhist beliefs that souls reincarnate, and that a human soul may be reborn to a new life as a different species. It is present in the belief of Native Hawaiians that they were created as part of the same family as the mountain Maunakea.

Answering questions about what steps represent a path forward will rely on finding a synthesis of scientific and technological possibilities with insights into justice and ethics that religion can provide. Looking to the future, there is every reason to believe that ideas about science and religion will continue to shape those discussions. It is to be hoped that with greater awareness of what science and religion are, what their historical relationship has been, and who has controlled the dialogue between them, more fruitful interactions will follow.

References

Abbreviations for websites cited more than once:

CCEL   Christian Classics Ethereal Library: <http://www.ccel.org/>

CWCD   The Complete Works of Charles Darwin Online: <http:// darwin-online.org.uk/>

FT   Famous Trials website: <https://famous-trials.com/>

PG   Project Gutenberg: <http://www.gutenberg.org/>

TP   Thomas Paine National Historical Association: <http:// www.thomaspaine.org/>

This list gives references for material directly quoted in the text. The
Further reading section gives suggested background reading and
additional sources.
Where reputable online editions of works are available, these have
been cited in addition to the original published source. Different
English translations of biblical passages can be compared online at
The Bible Gateway: <http://www.biblegateway.com/>

Chapter 1: What are science–religion debates really about?

Galileo's condemnation: Mario Biagioli, *Galileo, Courtier: The Practice
of Science in the Culture of Absolutism* (Chicago, 1994), quotation
at pp. 330–1. Documents relating to Galileo's trial and
condemnation can be found online at FT. Psalm 102:25. Thomas
Huxley's review of *The Origin of Species* was originally published in

1860 in the *Westminster Review* and was reprinted in Volume 2 of his *Collected Essays* (9 volumes, London, 1893–4), pp. 22–79, quotation at p. 52; available online at The Huxley File at Clark University: <http://aleph0.clarku.edu/huxley/>. John Hedley Brooke, *Science and Religion: Some Historical Perspectives* (Cambridge, 1991), quotation at p. 5.

Quotation from Galileo Galilei, *Dialogue Concerning the Two Chief World Systems* (1632), in William Shea, 'Galileo's Copernicanism: The Science and the Rhetoric', in *The Cambridge Companion to Galileo*, ed. Peter Machamer (Cambridge, 1998), pp. 211–43, quotation at p. 238. Psalm 19:1. Thomas Paine, *The Age of Reason, Part I* (1794), in *Thomas Paine: Political Writings*, ed. Bruce Kuklick (Cambridge, 1989), quotations from chapters 7, 11, and 16; available online at TP.

Chapter 2: Galileo and the philosophy of science

Documents relating to Galileo's trial and condemnation can be found at FT. Francis Bacon, *The New Organon, or True Directions Concerning the Interpretation of Nature* (1620), Aphorism III; *Valerius Terminus: Of the Interpretation of Nature* (1603), chapter 1. Both these works are available in modern editions, and also online at the University of Adelaide: <http://etext.library.adelaide.edu.au/>. Thomas Paine, *The Age of Reason, Part I* (1794), in *Thomas Paine: Political Writings*, ed. Bruce Kuklick (Cambridge, 1989), chapter 2; available online at TP. Joshua 10:12–14. Council of Trent declaration: Richard Blackwell, 'Could There Be Another Galileo Case?', in *The Cambridge Companion to Galileo*, ed. Peter Machamer (Cambridge, 1998), pp. 348–66, quotation at p. 353. Romans 1:20.

Chapter 3: God and nature

Milk miracle: 'Right-Wing Hindus Milk India's "Miracle"', *The Independent* (London), 25 September 1995, p. 11. Olive oil: 'A Virgin Mary Statue has been "Weeping" Olive Oil. Church Leaders Can't Explain it', *The Washington Post*, 18 July 2018. Friedrich Schleiermacher, *On Religion: Speeches to its Cultured Despisers*, ed. Richard Crouter (Cambridge, 1996), Second Speech, quotation at p. 49; first published in German in 1799; available online at CCEL. Henry Drummond, *The Lowell Lectures on the Ascent of*

Man (1894), chapter 10; available online at CCEL. G. W. Leibniz, 'Mr Leibnitz's First Paper', in Samuel Clarke, *A Collection of Papers, Which passed between the late Learned Mr. Leibnitz, and Dr. Clarke, In the Years 1715 and 1716* (1717); available online at The Newton Project at Sussex University: <http://www.newtonproject. sussex.ac.uk/>. Laplace and Napoleon: Roger Hahn, 'Laplace and the Mechanistic Universe', in *God and Nature: Historical Essays on the Encounter between Christianity and Science*, ed. David C. Lindberg and Ronald L. Numbers (Berkeley, 1986), pp. 256–76, quotation at p. 256. Descartes to Mersenne: quoted in Carolyn Merchant, *The Death of Nature: Women, Ecology, and the Scientific Revolution* (San Francisco, 1983), p. 205. Nancy Cartwright uses the phrase 'dappled world' to echo Gerard Manley Hopkins's poem 'Pied Beauty', which starts with the line 'Glory be to God for dappled things'; Nancy Cartwright, *The Dappled World: A Study of the Boundaries of Science* (Cambridge, 1999), Part I, quotation from Hopkins at p. 19. Einstein made comments about God not playing dice on several occasions, including in a letter to the physicist Max Born in 1926; Abraham Pais, *Subtle is the Lord: The Science and the Life of Albert Einstein*, new edition (Oxford, 2005), chapter 25. Pius XII, 'The Proofs for the Existence of God in the Light of Modern Natural Science', address delivered 22 November 1951, published in English as 'Theology and Modern Science', *The Tablet* (1 December 1951), p. 392. Francis Bacon, *The Advancement of Learning*, Book II (1605). Steven Shapin and Simon Shaffer, *Leviathan and the Air Pump: Hobbes, Boyle, and the Experimental Life* (Princeton, 1985). J. Topham, 'Science and Popular Education in the 1830s: The Role of the Bridgewater Treatises', *The British Journal for the History of Science*, vol. 25, issue 4 (1992), pp. 397–430 doi:10.1017/S0007087400029587. David Hume, *Dialogues Concerning Natural Religion* (1779), Part II; available in several modern editions, and online at PG. Thomas Malthus, *An Essay on the Principle of Population* (London, 1798), chapter 18; available on PG.

Chapter 4: Darwin and evolution

Charles Lyell used the phrase 'go the whole orang' in a letter to Darwin in March 1863. Frederick Burkhardt and Sydney Smith (eds), *The Correspondence of Charles Darwin, Volume 11: 1863* (Cambridge, 1985), pp. 230–3; this letter is available online at The Darwin

Correspondence Project: <http://www.darwinproject.ac.uk/>. Quotations from Darwin's *Beagle* notebooks: Adrian Desmond and James Moore, *Darwin* (London, 1991), pp. 122, 176. Darwin's comments on the 'damnable doctrine' of damnation, and on preferring the label 'agnostic', are made in the section of his autobiography concerning religious belief, *The Autobiography of Charles Darwin*, ed. Nora Barlow (London, 1958), pp. 85–96, quotations at pp. 87, 94; available online at CWCD. *The Origin of Species by Means of Natural Selection* (1859) is available in many modern editions, and online at CWCD, where changes between editions can also be compared, such as the insertion of 'by the Creator' at the end of the 1860 second edition, at p. 490. On Darwin's attitudes towards Paley, *The Autobiography of Charles Darwin*, p. 87. Charles Kingsley, *The Water Babies* (1863), chapter 7, p. 315; available online at PG. Samuel Wilberforce's review of *The Origin of Species* in the *Quarterly Review* 108 (1860), pp. 225–64, quotations at pp. 231, 259–60; available online at CWCD. Huxley's and others' recollections of the 1860 Oxford debate are discussed in Frank James, 'An "Open Clash between Science and the Church"? Wilberforce, Huxley and Hooker on Darwin at the British Association, Oxford, 1860', in *Science and Beliefs: From Natural Philosophy to Natural Science, 1700–1900*, ed. D. Knight and M. Eddy (Aldershot, 2005), pp. 171–93, quotation from Huxley at p. 185. See also Leonard Huxley, *The Life and Letters of Thomas Henry Huxley*, 2 vols (London, 1900); selections available online through the '20th Century Commentary' section of HF. Tennessee's 1925 anti-evolution statute is quoted in Edward J. Larson, *Summer for the Gods: The Scopes Trial and America's Continuing Debate over Science and Religion* (Cambridge, Mass., 1997), p. 50. The text of the statute is available online at FT. Bryan's comments on 'the little circle entitled "Mammals"' come from the speech he intended to deliver to the jury as the closing argument for the prosecution in the Scopes trial. Darrow's decision to submit the case to the jury without argument prevented Bryan from delivering the speech, which is included as an appendix to William Jennings Bryan and Mary Baird Bryan, *The Memoirs of William Jennings Bryan* (Philadelphia, 1925), quotation at p. 535. Genesis 1:26. Extracts from the transcript of the Scopes trial, including the cross-examination of Bryan by Darrow, are available online at FT. Text of Arkansas 'Balanced Treatment' law quoted in the court ruling *McLean v. Arkansas*

Board of Education (1982) included as an appendix to Langdon
Gilkey, *Creationism on Trial: Evolution and God at Little Rock*
(Charlottesville, Va., 1998), quotation at p. 295. The full text of
Judge John E. Jones III's ruling in the Dover case in 2005 is
available on the NCSE website: <https://ncse.ngo/files/pub/legal/
kitzmiller/highlights/2005-12-20>_Kitzmiller_decision.pdf>.
Peter Gottschalk, *Religion, Science, and Empire: Classifying
Hinduism and Islam in British India* (Oxford 2013), quotation
on p. 44. On Havasupai: Robyn L. Sterling, 'Genetic Research
Among the Havasupai: A Cautionary Tale', *American Medical
Association Journal of Ethics* (February 2011), pp. 113–17. Kim
TallBear, 'Tell Me a Story: Genomics vs. Indigenous Origin
Narratives', *GeneWatch* (August–October 2013).

Chapter 5: Mind, brain, and morality

Mario Beauregard and Vincent Paquette, 'Neural Correlates of a
Mystical Experience in Carmelite Nuns', *Neuroscience Letters*,
vol. 405, issue 3 (25 September 2006), pp. 186–90; reported in *The
Daily Telegraph* (London), 30 August 2006, p. 12, as 'Nuns Prove
God Is Not Figment of the Mind'; available online via <http://
www.telegraph.co.uk/>. 'Let us eat and drink for tomorrow we die'
is a biblical phrase: 1 Corinthians 15:32; see also Ecclesiastes 8:15,
Isaiah 22:13, Luke 12:19–20. Francis Collins on altruism: *The
Language of God: A Scientist Presents Evidence for Belief* (New
York, 2006), pp. 21–31. Biology, politics, and race: Dorothy
Roberts, *Fatal Invention: How Science, Politics, and Big Business
Re-create Race in the 21st Century* (New York, 2011). On situated
knowledge: Donna Haraway, 'Situated Knowledges: The Science
Question in Feminism and the Privilege of Partial Perspective',
Feminist Studies, vol. 14, no. 3 (Autumn 1988), pp. 575–99.

Chapter 6: The worlds of science and religion

On TMT and protests: Iokepa Casumbal-Salazar, 'A Fictive Kinship:
Making "Modernity," "Ancient Hawaiians," and the Telescopes on
Mauna Kea', *Native American and Indigenous Studies* (2017).
Korey Haynes, 'Protests Resume in Hawaii with Start of Thirty
Meter Telescope Construction', *Discover*, 16 July 2019; available
online via <http://www.discovermagazine.com>. George Johnson,
'Seeking Stars, Finding Creationism', *The New York Times*, 20

October 2014; available online via <http://www.nytimes.com>. Adrienne LaFrance, 'The Thirty Meter Telescope and the Fight for Hawaii's Future', *The Atlantic*, 30 October 2015; available online via <http://www.theatlantic.com>. On colonial medicine: Megan Vaughn, *Curing Their Ills: Colonial Power and African Illness* (Cambridge, 1991). C. Clifton Roberts, 'Witchcraft and Colonial Legislation', *Africa: Journal of the International African Institute* (October 1935). Damien Droney, *Weedy Science: Projects of Herbal Medicine in Postcolonial Ghana* (forthcoming). Jennifer Lee Carrell, *The Speckled Monster: A Historical Tale of Battling Smallpox* (New York, 2003). Adam Shapiro, 'Are Pandemic Protests the Newest Form of Science-Religion Conflict?', *Religion & Politics*, 14 July 2020; available online via <http://www.religionandpolitics.org>. Robert N. Proctor, *Cancer Wars: How Politics Shapes What We Know and Don't Know about Cancer* (New York, 1995). Mark V. Barrow, *Nature's Ghosts: Confronting Extinction from the Age of Jefferson to the Age of Ecology* (Chicago, 2009). Rachel Carson, *Silent Spring* (New York, 1962). Mark R. Stoll, *Inherit the Holy Mountain: Religion and the Ride of American Environmentalism* (Oxford, 2015). Holmes Rolston III, *Genes, Genesis and God: Values and their Origins in Natural and Human History* (Cambridge, 1999); quotation on page 288. Naomi Oreskes and Erik M. Conway, *Merchants of Doubt: How a Handful of Scientists Obscured the Truth on Issues from Tobacco Smoke to Global Warming* (New York, 2010).

Further reading

General

Reference works

Philip Clayton and Zachary Simpson (eds), *The Oxford Handbook of Religion and Science* (Oxford and New York, 2006).

Gary B. Ferngren (ed.), *The History of Science and Religion in the Western Tradition: An Encyclopedia* (New York and London, 2000).

J. Wentzel van Huyssteen (ed.), *Encyclopedia of Science and Religion*, 2 vols (New York, 2003).

Historical studies

John Hedley Brooke, *Science and Religion: Some Historical Perspectives* (Cambridge, 1991).

John Brooke and Geoffrey Cantor, *Reconstructing Nature: The Engagement of Science and Religion* (Edinburgh, 1998).

Peter Harrison, *The Territories of Science and Religion* (Chicago, 2015).

David Knight and Matthew Eddy (eds), *Science and Beliefs: From Natural Philosophy to Natural Science* (Aldershot, 2005).

Bernard Lightman (ed.), *Rethinking History, Science, and Religion: An Exploration of Conflict and the Complexity Principle* (Pittsburgh, 2019).

David C. Lindberg and Ronald L. Numbers (eds), *God and Nature: Historical Essays on the Encounter between Christianity and Science* (Berkeley, 1986), and *When Science and Christianity Meet* (Chicago and London, 2003).

Overviews from Christian perspectives

Ian Barbour, *Religion and Science: Historical and Contemporary Issues* (San Francisco, 1997).

Alister E. McGrath, *Science and Religion: An Introduction* (Oxford, 1998).

Arthur Peacocke, *Creation and the World of Science: The Reshaping of Belief*, revised edition (Oxford and New York, 2004).

John Polkinghorne, *Theology and Science: An Introduction* (London, 1998).

Islamic science

Taner Edis, *An Illusion of Harmony: Science and Religion in Islam* (Amherst, NY, 2007).

Muzaffar Iqbal, *Islam and Science* (Aldershot, 2002), and *Science and Islam* (Westport, Conn., 2007).

Seyyed Hossein Nasr, *Science and Civilisation in Islam*, 2nd edition (Cambridge, 1987).

George Saliba, *Islamic Science and the Making of the European Renaissance* (Cambridge, Mass., 2007).

M. Alper Yalçinkaya, *Learned Patriots: Debating Science, State and Society in the Nineteenth-Century Ottoman Empire* (Chicago, 2015).

Judaism and science

Geoffrey Cantor, *Quakers, Jews, and Science: Religious Responses to Modernity and the Sciences in Britain, 1650–1900* (Oxford and New York, 2005).

Noah J. Efron, *Judaism and Science: A Historical Introduction* (Westport, Conn., 2007).

Jonathan Sacks, *The Great Partnership: Science, Religion, and the Search for Meaning* (New York, 2011).

Hinduism and science

Cheever Mackenzie Brown, *Hindu Perspectives on Evolution: Darwin, Dharma, and Design* (London, 2012).

Global perspectives

John Hedley Brooke and Ronald L. Numbers (eds), *Science and Religion Around the World* (Oxford, 2011).

Catherine Keller and Mary-Jane Rubenstein (eds), *Entangled Worlds: Religion, Science, and New Materialisms* (New York, 2017).

Fraser Watts and Kevin Dutton (eds), *Why the Science and Religion Dialogue Matters: Voices from the International Society for Science and Religion* (Philadelphia and London, 2006).

Websites

American Association for the Advancement of Science Dialog on Science, Ethics and Religion: <http://www.aaas.org/programs/dialogue-science-ethics-and-religion

Center for Islam and Science: http://www.cis-ca.org/>

Center for Theology and the Natural Sciences: <http://www.ctns.org/>

International Society for Science and Religion: <http://www.issr.org.uk/?>

John Templeton Foundation: <http://www.templeton.org/>

National Center for Science Education: <http://www.ncse.org/>

Stanford Encyclopedia of Philosophy: <http://plato.stanford.edu/?>

TalkOrigins Archive: Exploring the Evolution/Creation Controversy: <http://www.talkorigins.org/?>

Chapter 1: What are science–religion debates really about?

Religious belief and the birth of modern science

Peter Dear, *Revolutionizing the Sciences: European Knowledge and its Ambitions, 1500–1700* (Basingstoke, 2001).

Peter Harrison, *The Bible, Protestantism, and the Rise of Natural Science* (Cambridge, 2008).

Steven Shapin, *The Scientific Revolution* (Chicago, 1996).

Books by religious scientists

Francis Collins, *The Language of God: A Scientist Presents Evidence for Belief* (New York, 2006).

Guy Consolmagno, *God's Mechanics: How Scientists and Engineers Make Sense of Religion* (San Francisco, 2007).

Owen Gingerich, *God's Universe* (Cambridge, Mass., 2006).

John Polkinghorne, *Belief in God in an Age of Science* (New Haven, 1998).

Thomas Paine

Thomas Paine, *Political Writings*, ed. Bruce Kuklick (Cambridge, 1989); Paine's major works are available online at TP.

Gregory Claeys, *Thomas Paine: Social and Political Thought* (Boston and London, 1989).

John Keane, *Tom Paine: A Political Life* (London, 1996).

Leigh Eric Schmidt, *The Church of Saint Thomas Paine: A Religious History of American Secularism* (Princeton, 2021).

Science and atheism

Elaine Howard Ecklund and David R. Johnson, *Varieties of Atheism in Science* (Oxford, 2021).

Nathan Johnstone, *The New Atheism, Myth, and History. The Black Legends of Contemporary Anti-Religion* (London, 2018).

Shoaib Ahmed Malik, *Atheism and Islam: A Contemporary Discourse* (Abu Dhabi, 2018).

Victor J. Stenger, *God: The Failed Hypothesis. How Science Shows that God Does Not Exist* (Amherst, 2007).

Natural theology

John Hedley Brooke, *Science and Religion: Some Historical Perspectives* (Cambridge, 1991).

Russell Re Manning (ed.), *The Oxford Handbook of Natural Theology* (Oxford, 2013).

Chapter 2: Galileo and the philosophy of science

Philosophy of science

A. F. Chalmers, *What Is This Thing Called Science?*, 3rd edition (Buckingham, 1999).

Peter Godfrey-Smith, *Theory and Reality: An Introduction to the Philosophy of Science* (Chicago, 2003).

Samir Okasha, *Philosophy of Science: A Very Short Introduction* (Oxford, 2002).

Philosophy of science in theological perspective

Philip Clayton, *Explanation from Physics to Theology: An Essay in Rationality and Religion* (New Haven, 1989).

Christopher Knight, *Wrestling with the Divine: Religion, Science, and Revelation* (Minneapolis, 2001).

Galileo and the Church

John Brooke and Geoffrey Cantor, *Reconstructing Nature: The Engagement of Science and Religion* (Edinburgh, 1998).

J. L. Heilbron, *The Sun in the Church: Cathedrals as Solar Observatories* (Cambridge, Mass., 1999).

Peter Machamer (ed.), *The Cambridge Companion to Galileo* (Cambridge, 1998).

Ernan McMullin (ed.), *The Church and Galileo* (Notre Dame, Ind., 2005).

Realism, philosophy, and science

Ian Hacking, *Representing and Intervening* (Cambridge, 1983).

Thomas Kuhn, *The Structure of Scientific Revolutions*, 3rd edition (Chicago and London, 1996); first published 1962.

Peter Lipton, *Inference to the Best Explanation*, 2nd edition (London, 2004).

Richard Rorty, *Philosophy and Social Hope* (London, 1999).

Bas van Fraassen, *The Scientific Image* (Oxford, 1980).

Realism and theology

Colin Crowder (ed.), *God and Reality: Essays on Christian Non-Realism* (London, 1997).

Don Cupitt, *Taking Leave of God* (London, 1980).

Michael Scott and Andrew Moore (eds), *Realism and Religion: Philosophical and Theological Perspectives* (Aldershot, 2007).

Janet Soskice, *Metaphor and Religious Language* (Oxford, 1985).

Chapter 3: God and nature

Miracles

David Corner, *The Philosophy of Miracles* (London, 2007).

John Earman, *Hume's Abject Failure: The Argument Against Miracles* (New York, 2000).

Robert J. Fogelin, *A Defense of Hume on Miracles* (Princeton, 2003).

Robert B. Mullin, *Miracles and the Modern Religious Imagination* (New Haven and London, 1996).

Jane Shaw, *Miracles in Enlightenment England* (New Haven and London, 2006).

God and physics

Philip Clayton, *God and Contemporary Science* (Edinburgh, 1997).

Paul Davies, *The Mind of God: Science and the Search for Ultimate Meaning* (London, 1992).

Willem B. Drees, *Beyond the Big Bang: Quantum Cosmologies and God* (La Salle, Ill., 1990).

John Polkinghorne, *The Faith of a Physicist* (Princeton, 1994), also published as *Science and Christian Belief* (London, 1994).

Nicholas Saunders, *Divine Action and Modern Science* (Cambridge, 2002).

Laws of nature

Nancy Cartwright, *How the Laws of Physics Lie* (Oxford, 1983), and *The Dappled World: A Study of the Boundaries of Science* (Cambridge, 1999).

John Dupré, *The Disorder of Things: Metaphysical Foundations of the Disunity of Science* (Cambridge, Mass., 1993).

Bas van Fraassen, *Laws and Symmetry* (Oxford, 1989).

Ursula Goodenough, *The Sacred Depths of Nature* (Oxford, 1998).

Quantum physics

Karen Barad, *Meeting the Universe Halfway: Quantum Physics and the Entanglement of Matter and Meaning* (Durham, 2007).

George Johnson, *Fire in the Mind: Science, Faith, and the Search for Order* (New York, 1995).

John Polkinghorne, *Quantum Theory: A Very Short Introduction* (Oxford, 2002), and *Quantum Physics and Theology: An Unexpected Kinship* (London, 2007).

Chapter 4: Darwin and evolution

Charles Darwin

Janet Browne, *Darwin: A Biography*, 2 vols (London, 1995, 2002).

Charles Darwin, *The Autobiography of Charles Darwin*, ed. Nora Barlow (London, 1958), available online at CWCD.

Adrian Desmond, James Moore, and Janet Browne, *Charles Darwin* (Oxford, 2007).

Jonathan Hodge and Gregory Radick (eds), *The Cambridge Companion to Darwin* (Cambridge, 2003).

History of biology

Peter J. Bowler, *Evolution: The History of an Idea*, 3rd edition (Berkeley and London, 2003), and *The Eclipse of Darwinism: Anti-Darwinian Evolution Theories in the Decades around 1900* (Baltimore, 1992).

Jim Endersby, *A Guinea Pig's History of Biology: The Plants and Animals Who Taught Us the Facts of Life* (London, 2007).

Darwinism and religion

Peter J. Bowler, *Monkey Trials and Gorilla Sermons: Evolution and Christianity from Darwin to Intelligent Design* (Cambridge, Mass., and London, 2007).

C. Mackenzie Brown (ed.), *Asian Religious Responses to Darwinism* (Cham, 2020).

Marwa Elshakry, *Reading Darwin in Arabic* (Chicago, 2013).

David N. Livingstone, *Dealing with Darwin: Place, Politics, and Rhetoric in Religious Engagements with Evolution* (Baltimore, 2014).

James Moore, *The Post-Darwinian Controversies: A Study of the Protestant Struggle to Come to Terms with Darwin in Great Britain and America, 1870–1900* (Cambridge, 1979), and *The Darwin Legend* (Grand Rapids, Mich., 1994).

Michael Ruse, *Darwin and Design: Does Evolution Have a Purpose?* (Cambridge, Mass., 2003).

Thomas Huxley and Victorian science

Adrian Desmond, *Huxley: From Devil's Disciple to Evolution's High Priest* (London, 1998).

Bernard Lightman (ed.), *Victorian Science in Context* (Chicago, 1997).

Frank M. Turner, *Contesting Cultural Authority: Essays in Victorian Intellectual Life* (Cambridge, 1993).

Paul White, *Thomas Huxley: Making the 'Man of Science'* (Cambridge, 2003).

Theology and evolution

Geoffrey Cantor and Marc Swelitz (eds), *Jewish Tradition and the Challenge of Darwinism* (Chicago, 2006).

Johan De Smedt and Helen De Cruz, *The Challenge of Evolution to Religion* (Cambridge, 2020).

John F. Haught, *God After Darwin: A Theology of Evolution* (Boulder, Colo., and Oxford, 2000).

Nancey Murphy and William R. Stoeger, SJ (eds), *Evolution and Emergence: Systems, Organisms, Persons* (Oxford, 2007).

Arthur Peacocke, *Theology for a Scientific Age: Being and Becoming—Natural, Divine, and Human*, enlarged edition (Minneapolis and London, 1993).

Michael Ruse, *Can a Darwinian Be a Christian? The Relationship between Science and Religion* (Cambridge and New York, 2001).

Creationism

Dorothy Nelkin, *The Creation Controversy: Science or Scripture in the Schools?* (New York, 1982).

Ronald L. Numbers, *The Creationists: From Scientific Creationism to Intelligent Design*, expanded edition (Cambridge, Mass., and London, 2006).

Eugenie C. Scott, *Evolution versus Creationism: An Introduction* (Westport, Conn., 2004).

The Scopes trial

Edward J. Larson, *Summer for the Gods: The Scopes Trial and America's Continuing Debate over Science and Religion* (New York, 1997).

Adam R. Shapiro, *Trying Biology: The Scopes Trial, Textbooks, and the Antievolution Movement in American Schools* (Chicago, 2013).

Legal aspects

Langdon Gilkey, *Creationism on Trial: Evolution and God at Little Rock* (Charlottesville, Va., 1998).

Marcel La Follette (ed.), *Creationism, Science, and the Law: The Arkansas Case* (Cambridge, Mass., 1983).

Edward J. Larson, *Trial and Error: The American Controversy over Creation and Evolution*, 3rd edition (New York and Oxford, 2003).

Nicholas J. Matzke, 'The Evolution of Antievolution Policies after Kitzmiller v. Dover', *Science*, vol. 351, 6268 (1 January 2016), pp. 28–30.

Intelligent design

Michael J. Behe, *Darwin's Black Box: The Biochemical Challenge to Evolution* (New York, 1996), and *The Edge of Evolution: The Search for the Limits of Darwinism* (New York, 2007).

William Dembski and Michael Ruse (eds), *Debating Design: From Darwin to DNA* (Cambridge, 2004).

Kenneth R. Miller, *Finding Darwin's God: A Scientist's Search for Common Ground between God and Evolution* (New York, 1999).

Robert T. Pennock (ed.), *Intelligent Design Creationism and its Critics: Philosophical, Theological, and Scientific Perspectives* (Cambridge, Mass., 2001).

Chapter 5: Mind, brain, and morality

Brain and mind

Antonio Damasio, *Descartes' Error: Emotion, Reason, and the Human Brain*, revised edition (London, 2006).

John Searle, *Mind: A Brief Introduction* (Oxford, 2004).

Neuroscience, psychology, and religion

C. Daniel Batson, Patricia Schoenrade, and W. Larry Ventis, *Religion and the Individual: A Social-Psychological Perspective* (New York and Oxford, 1993).

Warren S. Brown, Nancey Murphy, and H. Newton Malony, *Whatever Happened to the Soul? Scientific and Theological Portraits of Human Nature* (Minneapolis, 1998).

John Lardas Modern, *Neuromatic Or, A Particular History of Religion and the Brain* (Chicago, 2021).

Nancey Murphy and Warren S. Brown, *Did My Neurons Make Me Do It? Philosophical and Neurobiological Perspectives on Moral Responsibility and Free Will* (Oxford, 2007).

Andrew Newberg, Eugene d'Aquili, and Vince Rause, *Why God Won't Go Away: Brain Science and the Biology of Belief* (New York, 2002).

Fraser Watts, *Theology and Psychology* (Aldershot, 2002).

Cognitive science and anthropology of religion

Scott Atran, *In Gods We Trust: The Evolutionary Landscape of Religion* (London and New York, 2002).

Pascal Boyer, *Religion Explained: The Human Instincts that Fashion Gods, Spirits and Ancestors* (London, 2001).

Steven Mithen, *The Prehistory of the Mind: The Search for the Origins of Art, Religion and Science* (London, 1996).

Wentzel van Huyssteen, *Alone in the World? Human Uniqueness in Science and Theology: The Gifford Lectures* (Grand Rapids, Mich., 2006).

Evolution and ethics

Stephen R. L. Clark, *Biology and Christian Ethics* (Cambridge, 2000).

Daniel C. Dennett, *Darwin's Dangerous Idea: Evolution and the Meanings of Life* (London and New York, 1995).

Frans de Waal, *Primates and Philosophers: How Morality Evolved* (Princeton and Oxford, 2006).

Thomas Huxley, *Evolution and Ethics, and Other Essays*, in *Collected Essays* (London, 1893–4), vol. 9; available online at HF.

Mary Midgley, *Beast and Man: The Roots of Human Nature*, new edition (London and New York, 1995).

Altruism and selfishness

Richard Dawkins, *The Selfish Gene* (New York and Oxford, 1976).

Thomas Dixon, *The Invention of Altruism: Making Moral Meanings in Victorian Britain* (Oxford, 2008).

Stephen G. Post, Lynn G. Underwood, Jeffrey P. Schloss, and William B. Hurlbut (eds), *Altruism and Altruistic Love: Science, Philosophy and Religion in Dialogue* (Oxford and New York, 2002).

David Sloan Wilson, *Does Altruism Exist? Culture, Genes, and the Welfare of Others* (New Haven, 2015).

Gender, sexuality, and society

Austen Hartke, *Transforming: The Bible and the Lives of Transgender Christians* (Louisville, Ky., 2018).

Roy Porter and Lesley Hall, *The Facts of Life: The Creation of Sexual Knowledge in Britain, 1650–1950* (New Haven, 1995).

Kathleen M. Sands (ed.), *God Forbid: Religion and Sex in American Public Life* (Oxford, 2000).

Jeffrey Weeks, *Sex, Politics and Society: The Regulation of Sexuality since 1800*, 2nd edition (London, 1989), and *Coming Out: Homosexual Politics in Britain from the Nineteenth Century to the Present*, revised edition (London, 1990).

The naturalistic fallacy

Alasdair MacIntyre, *After Virtue: A Study in Moral Theory*, 2nd edition (Notre Dame, Ind., 1984).

G. E. Moore, *Principia ethica*, edited with an introduction by Thomas Baldwin (Cambridge, 1993); first published 1903.

Feminist epistemology of science

Donna Haraway, *Simians, Cyborgs, and Women* (New York, 1991).

Sandra Harding, *Whose Science? Whose Knowledge?* (Ithaca, NY, 1991).

Evelyn Fox Keller, *Reflections on Gender and Science* (New Haven, 1985).

Helen E. Longino, *Science as Social Knowledge* (Princeton, 1990).

Londa Schiebinger *The Mind Has No Sex?* (Cambridge, Mass., 1989).

Science and the future

Stephen R. L. Clark, *How to Live Forever: Science Fiction and Philosophy* (London and New York, 1995).

Mary Midgley, *Science as Salvation: A Modern Myth and its Meaning* (London and New York, 1992), and *Evolution as a Religion: Strange Hopes and Stranger Fears*, revised edition (London and New York, 2002).

John Polkinghorne and Michael Welker (eds), *The End of the World and the Ends of God: Science and Theology on Eschatology* (Harrisburg, 2000).

Chapter 6: The worlds of science and religion

Hawaii/Thirty Meter Telescope

Noelani Goodyear-Kaopua, Ikaika Hussey, and Erin Kahunawaika 'ala Wright (eds), *A Nation Rising: Hawaiian Movements for Life, Land, and Sovereignty* (Durham, NC, 2014).

Chanda Prescod-Weinstein, *The Disordered Cosmos: A Journey into Dark Matter, Spacetime, & Dreams Deferred* (New York, 2021).

Michael J. West, *A Sky Wonderful with Stars: 50 Years of Modern Astronomy on Maunakea* (Honolulu, 2015).

Colonial medicine and bioscience

Hartford Institute for Religion Research, *Navigating the Pandemic: A First Look at Congregational Responses* (Hartford, Conn., 2021).

Suman Seth, *Difference and Disease: Race and the Eighteenth-Century British Empire* (Cambridge, 2018).

Kim TallBear, *Native American DNA: Tribal Belonging and the False Promise of Genetic Science* (Minneapolis, 2013).

Helen C. Tilley, *Africa as a Living Laboratory: Empire, Development, and the Problem of Scientific Knowledge* (Chicago, 2011).

Environmentalism and religion

Celia E. Deane-Drummond, *The Ethics of Nature* (Malden, Mass., 2004).

Katherine Hayhoe, *Saving Us: A Climate Scientist's Case for Hope and Healing in a Divided World* (New York, 2021).

Bron Taylor (ed.), *Encyclopedia of Religion and Nature* (London, 2005).

Science denial

Michael Gordin, *The Pseudoscience Wars: Immanuel Velikovsky and the Birth of the Modern Fringe* (Chicago, 2013).

Naomi Oreskes, *Why Trust Science?* (Princeton, 2019).

Index

For the benefit of digital users, indexed terms that span two pages (e.g., 52–53) may, on occasion, appear on only one of those pages.

Index

Science and Religion

Science and Religion

RELIGION
IN AMERICA
A Very Short Introduction
Timothy Beal

Timothy Beal describes many aspects of religion in contemporary America that are typically ignored in other books on the subject, including religion in popular culture and counter-cultural groups; the growing phenomenon of "hybrid" religious identities, both individual and collective; the expanding numbers of new religious movements, or NRMs, in America; and interesting examples of "outsider religion." He also offers an engaging overview of the history of religion in America, from Native American traditions to the present day. Finally, Beal highlights the three major forces shaping the present and future of religion in America.

www.oup.com/vsi

SCIENTIFIC REVOLUTION
A Very Short Introduction
Lawrence M. Principe

In this *Very Short Introduction* Lawrence M. Principe explores the exciting developments in the sciences of the stars (astronomy, astrology, and cosmology), the sciences of earth (geography, geology, hydraulics, pneumatics), the sciences of matter and motion (alchemy, chemistry, kinematics, physics), the sciences of life (medicine, anatomy, biology, zoology), and much more. The story is told from the perspective of the historical characters themselves, emphasizing their background, context, reasoning, and motivations, and dispelling well-worn myths about the history of science.

www.oup.com/vsi

CATHOLICISM
A Very Short Introduction
Gerald O'Collins

Despite a long history of external threats and internal strife, the Roman Catholic Church and the broader reality of Catholicism remain a vast and valuable presence into the third millennium of world history. What are the origins of the Catholic Church? How has Catholicism changed and adapted to such vast and diverse cultural influences over the centuries? What great challenges does the Catholic Church now face in the twenty-first century, both within its own life and in its relation to others around the world? In this Very Short Introduction, Gerald O'Collins draws on the best current scholarship available to answer these questions and to present, in clear and accessible language, a fresh introduction to the largest and oldest institution in the world.

www.oup.com/vsi

PENTECOSTALISM
A Very Short Introduction
William K. Kay

In religious terms Pentecostalism was probably the most vibrant and rapidly-growing religious movement of the 20th century. Starting as a revivalistic and renewal movement within Christianity, it encircled the globe in less than 25 years and grew in North America and then in those parts of the world with the highest birth-rates. Characterised by speaking in tongues, miracles, television evangelism and megachurches, it is also noted for its small-group meetings, empowerment of individuals, liberation of women and humanitarian concerns. William K Kay outlines the origins and growth of Pentecostalism, looking at not only the theological aspects of the movement, but also the sociological influences of its political and humanitarian viewpoints.

www.oup.com/vsi

PAGANISM
A Very Short Introduction
Owen Davies

This *Very Short Introduction* explores the meaning of paganism - through a chronological overview of the attitudes towards its practices and beliefs - from the ancient world through to the present day. Owen Davies largely looks at paganism through the eyes of the Christian world, and how, over the centuries, notions and representations of its nature were shaped by religious conflict, power struggles, colonialism, and scholarship. Despite the expansion of Christianity and Islam, Pagan cultures continue to exist around the world, whilst in the West new formations of paganism constitute one of the fastest-growing religions.

www.oup.com/vsi

THE REFORMATION
A Very Short Introduction
Peter Marshall

The Reformation transformed Europe, and left an indelible mark on the modern world. It began as an argument about what Christians needed to do to be saved, but rapidly engulfed society in a series of fundamental changes. This *Very Short Introduction* provides a lively and up-to-date guide to the process. Peter Marshall argues that the Reformation was not a solely European phenomenon, but that varieties of faith exported from Europe transformed Christianity into a truly world religion. It explains doctrinal debates in a clear and non-technical way, but is equally concerned to demonstrate the effects the Reformation had on politics, society, art, and minorities.

www.oup.com/vsi